On Being a
Language Teacher

On Being a Language Teacher

A Personal and Practical Guide to Success

• • • • • • • • • • • • • • • • • • •

Norma López-Burton
University of California at Davis

Denise Minor
California State University, Chico

Yale
UNIVERSITY PRESS

New Haven and London

Yale University Press books may be purchased in quantity for educational, business, or promotional use. For information, please e-mail sales.press@yale.edu (U.S. office) or sales@yaleup.co.uk (U.K. office).

Editor: Tim Shea
Publishing Assistant: Ashley E. Lago
Manuscript Editor: David Pritchard
Production Editor: Ann-Marie Imbornoni
Production Controller: Aldo Cupo

Set by Newgen North America, Inc.
Printed in the United States of America.

Library of Congress Cataloging-in-Publication Data

López-Burton, Norma, 1957–
   On being a language teacher : a personal and practical guide to success / Norma López-Burton, University of California at Davis ; Denise Minor, California State University, Chico.
      pages cm
   Includes bibliographical references and index.
   ISBN 978-0-300-18689-5 (pbk. : alk. paper)   1. Language teachers—Training of.   2. Language teachers—Vocational guidance.   3. Language and languages—Study and teaching.   I. Minor, Denise Earla.   II. Title.
   P53.85L67 2013
   418.00711—dc23

                                                                2013031356

A catalogue record for this book is available from the British Library.

This paper meets the requirements of ANSI/NISO Z39.48-1992 (Permanence of Paper).

10 9 8 7 6 5 4 3 2 1

To my husband, Thomas P. Burton, the love of my life
Norma López-Burton

To my family, the Milgrams and the Minors
Denise Minor

To view the videos indicated by the symbol , please go to **yalebooks.com/languageteacher**. The **password** required to view the videos is: learn.

Contents

PART III · BEYOND THE BASICS

PART IV · THE FUTURE

To the Reader

DENISE MINOR

It has been almost three decades since I first stepped into a classroom as a language teacher. I can still see the stairs leading up to the tiny language academy on the second story above a clothing shop in downtown Irún, Spain. I can still picture the bespectacled receptionist sitting at the top of the stairs monitoring the comings and goings of the students and teachers. I clearly remember my classroom with its half-size blackboard and fifteen wooden desks jammed into a space that probably had previously been a living room.

The Academy of Irún had hired me to teach a one-hour English class four nights a week based on one singular skill that I brought to the bargaining table: I was a native speaker. The reason I had not been hired at any of the more prestigious language academies in nearby San Sebastián (where I lived) was based on one singular characteristic that I did not possess: I was not British. Almost everyone wanted to learn the "real" English of England. Apparently, the students of the more economically priced Academy of Irún were not so picky.

The textbook we used told the story of a lackadaisical young man named Arthur who rented a room from an aging landlady somewhere near London. Arthur was good-natured but forgetful and was always getting into trouble. Each day before class I sat in the cafés of San Sebastián studying the British vocabulary of my book about Arthur. One took a "lift" instead of an elevator and used a "rubber" to erase a paper. If I ever messed up and used an American word, I could count on the twelve-year-old boy with the pale red hair who sat in the back of the room to correct me.

I had taken the job simply because I needed the money. My true calling was as a writer, and this year in Spain would serve two purposes: to help me become bilingual and to provide me with fuel for future storytelling. But a funny thing happened during that first month at the Academy of Irún. I fell in love with teaching, and there was nothing gradual about my fall.

Of course the first few nights at the school were terrifying because I did not have a clue what I was doing. To make matters worse (or better, when looked at in hindsight), I could barely speak Spanish. I had neglected to learn the language before quitting my job as a newspaper reporter the previous month and moving to Spain. In my class, I had to rely upon the textbook, pantomimes, and my ability to draw with the tiny stubs of chalk that were left there at the end of the day.

But the thrill I felt each night as I saw the faces of my students—from the twelve-year-old boy to the octogenarian in the front row—as they registered comprehension, was addicting. The same creativity I put to use in writing stories was channeled into creating games and interactive activities, things that I learned only years later were officially known as "communicative activities." Sometimes my plans fell flat. But usually they went very well, and after class I bounded down those stairs to relive the success of the evening in my mind as I took the slow bus home.

There is no way I could ever have imagined those many years ago that I would someday get a PhD in Spanish linguistics, become a trainer of future Spanish teachers, and coauthor a book about language teaching. For this book, Norma and I have teamed up to try to address what we see as the enormous gap that exists between the pedagogical training of many beginning language teachers and the responsibilities that they assume when they step into their classrooms the first day. This gap is built into the system of beginning language instruction at most research universities in the nation. Graduate students, simply by virtue of having been accepted into an MA or a PhD program, are handed the roster and the responsibility for thirty beginning students. Most of them receive concurrent training in pedagogy, and they learn much of what they need to know by the end of their first semester. But for the first couple of months many feel as if they have been thrown into the deep end of a swimming pool without ever having had swim lessons.

There are many other teachers who struggle at first: people with master's degrees hired to teach at community colleges; heritage speakers of languages hired to teach at night schools simply because of their fluency; and credentialed high school teachers who, by the time they land their first job, look back in a fog on their class-planning seminars. There are, of course, those teachers like I was years ago that have been hired to teach abroad simply because they possess the abilities of a native speaker. They all ask themselves, "What am I going to do the first day, the first week, the first month?"

This book is essentially a how-to manual that will not only guide new teachers through their first months of instruction but will also ground them in the research and theory that underpins good language pedagogy. In addition, there are chapters on a variety of topics ranging from culture to technology to assessment that will be useful to even the most veteran teachers.

We have designed a four-part book that can be used differently by different groups of teachers or professors. For supervisors of beginning language courses at research universities, the book could be used in the order in which it is written, beginning with Part I and the step-by-step instructions for running a language classroom. For professors and teacher trainers in credential programs or linguistic departments, the book could be used beginning with Part II to give future teachers a foundation in theory and research. Experienced teachers might be interested primarily in Part III and the chapters that provide guidance in technology, assessment, the inclusion of students with disabilities, and the strategies for teaching classes that serve both heritage speakers and students learning a second language. Recent graduates of credential and graduate programs could start at the end with Part IV and the chapters providing recommendations for getting a job and for negotiating workplace politics during the first year. After finding a job, they might go back to study the other sections.

Our primary goal has been to write a book that is as readable as good fiction and as informative as the best teaching methodology texts. In addition, we have aimed to provide both teachers and teachers-in-training with some of the kinds of information that they will not find anywhere else except in intimate conversations with seasoned professionals. Finally, we hope that we have written a touchstone of sorts, the kind of book that teachers will keep for years to pull out occasionally to remind themselves about issues essential to the art and profession of language instruction.

Introduction
Impressions Left by Teachers

NORMA LÓPEZ-BURTON

Being a painfully shy child, I found my time at school to be an ordeal. I never understood what compelled adults to repeatedly ask, "Do you like school?" What kind of a question was that?! What kind of kid likes to sit quietly in a chair all day fearing the moment she gets picked on by the all-powerful teacher? And as if that were not enough torture, being sent home with homework was a reminder of the stress of the day. It never ended, not even on weekends. The only refuge was summer. "Do you like school?" That was the stupidest question! It was also cruel, because to be polite you were forced to lie. I was afraid to lie, so I just cocked my head, shrugged my shoulders, and smiled.

In my view—and maybe I just had more than my fair share of bad teachers—teachers were a mean version of parents. They were similar in the sense that they controlled you and were able to punish you with a bad grade, but meaner because they had the power to embarrass you in front of your peers. I lived in constant fear of being ridiculed. Children want above all to be cool, or at least to fit in, and the teacher laughing at you is the worst because it gives permission to the rest of the class to do the same.

Many of my teachers used the "humiliation approach." As children, they had gone through it and survived. Now it was their turn to do unto others—kind of a rite of passage. I had a social science teacher—let's call her Mrs. Narvaez, may God have mercy on her soul—who loved this approach.

She would return the graded exams in order of score from best to worst, and her demeanor and comments would get more sarcastic as she announced lower and lower scores. I remember chanting under my breath, "Mine is next, mine's got to be next, please, please, let mine be next!" But as bad as that teacher was, I had one that was worse. I had a teacher in the eighth grade who not only handed out the exams in order of scores, but reseated all the students after each exam according to their scores from left to right in the room. On the left were the best students (her desk was on the left), and the students with progressively lower scores would fill up the right side of the classroom. This teacher would not make any comments as she assigned your new seat. It was all handled matter-of-factly: you are the better student, you get to sit close to me, you are not, you sit over there. I would study a lot, not because I wanted to sit close to this monster, but because I did not want to be seated toward the right and be taunted and looked down upon by my classmates until the next test.

The "humiliation approach" did work with me, in a perverse way. The end result was that I studied and got good grades, but I never felt the joy and love of learning. I hated school and I disliked and resented the teachers who used this method. I studied to do well on a test, and I quickly forgot the material once I jumped each successive hurdle. Mission accomplished. Next test!

But, the fact that I am writing this book in a coherent way is a testament to my having had *some* good teachers, and I am grateful for that. They were such a great relief from the other stressful, misguided, and sadistic teachers that filled most of my day. As a result, I loved them and hence the material they were teaching, whether I was good at it or not. I have always found science somewhat interesting (I am more of a humanities person), but after having Mrs. García in the fifth grade, I wanted to become a scientist. She talked about genes and the information they carried with such passion! She would relate with wide eyes that the DNA in a single human body, if stretched out, could cover the whole world a couple of times. She would say, gesturing with her hands like an opera singer, "CAN YOU IMAGINE?! IT GIVES ME GOOSE BUMPS JUST TO THINK ABOUT IT! CAN YOU BELIEVE THAT?!" We would sit there, mouths open, mesmerized by these incredible revelations. Our eyes would widen with hers, and it felt like soon one of us was going to stand up and shout, "YES, I BELIEVE!!"

Other teachers, few and far between, also inspired me. Not knowing at the time that I was going to actually become a teacher, I felt that if I *were* to be one, I would like to be like them. I admired Mrs. Rivera's enthusiasm in class. I remember her almost marching in and with a big smile saying, "GOOD MORNING, CLASS!" Even on bad days, that greeting would pick you up. I admired Mrs. Ayala, my Spanish teacher, for always raising the bar in a kind but firm way. She would make us read so much, and memorize poems and soliloquies. When some students would question their own abilities, she was very encouraging and optimistic about our potential. "Too long to memorize? Oh, no, you can do it. I am convinced you can do it, no doubt." And she would walk away muttering, "No doubt, uh, uh, no doubt." I also remember a funny microbiology teacher in college. She was so down-to-earth, so disarming, so person-next-door instead of acting like a lofty pro-fessor. She would come up with some random outrageous comments: "Now the mitochondrion is the source of . . . oh my goodness I forgot to look at the expiration date on my milk, I think it expired, I have to buy milk, my cat is going to be hungry and she can be a demanding little bugger, the other day, well . . . anyway, the mitochondrion, yes, the mitochondrion, don't ever mess with it because it is a tricky little thing, it can . . ." She was not crazy. She was just a natural comedian and would digress on purpose to make us laugh and stay alert. Her personality added so much life to the class. There was no falling asleep there.

Those human beings, the good, the bad, and the funny, influenced my life as a teacher. From the bad I learned what never to do, and from the good and funny, the art of being a good teacher: to be enthusiastic, passionate, patient, to keep my cool, and to do the right thing even in the face of trying students.

I have been teaching at the University of California at Davis for over thirty years now, and a few years ago I had a pretty good Spanish 2 class except for the one proverbial bad apple. Let's call him Ricardo. He was the type of student who was "not amused" by anything I did. That boy made my life dif-ficult for three months. I could always count on him to have a snide remark about every activity. Right after giving directions I would hear "We have to do what?! God!" or a loudly muttered "This is boring!" If it weren't illegal I would have grabbed him by the neck, but I knew he was immature, a work in progress. I kept my cool and just pleaded with my eyes, "Come on, Ricardo, cooperate." But he seldom did. I can usually change a student's attitude with my smile and charm, but not this one. He stubbornly continued to be a pill from the beginning to the end of the course. I was glad when that quarter was over.

A few years later, I went to pick up my twelve-year-old son at soccer practice, and out on the field I saw their new assistant coach directing the kids on the last exercise of the day. He was having a lot of trouble and was obviously very frustrated. They weren't paying attention, and some were complaining, "This is boring!" I pity the poor soul who has to deal with eighteen twelve-year-old boys. As I got closer to the field I thought I recognized him. Yes, it was he, my old friend Ricardo! At that moment I looked up to the sky and thanked the Lord for letting me live long enough to see this! Poetic justice! Oh man oh man, how sweet it is! It did the soul good! He ended the practice and when he looked my way, he recognized me. I tried to hide my grin, but I guess I was unsuccessful because he came straight to me and said sheepishly, "I guess I am paying for everything I did to you, huh?" "You weren't that bad," I lied. And then he said emphatically and with surprising sincerity, "Yes, I was. I was a jerk. You were the best teacher I've ever had and I acted like a jerk!" I couldn't believe my ears. This guy gave me so much grief all quarter long, and now he tells me I was the best teacher he'd ever had?! That quarter he had made me doubt my abilities and my belief that I was a pretty good teacher. When he left my Spanish class with an I-am-glad-this-stupid-class-is-over smirk on his face at the end of that quarter, I thought I had failed, but, wow, what do you know!

I learned you never know what is really happening in those heads. Many young people say one thing but mean another. As a teacher you may never know if you have made a difference, but I marvel at those rare occasions when fortune lets you see some students, years after they leave your class, even when you don't remember their names or their faces. They tell you how much they enjoyed your class and how much you have influenced their lives. It is like a little form of immortality or even time travel. Your effort, dedication, sincerity, patience, passion, and love of teaching may not have an obvious payoff right away, but know, without a doubt, that you are influencing the future. Just make sure that influence is for the good.

Acknowledgments

Norma López-Burton would like to thank:

Thomas Burton
Leslie Burton
Kelly Bilinski
Caleb Bloodworth
María Cetto
Robert Craig
Annabelle Dolidon
Emily Foss
Andronike Halbrook
Miriam Hernández-Rodríguez
Tasha Lewis
Laura Marqués
Kimberly Morris
Cristina Pardo Ballester
Jill Pellettieri
Tracy Quan
Kathy Robertson
Katie Stafford
Carolina Viera
My top-notch Teaching Assistants at UCD

A special thanks to the two graduate students who made my life a little harder a few years ago. Their antics inspired me to write this book. *No hay mal que por bien no venga.*

Denise Minor would like to thank:

Patricia Black
Kate Buckley
Connie Chrysler
Lamia Djeldjel
Laurie Evans
Holly Johnson
Aimin Lu
Laura Marqués
Al Shademan
Jennifer Smith
Niel Stevens
Denise Tracy
Eve Zyzik
The present and future language teachers trained at Chico State

Part I • In the Classroom

1 • The First Day of Class and Lesson Planning

NORMA LÓPEZ-BURTON

I was admitted to the master's degree program at the University of California, Davis, in January 1981. Most graduate students start in September. At UCD most graduate students have no teaching experience at all. Back in the day, the only requirements to be in charge of a language class were that one be a graduate student and be fairly fluent in the language one was about to teach. New graduate students got a three-day orientation before they met their class for the first time, and they also had to attend a methodology class that met four hours a week for ten weeks. Since I started in January, I missed all that. For some reason my supervisor did not feel the need to update me in any way, and he made no effort to educate me about teaching beforehand or to give me any warning about what I was about to face.

At the beginning-of-the-quarter meeting, he gave the new teacher assistants (TAs) their teaching assignments, room numbers, and materials. He called my name: "López-Burton, Norma. Hmm, López, you are a native speaker, right? That should make it easier for you! Well, you'll be teaching Spanish 1 in 103 Wellman Hall. That's a brick building in front of the Quad. Just exit through that door there, turn left, walk toward the Quad, and you'll see Wellman Hall right in front. Room 103 is on the left hallway of the building. Here is the book. Go get 'em!" He gave me more instruction on how to get to the room than what to do once I got there. Not only that, he assumed that because I was a native speaker, it was going to be easier for me, when the opposite is actually true.

I remember not being able to sleep well the night before my first day of class. I had an 8:00 a.m. class, so I chose what I was going to wear the night before and double-checked the alarm (made sure it was 6:00 a.m. and not 6:00 p.m.—a classic mistake). I was all set to go, nervous, but ready. "Hey, I'm a native speaker, how hard can this be? The students don't know anything."

Come morning, I checked the room number again, got there at 7:59, and opened the door to my classroom. It is hard to describe the feeling of all those eyes lifting to the door and watching my every step as I walked the long mile it took to get to the front of the classroom. I was petrified, but managed to write my name on the board as I'd programmed myself to do in my notes, and with a "Good morning" instead of a *Buenos días,* I started my first Spanish class . . .

That first day, and in fact that whole quarter, did not go very well, to put it mildly. Not having learned Spanish in a classroom, I was not familiar with my own language's grammar rules, and therefore I was completely ill-prepared to explain anything linguistic. I didn't even know that verbs in Spanish were grouped in *–ar, -er*, and *–ir* endings! I tried to respond to questions like "Why do you say '*Buenos días*' (Good days) instead of '*Buena mañana*' (Good morning)?" Or "Why do you say '*Me llamo*' (I am called) instead of 'Mi nombre es' (My name is)?" My lowest point was when one student asked me, "Why is it that we have to say '*Yo hablo*,'" and I blurted out, "Because you are male and your words should end in '*o*,' like '*guapo*.'" But then I immediately realized that I am female and I say "*Yo hablo*" too! That was a learning-impaired moment.

I was very stressed out that whole first quarter. My supervisor did not help me, and to be honest, I didn't seek his help either. I didn't want him to think I was a moron. Nor did I get help from my fellow TAs. Being a newcomer in January put me out of sync with the September group. Besides, they were all in their own little worlds, and sharing materials and ideas was like sharing underwear: it was just not done. The book was not what we now call "TA friendly." The book we were using back then was called *Beginning Spanish*, which was pretty old-school compared to what we have nowadays (I feel old when I say that). Now we have blue teacher's notes in the margin, an instructor's manual, teacher activity files, an instructor's resource kit, and all kinds of online help. *Beginning Spanish* was a bare-bones book. I keep a copy in my office to remind me of the dark ages of teaching. It was a two-color book, with long dialogues typical of the audio-lingual method, with exercises consisting of unrelated lists of vocabulary for translation or items to be changed into something else. There was no context to speak of and almost nothing was authentic. Culture was limited to the occasional author-generated "*Lectura Cultural*" (Cultural Reading), which I often skipped because I could hear audible sighs from the students when we did them. Those readings were pretty dry and tedious. There were some comprehension questions, but there was no cross-cultural contrast. Lacking any methodology instruction, I did a lot of "repeat after me" from the book and advised them to memorize phrases and vocabulary every night.

I taught in English about 90 percent of the time, reasoning that since they couldn't speak Spanish, naturally, they couldn't understand it either. I worked hard, and slowly started learning the grammar of my own language, but my confidence—what little I had—would still be shaken every day because invariably, one student would come up with a question I could not answer. Some questions, like the gender of words, had no logical explanation, and I would end up apologizing to the students for my language being so difficult. My raised eyebrows and the meek tone of my voice expressed eloquently my sympathy for their having to learn Spanish!

I was so inexperienced, and so young, too. I had just turned twenty-three three months before. I was 5'3", weighed 102 pounds soaking wet, and did not look twenty-three, but more like twelve. Looking young is a blessing now, but back then, the combination of being young, small, and unsure was deadly. Students smell insecurity like sharks smell blood in the water. They'll circle menacingly for a while before they grab your leg and pull you under for the death dive.

I felt I did just about everything wrong that first quarter. The students had a very young, nervous, unknowledgeable, English-speaking Spanish teacher who couldn't even explain the most basic language concepts. I cringe when I think of those times, but as always in life, you take your lumps and with luck you learn to improve. I read my student evaluations at the end of each quarter and took notes of the good, the bad, and the ugly. I visited teachers of other languages and learned many tricks that way. It took me several years of doing things the wrong way to start doing them right. With this book, I hope to shorten the reader's learning curve, and to make learning the ins and outs of this profession a better process for you than it was for me. Some people say "No pain, no gain," but it doesn't necessarily have to be like that. "No pain, no pain" is good too.

ANXIETY

Thinking back, there are some things I could have done to appear less like a newbie, less of a prey. Anxiety is the first giveaway. We all feel a little nervous, but as a first-time teacher that becomes magnified. There are chemical ways to deal with it, of course, but how long do you want to be dependent on anxiety pills before learning to naturally calm down? If this is going to be your profession, you have to find other ways.

Here is what has worked for me. As soon as you know where your classroom will be, go there, stand in front of the empty chairs, and imagine how it would be full of students. Some people recommend imagining them naked. I wouldn't go that far, but imagining twenty-five pairs of eyes staring at you, which is what you will actually experience, is a better rehearsal. Keep visualizing those virtual stares until you get comfortable. Get familiar with all the equipment. Know where the electric outlets are, how to work the projector, where and how to connect the laptop. The more familiar you are with the room, the less chance you'll fumble and look flustered.

When you arrive the first day of class, you have to remember that THEY are nervous too. Students are usually concerned about the impact you and the course are going to have on them: "Am I good enough to pass the class?" "Will the class be difficult?" "Will I be able to understand the teacher?" "Will I get a good grade?" Contrary to what you may feel, the students won't care about YOU, or your hair, your pimples, or your big hips. They will be listening for information about the class: your office hours, how many exams there will be, how much the exams will be worth, whether there's going to be a lot of homework, whether they'll be able to carry that study load and possibly work too, etc. They have their own agenda and you are not in it. It's not all about you!

But if you are not convinced about your students' own self-absorption, start speaking in the target language and only the target language. Their eyes will widen, they will lean forward, and they will concentrate hard on what you are *saying* and not on you as a person.

The trick to this whole thing is to act and look normal enough so their attention does not go from their agenda and concerns to you. To look "normal" you have to minimize the physical distractions. Wear something nice but casual, something that is comfortable to you and that your friends think you look good in: Look good, feel good, do good. Don't give the students an easy reason to think you are a nerd (wearing a necktie), a slob (wearing dirty or wrinkled clothes), or a tart (spaghetti-strap tank top with distracting cleavage).

One minor detail that can save you embarrassment is to bring a couple of wet wipes to wipe your chalky fingers every once in a while. Especially if you are wearing black, the chalk will show all over your clothing. If you forget the wet wipe, remember not to scratch your face or pick a wedgie with fingers full of chalk.

Acting "normal" comes with confidence, and confidence comes with practice and preparation. Practice at home what you are going to say. The more prepared you are, the more confident you'll feel. Have a written detailed lesson plan so you don't forget what you are going to say or do. It is also OK to take a few seconds to silently read what your lesson plan says you are going to do next in front of the students. Brief silences are not bad, and it actually makes you look organized. It tells the students, "I took time to write down and organize what I am going to do today in class. I am not ad-libbing. I put some thought into this."

Bottom line, you will feel a little self-conscious at the beginning, but not to worry—this too shall pass! You will feel more comfortable with each passing day.

YOUR FIRST DAY OF CLASS

Start your class with a confident smile and a greeting in the target language to set the tone. You will feel somewhat nervous, but remember, the students don't know that. Secretly transfer that nervous feeling to them. I know of a trick that may be considered a little mean, but I think it's fair game. We are talking first-day survival here! I start by saying, *"Hola, buenos días, ¿cómo están?"* (Hi, good morning, how are you?), and I wait a little for a response that usually does not come because it is only Spanish 1. They don't know how to answer, and their eyes start shifting. Then I hold three fingers up and say, *"Este es Español 3, ¿no?"* (This is Spanish 3, right?) Their eyes get big, some check their notes, and some ask each other nervously, "Did she just say Spanish 3? This is Spanish 1, right?? I have Spanish 1 written down." Then I hold my index finger up and I say, smiling, *"Sí, sí, es Español 1."* (Yes, yes, this is Spanish 1.) There, with that little harmless joke, I just transferred my anxiety to them. I am in control and they are the ones that are nervous.

After writing my name on the board, I used to speak English to go over the administrative side of the course—the syllabus, lab, absences, homework, university policies, etc.—but I later discovered that it was not necessary to say it in English if I made it crystal clear in Spanish. Doing it this way has three main advantages. First, as I said earlier, it shifts the students' attention from my nervous self to what I am saying. Second, it conveys the message that this is a Spanish class and that the student is going to hear information in this new language and is expected to make sense of what is being said. And third, and most importantly, it empowers the student. I noticed that if I spoke in Spanish the very first day and they were able to understand, they left that class with a sense of respect for the course (this is not going to be an easy A, they are going to have to focus) and a belief that they were going to be able to learn this language. It was doable. They understood most of what I was saying: "Cool. All right, I can do this."

To make this positive feeling possible, it is important to make what you say crystal clear with the use of the board, cognates, repetition, and body language. It doesn't mean that we are exclusively using cognates or using gestures for every single little word; that would be silly. We just have to make sure that the essential part of the sentence we utter is understandable. So those particular words must be either a cognate, a drawing, a symbol, or something they will understand. In the sentence *El examen número uno vale 15 por ciento de la nota* (Exam number one is worth 15 percent of the grade), the essential and most important words here to convey the message are *examen* and *15 por ciento*. The word *examen* is a cognate; they will understand it. The number "fifteen" and the word "percent" they won't know, but you can write them on the board. So the sentence can be said in its entirety in normal sounding Spanish—"*El examen número uno vale 15 por ciento de la nota*"—as you write on the board: *Examen #1 = 15%*. The students will be listening to a new language, and with the help of what you write on the board, they will be getting what you say.

Go on talking about the syllabus, using cognates, simple drawings, and body language as shown in the video. Occasionally there will be a word or two that are not easy to explain, like the word *asistencia* (attendance). I can't draw it, I can't make a simple gesture for it, and there is no cognate to match it. If there is no easy way out, I ask, *"Asistencia, ¿saben qué es asistencia?"* (Attendance, do you know what attendance means?) Maybe a false beginner will provide the answer, but if no answer comes from the class, you say "attendance" and move on. The students, not knowing there is a hard copy coming later, will be focused on the information and will take notes. That is when you see that they are understanding what you are saying in the target language. Otherwise, they would be confused and be asking each other, "What did she say?" Only after going through the syllabus do I distribute a hard copy. I ask them to read the syllabus at home: *"Es importante leer todo el papel."* (It is important to read the whole paper.) I repeat this phrase in Spanish as I gesture reading and looking at the paper, eyeglasses down to my nose, sweeping through the text with my index finger and saying, *"Uh huh, uh huh . . . ahh, uh huh, oh . . .* (change page) *uh huh, uh huh. Es importante leer todo el papel. Uh huh . . . ahh, uh huh, oh . . . aha . . . Si tienen preguntas . . ."* (If you have any questions)—I write a couple of question marks on the board and also chew on my index fingernail and frown

To view the videos, go to yalebooks.com/languageteacher. The password is: learn.

in concentration—"*Si tienen preguntas, aquí está mi e-mail . . .*" (here is my e-mail), and I write it on the board. "*¿Bien? ¿Una pregunta, dos preguntas, tres preguntas . . . ?*" (OK? One question, two questions, three questions?)—I signal with one finger, two fingers, three fingers—"*Muchas preguntas . . . por e-mail*" (A lot of questions . . . by e-mail), and I point to my e-mail address. The more you repeat a word in context, the better it will stick.

After most administrative issues have been addressed, I start using the language head-on. I work the crowd:

> Putting my hand on my chest, I say, "*Hola, me llamo Norma. ¿Cómo te llamas?*" (Hi, my name is Norma. What is your name?)
>
> "*Mark.*"
>
> Emphasizing *me llamo* with hand on chest, I continue, "*Me llamo Norma. ¿Cómo te llamas?*"
>
> "*Me llamo Mark.*" They usually put their hand on their chest too—funny.
>
> "*Ah, Mark,*" I say, shaking his hand, "*mucho gusto*" (nice to meet you). Then I write on the board the usual response to "nice to meet you," which is *igualmente,* so I can point to it when they don't know how to respond.
>
> "*Igualmente,*" I say, and point to the board.
>
> "*Igualmente,*" the student reads and repeats.

I do this with several students, showing true interest in meeting them, sometimes commenting on their names:

> "*Hola, me llamo Norma. ¿Cómo te llamas?*"
>
> "*Me llamo Leilani.*"
>
> "*Leilani, Leilani, hmmm, muy bonito*" (very pretty), I say with a smile.

Or,

> "*Hola, me llamo Norma. ¿Cómo te llamas?*"
>
> "*Me llamo Jennifer.*"

"¿Jennifer? ¡¿Jennifer López?!"

"No . . ."

"Jennifer López . . . ¡¡mucho gusto!! ¡Clase, Jennifer López!"

I encourage the class to say *mucho gusto*. *"¡Increíble, una persona famosa en mi clase de español!"* These are all cognates and the students understand.

"No, me llamo Jennifer . . ."

▶️🎞️ After doing this, I ask the students to go meet five new classmates so they can use what I have just demonstrated several times. Then I have a follow-up:

"¿Cómo se llama él?" (What is his name?), I say to a female student, pointing to a male.

She hesitates. I lead on with *"Se llama . . . Se llama . . ."*

"Se llama Sean." (His name is Sean.)

"Y tú, ¿cómo te llamas?" (And you? What is your name?)

"Me llamo Anne."

"¿Cómo se llama ella?" I say, pointing at a female student.

"Se llama . . . ," I lead on,

"Se llama Brooke." (Her name is Brooke.)

While doing this activity I start memorizing everybody's name, which takes a few classes to do, but memorizing names shows that you care and that you are interested in them as people, not just as students. It establishes a good connection with the students. I sometimes memorize their middle and last names too (from the roster), so when they make a funny mistake or do something unusual I can call them by their full name just like parents do: *"¡Jillian Rochelle Pearlmutter, ay caramba!"* Try it, it's funny.

▶️🎞️ Another useful and fun activity is pretending to be a famous person. These are the directions I give: *"Asume la personalidad de alguien famoso, por ejemplo, yo soy Penélope Cruz"* (Assume the personality of a famous person, for example, I am Penelope Cruz). Notice the essential words for understanding the directions are all cognates which can be easily understood. Still, you should demonstrate the activity first:

>*"Hola, me llamo Penélope Cruz. ¿Cómo te llamas?"*

>*"Me llamo Lady Gaga."*

>*"¿Lady Gaga? ¡Mucho gusto!"*

>*"Igualmente."*

Give the students a few minutes to think about their new personality, then instruct them to go meet five new people. This is a fun way to practice the same thing. Students laugh out loud with some of the personalities their fellow students come up with. After a few minutes of this, continue with a follow-up:

>*"¿Cómo se llama él? ¿Cómo se llama ella?"*

>*"Él se llama Barack Obama, ella se llama Cristina Aguilera."*

And I, starstruck, go meet them.

Your first day should set the tone of the course. These activities say: "I will speak in the target language as much as possible. I will use the language in context rather than dissect it grammatically. I will provide opportunities for you to practice what is being presented. I will include humor in the activities whenever possible."

LESSON PLANNING

The lesson plan—don't leave home without it. Excellent teachers always, no matter how many years of experience and how many times they have taught the course, have a lesson plan. But especially for a new teacher, thinking step-by-step about what one is going to do is essential. A lesson plan gives teachers confidence and makes them look organized.

There are different types of lesson plans. They vary depending on one's style and experience. As a novice teacher I remember writing down with great detail just about everything I was going to say or do in class. It would take up several pages. Ten years later, it shrunk to an outline, to something more like a road map with just the class activities and their order. Ten years after that, it started to grow in length again. As you get older, you start for-getting things, imagine that. So now my lesson plans include reminders like: Collect homework, Return exams, or Take roll.

Spanish 2
Pura vida Chapter 7
Day four

7:55	*Connect laptop*
	Return old homework
8:00	*Warm-up*
	Ask about their weekend
	Tell them what happened to me at the mall
5 min.	*Go over yesterday's homework*
	*(*Collect homework!)*
10-12 min.	*Input -PowerPoint "My weekend with Antonio Banderas"*
5 to 8 min.	*Guided practice: Exercise 5, pg. 253*
15 min.	*Communicative activity: "Best vacation" group writing directly on the board.*
	Arrange groups of 4 (sign off 1 - 6)
	*(*Take roll during the activity!)*
	Follow-up: Vote for best and most creative
	*(*Bring prizes!)*
If there is more time:	*Do Exercise 6, pg. 255*
Last 5 min.	*Tomorrow: Comparisons/ give examples Read pages. 244-45*
	Project and read comic strip.
	*(*Bring comic strip!)*
	Remind the students about exam date.

Other teachers prefer more detailed lesson plans like the following:

Wednesday, May 9, 2012

Foods, Drinks, and Nutrition | Homework: Grammar 8.1, Ex. 1–2 (pp. 300–1)

:00 **Greeting / Warm-up:** Signature activity from the handout – *La comida*. Be sure to highlight that the sentences at the bottom of the page are in the preterit.

:07 **Homework:** Ex. 1–2, *Dos mundos* pp. 300–1. Do a very brief review of the direct object pronouns, emphasizing the difference in the third-person forms for direct (*lo, la, los, las*) and indirect (*le, les*) object pronouns.

:12 **Input (PowerPoint) / Guided practice (questions on bottom of slides):** The PowerPoint is essentially a list of different foods and drinks, reflecting the vocabulary-centric nature of the chapter. Sections: breakfast, lunch, dinner, seafood, vegetables, fruits, meat.

> PLAN B: Project pp. 276–77 in the textbook using the document camera to talk about meals from yesterday. Ask the following questions taken from the PowerPoint:
>
> • *¿Qué desayunaron esta mañana? ¿Qué desayunan normalmente?* (What did you all eat for breakfast this morning? What do you normally eat for breakfast?)
>
> • *¿Ya almorzaron? Si sí, ¿qué almorzaron? Si no, ¿qué quieren almorzar hoy?* (Did you already eat lunch? If yes, what did you eat for lunch? If no, what do you want to eat for lunch today?)
>
> • *¿Qué quieren cenar hoy? ¿Cuáles comidas cenan normalmente?* (What do you want to eat for dinner today? What foods do you normally eat for dinner?)
>
> • *¿A ustedes les gustan los mariscos? ¿Cuál es su marisco favorito?* (Do you all like seafood? What is your favorite type of seafood?)
>
> • *¿Les gustan las legumbres? ¿Cuáles legumbres no comen?* (Do you all like vegetables? What vegetables do you not eat?)
>
> • *¿Les gustan las frutas?* (Do you all like fruit?)
>
> • *¿Hay vegetariano/a(s) en la clase? Si sí, ¿hace cuánto tiempo que eres/son vegetariano/a(s)?* (Are there vegetarians in the class? If yes, how long have you been a vegetarian?)

:25 **Guided practice (PowerPoint):** Divide the students into groups of three or four and ask that they categorize a number of the foods and drinks from the presentation into groups that contain substantial amounts of the following: protein, carbohydrates, calcium, vitamin A, vitamin C, grease/fat, and sugar. Ask one student in each group to be the secretary and to write down the group's responses. At the end of the activity, ask a few volunteers to read the foods/drinks they chose to put in certain nutritional categories. Then ask the follow-up questions on the next slide about nutrition.

> PLAN B: Have the students do Activity 2, *La nutrición*, on p. 278 in groups. The activity on the PowerPoint is adapted from this activity, so the process will be the same as above, except that the follow-up questions below may only be shared orally with the students:
>
> • *¿Cuáles son las comidas más ricas?* (What are the richest foods?)
>
> • *¿Cuáles son unas bebidas muy deliciosas?* (What are some delicious drinks?)
>
> • *¿Qué contienen estos alimentos? ¿Son saludables o no? ¿Por qué?* (What do these items contain? Are they healthy for you or not? Why?)

:35 **Communicative activity (in pairs):** *Búscalo tú: Las comidas y bebidas favoritas* from the handout. This is an information-gap activity. The students have to work together and ask each other questions to discover the information they are missing about the people in the activity. Each student has a different set of information and cannot look at the other individual's sheet. A model is provided on the PowerPoint.

Extra time I: Grammar practice activity (whole class): Activity 1 – *Las comidas del día* (p. 278). The students have to use direct object pronouns to talk about whether or not they eat a certain food for breakfast, lunch, or dinner, or as a dessert.

Extra time II: Written / communicative activity (individually, then in pairs): Activity 3 – *¿Qué vamos a comer hoy?* (p. 279). The students will each prepare two different menus for the day (all three meals, plus dessert[s]), using the menus in the book as models. One menu should contain only their favorite foods and drinks, while the other should be very healthy. After the written portion of the activity, the students compare their menus using the questions in the book and decide which is best, healthiest, etc.

:45 **Pre-grammar (PowerPoint):** *gustar/encantar* and food. A full explanation of this construction is given on the PowerPoint, including a comparison between English and Spanish forms and a comparison between using the *gustar/encantar* constructions with verbs versus with nouns (here, foods). The most important thing to emphasize here is the agreement between the subject (the food—what, for English speakers, is usually the object of the "liking" action rather than the subject) and the verb.

:50 Last-minute questions / Goodbyes

Instructional Sequence

The instructional sequence in lesson plans varies from day to day and also depends on what is being introduced, but the following is a typical sequence:

Day 1
Greeting / Warm-up
Review / homework
Introduction of new material
Guided practice
Communicative task
Wind down

Day 2
Greeting / Warm-up
Review / homework
More input
Communicative tasks
Wind down

Warm-up

Start your class with a greeting and a few minutes of warm-up questions. A warm-up is a casual, personal extension of the greeting:

"Good morning!"

"How are you?" (The usual response is "tired.")

"How many classes do you have?"

"What class takes the most time?"

"What is your favorite class?"

"Do you have a lot of homework?"

A warm-up is not necessarily a review, although it could be cleverly combined. If you are going over descriptions, you can veer your questions toward describing someone. If daily activities, you can ask what students usually do on weekends, at night, or on long weekends. If preterit, ask what they did the day before. If future, ask what they are planning to do that day or that weekend. The content of the chat has to match their linguistic level and the vocabulary they already know. Nothing new should be introduced here, otherwise it would feel like starting a car in second gear or engaging in a philosophical discussion without first having coffee. Warm-up questions could include:

"What are your plans for today?"

"Do you have an exam coming up?"

"How many hours did you sleep last night?"

"That is a pretty sweater, where did you get it?"

"What is your favorite day of the week?"

"What is your favorite season?"

"What's the weather like today?"

"Have you heard anything interesting in the news?"

"What did you have for dinner last night?"

"Do you know what happened to me yesterday?"

"I have a joke . . ."

Providing Input

We dedicate the next chapter to this very important concept, but for now let's just say that "input" is when the teacher presents new material, be it vocabulary or grammar, in context. The new forms are presented in stories (real or fictional) or anecdotes (true or invented). This can be enhanced with technology (YouTube or PowerPoint) or with projected transparencies of drawings to aid comprehension. You can also go "no-tech" by going at it with good use of gestures, repetition, pauses, and drama. These stories should be briefly interrupted by comprehension checks, which are questions we ask the students to make sure they are following what we are saying. (More on this in Chapter 2.)

Guided Practice

After presenting the new forms, students start using them in an easy and controlled way, with simple and specific practice exercises like multiple choice or matching columns. Some of these exercises may be communicative, but they are not usually open-ended.

Communicative Tasks

At this stage, students are given the opportunity to use the language in a more open setting to achieve a real outcome. These tasks simulate scenes requiring true communication and provide a lot of opportunities for output. There will be much more about communicative tasks in Chapter 3.

Wind Down

To wrap things up, I usually say what we are going to learn the next day. And to end on a positive note, I project one of the many comic strips I collect. Even if the joke is lame, they will shake their heads and smile. I also say enthusiastically, *"¡Hasta mañana, clase!"* (Until tomorrow, class!), and demand the same response back: *"¡Hasta mañana!"*

Armed with a lesson plan, even the most anxious new teacher will feel his or her confidence increase day by day. Before you know it, going to your class will be like walking into a living room full of relatives, and standing in front of the class addressing your students will be no problem at all.

Summary Questions

1. What can you do to reduce your anxiety the first few days of teaching?

_____

_____

2. What are most students probably thinking the first day of class?

_____

_____

3. Should you use the target language the first day of class? Why? Why not?

_____

_____

4. What should you wear the first day of class?

_____

_____

Scenarios

Scenario 1

On your first day of class you check your e-mail right before leaving your house and you discover that there was a last-minute classroom change. You can't find your room for some time and when you finally do, you are late, sweaty, and breathing heavily because you were rushing to get there. Your "cool" and your well-rehearsed beginning have been ruined. What do you do?

_____

_____

_____

Scenario 2

You start class speaking in the target language. You are making sure every-thing is comprehensible by using cognates, drawings, or pointing at props. But one student rebels and speaks up complaining that he doesn't under-stand ANYTHING and asking you to please speak English. What do you do?

_____

_____

2 • Introducing Grammar and Vocabulary

NORMA LÓPEZ-BURTON

You have successfully survived the first day of class and have learned about the importance of lesson planning. Next in the instructional sequence is to start providing language input and to optimally present the grammar and vocabulary. In Part II we will tell you why this has been shown to be the best way to teach a second language, and we will describe the theories that support it, but for now, take my word for it.

COMPREHENSIBLE INPUT

One of the teacher's most important roles is to provide language input. What students hear and understand from the teacher, they will most likely repeat. But not just any input will have this salubrious effect. The input must be comprehensible. In other words, the teacher cannot talk about the meaning of life in a beginning language class. What the teacher says must be understandable by using material the students already know through the use of cognates, gestures, drawings, or images. But "comprehensible" is not the only requirement. The input must also engage the student by being humorous, sad, or interesting in some way. If it has these qualities, the student will have a better chance of *acquiring* the words or phrases and thereby of internalizing them subconsciously and producing them later on.

¿Entendéis? means "Do you understand?" but it sounds like "In ten days."

    In this chapter you will learn how to introduce grammar and vocabulary in context. I will also provide you with examples of how you can turn the events of your own life, stories you've read, and even your own students' lives into comprehensible input.

    Do you remember learning your second language? Did you ever surprise yourself by blurting out phrases you had not studied, or by making a clever statement that just seemed to come out of nowhere? Let me give you an example. I remember an old professor who one day lost his temper and stepped into the hallway swearing about a long e-mail he had received from a student. Who did these students think they were, anyway? How could any-body expect him to have the time to read such a long e-mail? He kept going on and on about it in a very funny way. People started coming out of their offices to watch him, and everyone was laughing. Another professor said, "You are just an old fuddy-duddy. Isn't he an old fuddy-duddy? Ha, ha, an old fuddy-duddy, I tell you." I stood there smiling and amused by the whole thing. He kept ranting and the woman kept chuckling and repeating the same thing. A few weeks later, my husband was complaining about some politician. He kept ranting at the newspaper. I thought it was pretty funny, and out of the blue I said, "You are just an old fuddy-duddy." I stopped, sur-prised: Why did I say that? Where did that come from? And then I realized—it was from the office a few weeks ago. I had no idea what "fuddy-duddy" meant; I hadn't written the word down, hadn't looked up its meaning or etymology. I hadn't even tried to remember the word so I could use it later. It just came out. The context of the two situations was similar, the linguistic component had been repeated in a meaningful way, and so my brain just came up with it subconsciously. I did not learn that phrase; I acquired it.

Acquisition occurs because humans remember things that are memo-rable. Routine is easily forgotten, but an incident, a break in the routine, is what is remembered. You don't remember every walk you took to school, but you do remember that one day you saw a cute puppy, and how he peed on his owner's leg, and how embarrassed and annoyed the owner looked, and how the other kids were laughing. You not only remember the situation, you remember the puppy, the weather, the way the kids started laughing and pointing at the man, etc., etc.

We remember funny, sad, interesting, or unusual things that we observe or do. If students are in a boring class, mechanically writing things down and allowed to be passive, they will not store much in their subconscious. They will go home, study, memorize, pass the test, and forget all the important things you were trying to teach them a few weeks later. We must connect any information we teach to meaningful, repetitive usage, or to something memorable, or else the student will forget.

But being in the classroom is not the same as being immersed in the language, and with the limited time we have with our students, we can't expect miracles. We can, however, try to mimic real life as much as possible by presenting situations in context with interesting, funny, or memorable ways that students remember. Our goal is to facilitate acquisition. What is the alternative? Go over vocabulary lists? Explain grammar rules and provide isolated examples to memorize?

Many teachers feel that teaching grammar or vocabulary Is their main role. We can't teach fluency—that is a process that just happens—but we can teach *something*: we can teach rules! As a result, students learn mostly rules and don't hear the language in context. The only problem is that when they later try to apply the rules to say something, they take too long digging them up and so lose the listener's interest.

Students will better remember what you *actually say* in class than what you *tell* them to say. This struck me one day when I was visiting a Spanish 101 teacher from Argentina. Each Spanish-speaking country has its own regionalisms and ways of speaking, and I always respect that, but I tell all my teachers that they must also use the standard vocabulary and structures presented in the text to ensure that they will be understood in all twenty-one Spanish-speaking countries. In this particular class, the Argentine teacher had a student write some sentences on the board, and instead of writing *¿Tienes mi libro?* (Do you have my book?), he wrote *¿Tenés mi libro?*, using the Argentine way of conjugating the verb *tener*. The teacher corrected the "mistake" out loud and said, *"¡Tienes, Mike, tienes!"* She went to the back to talk to me briefly and expressed her frustration: *"Tienes* is in the book, it's in their homework, I tell them all the time, I don't understand!" As we continued talking, a student tried to get our attention. The teacher interrupted our chat and asked the student if he had a question, saying, *"Che, Rob, ¿tenés una pregunta?"* Bingo! That is why the students were using that form and not the one in the book. She was saying: "Do as I tell you, not as I do."

That is the power of input over explicit instruction. Learners repeat what we say in class. Because of the way the brain and comprehensible input work together, students who find themselves in a similar context will automatically recall what they have heard many times in class and produce it. So we have to take advantage of this and use the language as much as possible, because it will be what the students will repeat.

In class I always use phrases like *¡No te lo creo!* (I don't believe it!) or *¡No me digas!* (You don't say!). I don't tell them that *digas* is the second person informal subjunctive form of *decir* or that *me* is a pronoun. Nothing. I just say it in context, and my body language and facial expression explain it all. Over time students learn not only to repeat it automatically but also to use it appropriately. Moreover, they will sense and subconsciously get the word order without my pointing it out. And they don't produce mistakes such as *Te no lo creo* (You don't it I believe) or *Lo te no creo* (It you don't I believe). I have said the phrase so many times that the syntax is familiar to them. It can't be anything but *no-te-lo-creo*. Repetition gives us a feeling of what sounds right or not.

Taking up French later in life, I have had the opportunity to reflect on my own learning and think about what helps me learn. As an adult learner I have benefited from grammar rules. They are useful to figure out what to say or write correctly. But to think about all these rules while you are trying to construct a simple sentence is unnerving. I would lose friends! In French, if I want to say "We will give it to her," I have to remember to say the subject (it is optional in Spanish), then conjugate the verb in the first person: *je vais, tu vas, il va, nous allons*. OK, I need "we": *Nous allons*. Now the pronouns; the direct pronoun goes first: *Nous allons le*. The indirect pronoun goes next: *Nous allons le lui*. Now the verb, which cannot be conjugated because there are two verbs together, so the second one has to be in the infinitive: *Nous allons le lui donner*. And if I want to say the same sentence in the negative, I have to insert two more words, *ne* and *pas* in the right order. The *ne* goes right after the subject and the *pas* after the *allons*: *Nous n'allons pas le lui donner*. (And sometimes it feels like the order will have to change if it is Wednesday or if it is raining!) The knowledge of these rules has helped me construct these sentences, but by the time the second hand makes a full rotation, I will have produced only half a sentence. I can't carry on a conversation like that. Even my own mother would not wait for me!

But repetition for input has to be used correctly. I remember as a child in Puerto Rico, I had an elementary school English teacher who used a song to introduce new vocabulary. I still remember it (see Figure 1).

After having us memorize it, the teacher would ask, *"Clase, ¿cómo se dice gallina en inglés?"* (Class, how do you say *gallina* in English?) So we would

Pollito-chicken, **gallina**-hen, **lápiz**-pencil *y* **pluma**-pen.
Ventana-window, **puerta**-door, **maestra**-teacher *y* **piso**-floor.

Figure 1

have to mentally go over the song: *Pollito*–chicken, *gallina*–hen. HEN! *"¡Muy bien! Y ¿cómo se dice pluma en inglés?"* (Very good! And how do you say *pluma* in English?) Again a quick reference to the song: *Pollito*–chicken, *gallina*–hen, *lápiz*–pencil y *pluma*–pen. PEN! *"¡Muy bien!"* But if she asked for *"piso,"* the last item in the song, we would have to sing the whole thing! Sure, a song like that does help you remember words for a test, and she probably had a "mission accomplished" feeling when we tested well. When we are writing we have more time to remember a song or any gimmick we use, but it is useless—counterproductive even—if we actually want to say something. The listener will walk away before we can get the words out.

Input from the teacher and repetition are essential for acquisition to occur, and the more words and structure the students acquire, the better, because it shortens the time they "take leave of the conversation" to look up rules in the computer files of their brains. So be sure to use the target language in class as much as possible. Remember, you are the main source of comprehensible input. The lion's share of class time has to be dedicated to input, whether it is telling a story, giving directions for an activity, a warm-up, a reminder, hellos, goodbyes, interjections, or exclamations . . . and all that must be in the target language so your students can hear how the language is normally used.

PROVIDING INPUT

What can we say to make a comprehensible input story memorable? It doesn't have to be all fun and games. Students are curious about your life (imagine that!), so take advantage of their voyeuristic interest. Introduce any grammar point in the context of your life or daily routine. And, by the way, what you tell them doesn't have to all be true—it could be, as they say in the movies, "based on" or "inspired by" an event in your life. Or if you are a private person, make the whole thing up! Just say it in a convincing way so they believe what you are saying. They will be super-motivated by learning about your tawdry life, and at the same time get the input.

There are many sources of input:

- Personal stories (real or made-up, sad, funny, interesting, shocking)

- Made-up stories

- Stories with your own students as protagonists

- A familiar children's story

- Comic strips

- Short Internet videos (discussed in Chapters 4 and 12)

- Songs (discussed in Chapter 4)

- Written short stories, poems, newspaper articles, or magazines

We'll now look at how you can go about mining these sources.

Personal Stories

Students are interested in your life, so talk about yourself, your routine, or something that happened to you, to a friend, or to your parents. Narrate something you dreamt, something you are going to do, something hypothetical you would like to do. Talk about your likes and dislikes, or your preferences. I heard a comedian say, "Everything that happens to you in life is either good or it's material."

One day I spoke about something that happened to me at an airport (I embellished the story a little, but the core was true). I was introducing narration in the past. This is what I told them in Spanish:

Last year something incredible happened to me. I was on a flight from Tucson to Sacramento. I was really thirsty, so I drank water, drank a can of soda, and drank and drank more water. (Note the repetition of the target structure). Pretty soon I wanted to go to the bathroom, but the big lady next to me sitting in the aisle seat was sleeping, snoring actually, so I decided to wait. I waited, and waited, and waited. (Again, repetition.) When the plane landed, I went directly to the bathroom. I went in and there was nobody. I was the only person in that huge bathroom. I was a little concerned, but I had to go, so I went ahead. Then suddenly I heard . . . Do you know what I heard? (Pause.) I heard the voice of a man! (I say this with big eyes and leaning forward. My students' eyes usually widen too.) Was it a man?! Was it a man or was it a woman with a deep voice? I opened the stall door just a little bit (I act this out) and I saw that it was a man! There was a man in the ladies' bathroom!! My heart <u>was</u> beating so fast! (Hand to my chest.) What do I do now? Suddenly, I <u>heard</u> another person come in. Perfect, I <u>thought</u>, two women against one man. I <u>opened</u> the door a little bit again (acting it out again) and to my horror, I <u>saw</u> that it <u>was</u> another man! How can that be? Then I <u>looked</u> carefully to the left side and guess what I <u>saw</u>? (Pause.) I <u>saw</u> urinals!! I <u>was</u> in the men's bathroom!

After the laughter dies down, I ask comprehension-check questions. If you think the story is too long, break it in half, ask questions in the middle, and then continue:

"Why <u>did I need</u> to go to the bathroom?"

"Because you <u>drank</u> a lot of water."

"What else <u>did I drink</u>?"

"You <u>drank</u> a soda."

"Why <u>couldn't I use</u> the bathroom in the plane?"

"Because the lady next to you <u>was asleep</u>." Etc.

With these questions, you check students' comprehension and they also practice producing the desired structure, with you gently correcting mistakes along the way. If the students are having difficulties producing the structure—after all, it is very new to them—then ask yes/no or other simple questions to help them out:

"<u>Did I drink</u> a lot of water or <u>did I drink</u> a lot of beer?"

"You <u>drank</u> a lot of water."

"<u>Was I</u> in a hurry to get out of the plane?"

"Yes, <u>you were</u> in a hurry."

You can also have a follow-up activity after any story, still focusing on the use of the new structure. For this one, try something like: "In groups of three students, guess what <u>happened</u> to me after I <u>discovered</u> I was in the men's bathroom. How <u>did</u> I get out of there?" Each group reaches a consensus and then reports to the class, at which time I divulge which group guessed what really happened while making sure to use the same vocabulary and grammar structures.

Made-up Stories

Sometimes teachers do not want to share their lives, so made-up stories are an alternative. To introduce food vocabulary, for example, narrate a date with a movie star of your choice and order food at an expensive restaurant. Make it funny. Have the movie star be in love with you and you be the one rejecting him or her. For events in the past, pick an important political figure, athlete, singer, artist, or TV personality, and say what you did on a trip you took together. Students will know it is made-up and will just relax and enjoy your creativity and imagination.

For family vocabulary, I tell my students that I am J-Lo's cousin, that her mom is my aunt and calls me N-Lo, and that J-Lo has always been jealous of me. The students know I am making this up and shake their heads smiling, but it is engaging because I keep going and describing our friendship and all the family connections. It's funny, they use *No me digas!* (You don't say!) on me!

Obviously made-up stories are funny, but you can also create an alter ego and sell your story without letting on to the students. A young teacher at our university thought her life was not so interesting. So, because she had just come out of a relationship, she decided to make up a new and im-proved boyfriend and contextualize everything around their new imaginary lives together. She excitedly introduced adjectives describing him and his family, taught activity verbs saying what they liked to do individually and as a couple, and introduced numbers by listing the prices of all the expen-sive trinkets he bought for her. The students were following all her stories with much interest, and every time she said she was going to tell the latest about her "Robert," they would put their pencils down and lean forward. The teacher's secret agenda every time was to introduce a new grammar point or vocabulary, and she was successful because the students were very atten-tive, and they understood almost everything.

One day she had to introduce the future tense and decided to tell her students about an upcoming trip to see her "boyfriend's" parents for the first time that weekend. She said she was very nervous and excited and told them—using the targeted future tense—a prediction of what was going to happen that weekend. The following Monday, the first thing her students said was, "SO . . . WHAT HAPPENED?!" The young teacher had forgotten about her made-up story, but quickly recovered and said she would tell them the next day. The students had swallowed the story hook, line, and sinker! She was surprised at the power of her storytelling. It made for a very animated and engaged class, with the side effect being the understanding of a new structure within the context of an interesting story.

Stories with Your Own Students as Protagonists

To add a little variety and shift the attention from you, make up stories using your students as the main characters. It is important to choose students who you know for sure can take a joke, or ask a student to pick a name from a hat so you are not accused of picking on somebody.

To introduce the present progressive, I told this story to the class in the historical present:

> Do you know what happened to Peter? (I point at Peter who is sitting in the front row.) It's in all the newspapers! First his parents decide to go on a trip and leave him home alone. Peter then decides to have a harmless little party for the class and invites . . . (I mention all the students in the class) . . . but he forgets one, Joe. Joe is offended and is mad (I gesture Joe being mad). So Joe goes to the store and buys a pair of binoculars to observe the party at a distance. The day of the party all the other students arrive. What is happening at the party? Well, Jane is dancing like Britney Spears (I use gestures for each of the actions I mention), Gina is eating a lot of chips and salsa , Rick and Charlie are singing, and what is Joe doing? He is watching! Veronica is sleeping, Nick is studying, as always, Melissa is talking and talking and talking. And what is Joe doing? He is watching! (I mention several more names and activities that are going on in the party, using gestures to aid comprehension.)

This is a good point to review by asking comprehension questions: "Class, who is Peter inviting to the party? Who is missing? Joe buys a pair of binoculars, why? He wants to see what people are doing at the party, right? What is Jane doing at the party? What is Gina doing? What is Veronica doing," etc.

Back to the story:

> . . . And what is Joe doing? He is watching! Then he has an idea. He calls all his buddies from the fraternity and says, "Hey, I am having a party, you are invited!" He calls a lot of people and tells them they are invited

to his party. But instead of telling them to go to his house, Joe sends them to Peter's house, and Peter asks, "What is happening?" And what is Joe doing? He is watching! At the house people are drinking, breaking things, being loud . . . Peter is saying, "What is happening!" And what is Joe doing? He is watching!

After several more actions in the progressive, I again stop for comprehension questions: "Who is arriving? What are they doing? And what is Joe doing?"

I continue the story:

Then, do you know who arrives? Peter's parents arrive and see the big disaster. OK, now in groups of three, guess what happens at the end. What do you see the parents doing? What does Peter do? What happens to Joe at the end?

Each group reports to class and together vote for the best ending.

Obviously, this is a made-up story, but the students always get into it because I am using them as the stars of the story.

A Familiar Children's Story

Sometimes I use familiar children's books as a source of input. I prefer that it be well-known because knowing the story line aids comprehension. I project the story images onto the screen without the words (I photocopy the story from a book, then delete the words), and narrate the story myself using the target language, asking comprehension questions along the way. Students are receptive to this because it reminds them of their childhood: "Oh, I used to read that so many times!" "That was my favorite story," or "Wow, I haven't heard that story in a long time."

I have used many different children's books, but one of my favorites is *Are You My Mother?*, by P. D. Eastman. This book is wonderfully repetitive, so it is perfect for providing input. I have used this story for the verb "to be" (which is a little troublesome in Spanish), for verbs in the present tense narrated in the historical present, for verbs in the past, for adjectives . . . Another good one is *Alexander and the Terrible, Horrible, No Good, Very Bad Day*, by Judith Viorst. This book is funny, and it is great to emphasize adjectives or events in the past. Some books are a little long, so I pick and choose the pages I want so as to keep the narration short and to the point.

Comic Strips

I always watch out for comic books with comic strips like the one in Figure 2. You know teaching has taken over your life when friends show you something funny and you respond, "That is great! I can use it for the future tense!" You can use one comic strip for several purposes at different levels (but with different students). I have used this particular strip for location adverbs, for adjectives/description, for verbs in the present tense, for narration in the past, and for future tense. When I use these, I show one or two frames at a time. If you show everything at once, the students get ahead of you and don't listen to what you have to say. So you can use a projector and cover the bottom frames with a piece of paper, revealing them when appropriate.

Using the comic strip in Figure 2 for location adverbs:

A man arrives at his apartment. He is <u>in front of</u> . . . (my pointer goes from the man to the door as I say "in front of") the door and he hears, "Goodness, my husband!" He comes in furious and slams the door and breaks a picture frame. Do you see where the picture frame is? Yes, it is <u>behind</u> the door. (Again, I show location with a pointer every time I introduce a location adverb.) Where is his wife? She is <u>to the right of</u> the bed and the little bear is <u>on top of</u> the bed. He looks <u>under</u> the bed and nothing. He looks at the closet. The wife is <u>next to</u> the closet, then the wife gets <u>in front of</u> the closet and says, "Noooo!" The husband is now <u>in front of</u> the closet, opens it, and finds out what he suspected: his cookies!

Using the same comic strip for adjectives/general description:

An <u>old man</u> arrives at his house. He is <u>short</u>, looks like <u>he is tired</u>. What is he wearing? He is wearing an <u>old hat</u> and a <u>black suit</u>. He has <u>big ears</u>, doesn't he? He is wearing <u>small eyeglasses</u>. He comes in the house and sees his wife. What is she wearing? She is wearing pajamas and <u>comfortable slippers</u>. Is she <u>young or old</u>? She <u>is old</u>, like her <u>old husband</u>. He is <u>pretty mad</u> and she looks <u>worried</u>. Hmm, I wonder why? Is she wearing <u>small eyeglasses</u> too? She is not wearing <u>small eyeglasses</u>. (Repetition is very important. It may seem redundant to you, but beginners welcome repetition.) The <u>old man</u> looks everywhere and finally looks in the closet and finds what he suspected: his cookies!

Figure 2

Using the same comic strip for verbs in the present tense:

A husband <u>walks</u> to his apartment and <u>hears</u>, "Goodness, my husband!" The man <u>opens</u> the door and <u>comes in</u> furious and slams the door. His wife <u>looks</u> at him, worried. He <u>tries to find</u> something or someone. What <u>is</u> he <u>looking</u> for? He <u>looks</u> under the bed and <u>finds</u> nothing. <u>Looks</u> everywhere but <u>can't find</u> anything. The wife <u>looks</u> at the closet. He <u>looks</u> at the closet. (Again, repetition.) The wife <u>goes</u> to the closet and <u>says</u>, "Noooooo!" He <u>walks</u> to the closet and <u>opens</u> it. There he <u>finds</u> what he <u>is looking</u> for. What <u>is</u> he <u>looking</u> for? He <u>is looking</u> for his cookies!

For narrating in the past, just use the past where all the present is in the previous example. And finally, for future tense, predict what the man and the woman are going to do before each frame. Not all comic strips are this flexible, but many are. Collect and classify them for later use.

Other Sources of Input

Not all input is oral. Other sources of input include short stories, poems, newspaper or magazine articles, and short texts from the textbook. We will discuss these in Chapter 4, "Teaching Culture." Internet videos or songs are also sources of input; both are discussed in Chapter 4 and in Chapter 12, "The Use of Technology."

Clearly, there are numerous ways that students will get comprehensible input. But don't forget that YOU are the main source. You must provide input the whole class time, from the first greeting until "see you tomorrow." Class time is limited—make the most of it by using the target language as much as possible.

REVIEW: TIPS FOR PROVIDING INPUT

- Think of what you are going to say, keeping the new vocabulary or new grammar in mind. Don't feel you have to introduce every new vocabulary word or every possible grammar exception in the story. Think of something that will cover a lot of vocabulary that you can repeat over and over during the story. Remember, students won't recall something you mention only once.

- Use vocabulary and structures that have already been presented in the book before the current lesson. Students' understanding of the story will depend on this.

- Use images imaginatively: embellish, add drama, be wild, stretch the truth, lie . . . but make it memorable. Good teachers are good storytellers.

- Base your story on known material, so that the only "unknown" is what you are introducing. The majority of what you say must be comprehensible.

- Include fun and humor whenever possible.

- Find opportunities to repeat the vocabulary or the structure you are introducing. Remember, acquisition happens with input, repetition, and time.

- Ask comprehension-check questions to make sure the students are following you.

Summary Questions

1. What is comprehensible input?

_____

_____

_____

2. What does it mean to "acquire" a word or phrase?

_____

_____

_____

3. What are the sources of input?

_____

_____

_____

4. What elements must comprehensible input have in order to be effective?

_____

_____

_____

Scenarios

Scenario 1

A French teacher was going over the *passé composé*. Most past tense construc-tions need the verb *avoir* to form the past tense, but there are 17 pesky verbs that require *être*, not *avoir*. And the problem is that these are not obscure ut-terances; most are very high frequency verbs, and students make mistakes all the time. The teacher composed his input story emphasizing those verbs that require *être*, had his students repeat the structures, asked questions, did a follow-up, and went on to guided practice. Because it was fresh in their mem-ories, the students did well and chose *être* over *avoir*, but by the next day they were consistently forgetting which situation required which verb.

To help them, the instructor recalled that there was a way to remember all of the situations relatively easily, and taught his students the following mnemonic. Each letter in the words Dr. and Mrs. Vandertrampp stands for one of the verbs that require *être* as an auxiliary:

D – *devenir*

R – *revenir*

M –*mourir*

R – *retourner*

S – *sortir*

V – *venir*

A – *arriver*

N – *naitre*

D – *descendre*

E – *entrer*

R – *rentrer*

T – *tomber*

R – *rester*

A – *aller*

M – *monter*

P – *partir*

P – *passer*

1. Do you think this mnemonic helped the students remember the verbs that require *être* in the written exam? Why?

_____

_____

2. Do you think this helped the students remember during oral exchanges? Why?

_____

_____

3. What would you have done differently to help the students remember these verbs? Explain.

_____

_____

Scenario 2

A traditional language teacher who bases almost all of her classes on the instruction of grammar decides one day to give comprehensible input a chance. She starts her class with a greeting and a review of the structure covered the day before. This is done in English or the target language depending on the complexity of their questions, and takes about 15 minutes. Next, she creates a context, an interesting and engaging comprehensible input story. She carefully weaves through the story many different examples of double-object pronouns (the target structure) but, because there are many examples, she only gets to say each example once. She asks comprehension-check questions and the students seem to understand what she said, but very few of them can produce the phrases with double-object pronouns. She concludes that students have not acquired anything and proceeds to give a grammar explanation in English.

1. What is this teacher's idea of acquisition?

_____

_____

2. What is this teacher's idea of comprehensible input?

_____

_____

3. What could you have done better?

_____

_____

4. What needs to happen for acquisition to actually take place?

_____

_____

_____

_____

3 · Communicative Tasks

NORMA LÓPEZ-BURTON

In a student-centered classroom, communicative tasks are the main event. Communication is the reason why the students have memorized vocabulary and studied the grammar. As teachers, we have to distinguish between the knowledge of the rules and the capacity to use those rules in an efficient and appropriate way. Imagine yourself learning how to use a sewing machine, learning about the different fabrics, threads, and colors, but never being given the opportunity to sew a garment or make a quilt. Tasks are the hands-on creative stage of learning a language. We have to sit down in front of that sewing machine and see what we can do with it.

WHAT ARE TASKS?

A task is an activity with a goal in which students use language to achieve a real outcome. Well-designed tasks simulate scenes requiring true communication and provide many more opportunities for output than in a teacher-centered class. Because communicative tasks are more entertaining than a lecture format, they reduce anxiety, fight boredom, and bring a measure of spontaneity that textbook exercises can't provide.

Elements of a Communicative Task

Communicative tasks usually involve employing the language in an open-ended and creative way, using the lesson's new vocabulary and grammar

point and ideally including some useful cultural content. Here are the essential features that all such tasks should have.

- **Engaging content**: A communicative task must grab the students' attention and interest. It has to motivate the student to complete the task. One activity might be: "Talk to your partner and list all the items you each have in your backpack." But something more engaging could be: "Make a list of ten items you predict are in your partner's backpack and talk to him/her to find out how many you got right."

- **Discovery**: The goal of the communicative exchange is to have students find out something they didn't know before. For example, if two students are asking each other questions, the information cannot be evident to both; the activity will require that one of them obtain information that the other one does not have. The exchange cannot be obvious. Students should not be asked to pair up for the purpose of describing themselves physically; they can see each other. A better task would be to describe each other's personalities, or describe the characteristics of an ideal mate. That information is not evident, and what is discovered is new.

- **Personal significance**: Your students must feel it is possible that a particular situation could happen to them. Of course, we all know we are carrying out the activity in the classroom—we are not in Paris or Perú!—but the task should mimic real life as much as possible. With the exception of competitive games, which do not necessarily mimic real situations, and given the right context and a believable situation, many activities can be brought to life. If characters are called for in the script of a role play, it is best if they really exist or are relevant to the students. Pretending to be Sarkozy, Salma Hayek, or Antonio Banderas is closer to life than asking them to imagine they are Juanita, Dietrich, Giuseppina, or Jacques. Who are these people and why should I care?

- **Purpose**: You need to have a clear purpose in communication. Including one of the following words gives purpose to an activity: *list, decide, share, order, rank, exchange, determine, compare, vote, draw, find out, contrast, plan out,* etc. This forces the learner to do something with the gathered information. If activities lack purpose, students quickly label the activity "busywork" and react accordingly. Telling them to do Exercise 3 just doesn't cut it. Consider the following example:

  > In groups of three, talk to your classmates about what they usually eat in the campus cafeteria. Then, *decide* who of the three eats healthier items, OR *rank* each student in the group as to who is the biggest to least spender, OR *compare* who eats more and who eats less, OR *find out* what items are the group's favorite or least favorite foods in the campus cafeteria, OR *vote* for the top three delicious foods in the cafeteria, etc.

- **Follow-up**: Don't let tasks just die when time is up. Let students know that feedback, oral or written, is always expected. If you are asking the students to collect data, analyze it. If you ask that they come up with incredible vacation plans, have students vote for the best one. If you have a competitive game, give a prize—a piece of candy, applause, a standing ovation, your respect . . . ☺

General Guidelines

- **Preparation**: Make sure the students know the key words and phrases they will need to carry out the task. Write them on the board and ask the students if they understand them.

- **Directions**: Tell students in the target language what you want them to accomplish by activity's end in a clear and concise way, using the "purpose words" mentioned above: decide, determine, compare, vote, draw, find out, contrast, plan out, etc.

- **Model**: Telling students what to do is not enough. Some pay attention, some don't. Some may get the general idea of what they are supposed to do, but are not completely certain. Modeling the activity using a student as a partner helps remove all doubt.

- **Teacher's hidden agenda**: This is the real reason for which you planned the activity. It may seem like fun and games for the students, but your ulterior motive is that students produce a particular verb tense, practice a particular function, or use certain vocabulary while carrying out the activity. Once your students start their group work, make sure they are practicing the concepts you had in mind. Roam around, listen, and steer them toward what you want them to produce.

- **Grouping**: Vary the student groups. If you issue a general statement like "OK, let's form groups of three," students will slowly look around to see what group to join. Some students will avoid eye contact so they are not asked to work with a particular student they don't like. This group negotiation will waste a lot of class time. Another problem is that some students pair up with friends or with a neighbor, which results in students always sharing information with the same individual, and because they already know each other, the linguistic purpose to communicate is diminished. There are many ways to vary the groupings:

To view the videos, go to yalebooks.com/languageteacher. The password is: learn.

- For pair work, name the right side of the class "Student 1," the left "Student 2." Student 1 must seek out a Student 2 partner, so that they don't always talk to the person sitting nearby.

- If you organize small groups, know how many students you have (let's say 25 students), divide that number by the groups you want (let's say groups of four), have them sign off in the target language from one to six, then ask all 1s to get together, all 2s to get together, etc. You will have one group of five.

- Use the grammar point you are covering to group students. If the subject is ordinal numbers, ask them to sign off by saying "First, Second, Third," etc. If talking about family, sign off saying "Mother, Father, Cousin," etc., in the target language. Then group "Mothers" together, "Cousins" together, and so on.

- Form groups based on what students wear or something they have in common. You may say: "Form groups of three students. Everybody with the same or similar color of shirt, get together." The same can be done with other items like type of shoes, same height, same birth month, same first letter in their name or last name, similar color of backpack, same type of pants, etc. The important thing is that you are telling the students to stand up and group themselves as directed. This eliminates a lot of guess-work, hurt feelings, and wasted time.

- **Spatial arrangements**: Depending on the activity, determine whether you want students to stand up so they can walk around and ask questions, form circles so they can talk to each other face-to-face, or be seated back-to-back so they don't see each other's information. Each activity will dictate the arrangement.

- **Roles**: Establish roles right after grouping. For example, some activities require a leader, a secretary, and a spokesperson. Make sure roles get determined before starting the activity. It is not enough to tell the students to choose a leader. Invariably, some students will not be listening or will be distracted by their new cute classmate. To keep things moving, you have to ask each group (always in the target language): "Who is the leader here?

And the secretary? Good, thank you. How about here? Perfect, thank you."

- **Monitor**. While the students are busy with the communicative activity, you could quickly take attendance or return a few papers, but your main role is to roam around answering questions and making sure that students are on the same page, are doing the right exercise, are following directions, or are not getting off track talking about their private lives.

- **Time**: Keep a quick pace. Call "time" before things start to drag. Give a "two-minute warning" when three-quarters of the class has reached the exercise's objective. Then use a signal you've adopted to stop the activity. Some teachers ask students to raise their hands, asking others for silence until they all have their hands up; others have a hand-clapping rhythm, and others yell "time," but flipping the lights off and on works best for me. Students get used to the signal and go back to their seats automatically—no need to yell or struggle asking them to stop the activity.

- **Follow-up**: With the whole class, check what the students have done. Comment on the result. Be interested, amazed, or horrified by the "new findings." This validates the students' work and lets them see their communication as something purposeful, not just another exercise.

TYPES OF TASKS

There are many different types of communicative tasks; some require involving the whole class, but many call for small-group work. The double aim of including communicative tasks in the classroom is to *generate output* and to *lead to an outcome that can be shared with others*. Each of the types of tasks presented below has those two very important characteristics. Don't forget to add to each of those activities the other elements we have discussed before: explaining the objective, including purpose words, having a linguistic hidden agenda, giving simple and clear directions, modeling the activity, roaming, checking on students, giving a "two-minute warning," doing a whole-class check requiring the new structure or vocabulary in the students' answers, following up, and doing something with the data gathered.

Guided Conversations

Many textbooks have guided conversations. These are activities specifically designed to practice a grammar point or a particular set of vocabulary. The questions are not open-ended, but guided and to the point. The goal is to converse with a classmate or small group in order to find out about preferences in food, activities, weather, classes, entertainment, etc. Because of their close-ended nature, the responses to guided questions are usually short and don't resemble a real conversation. So that these guided conversations don't fall flat, you should write a short list of appropriate "conversational reactions" or "back-channeling phrases" on the board and include them when you model the activity—phrases like "That's great," "Is that right?," "You don't say," "That's too bad," "No kidding?," "Me too," "Me neither," "That's terrible," "That figures," "That's interesting," etc. Students get a kick out of this and always include them in other conversations. After the activity is done, the follow-up for these conversations and many other types of tasks is "share small, share big, and share bigger." This means that a student first shares the information in pairs or small groups (share small), then two groups get together to see what the larger group has in common (share big), then all share with the class in a "whole-class check" (share bigger).

For example, given a list of possible activities, students are told to ask each other in pairs, "What did you do last summer?," and to react to what the partner says. The list may include camping, waterskiing, studying, traveling, working, sleeping, swimming, and so forth:

Student 1: What did you do last summer?

Student 2: I traveled to China.

Student 1: Really? When?

Student 2: In July.

Student 1: Wow. That's interesting!

After sharing small, ask two couples to share big, then finally do a whole-class check to share bigger.

Reach a Consensus

In small groups, the idea is to negotiate the different opinions of the members of the group and to come up with a consensus (the price of an article, a date, a number, a ranking, an opinion, etc.). It is important to monitor this carefully so that students, in the heated debate of trying to convince each other, don't slip back into their native language. A follow-up to this activity could be writing the results on the board, comparing the different groups' opinions or findings, and possibly reaching a class-wide conclusion.

Reach a Consensus Example

The Price Is Right

Secret agenda: To practice numbers from 1 to 1,000 or more.

Materials: PowerPoint images of everyday objects or objects from home (electronic tablets, digital cameras, cans of spaghetti, yogurt).

Procedure:
1. Review numbers from 1 to 1,000 or more.
2. Ask students to form groups of three.
3. Ask each group's name and write them on the board.
4. Show the image, let the students think and reach a price consensus in the target language.
5. The spokesperson must give a dollar-and-cents amount (so they are required to say more numbers).
6. The number closest to the real price wins one point.
7. The group with the most points wins the prize.

Directions to students: In groups of three, decide what the price of each of the displayed objects is. Reach a consensus and report to the class. The group with the most correct guesses will win the prize.

Follow-up: Announce the winner and deliver the promised prize.

Variations:
1. If technology fails, grab items from your briefcase.
2. Ask each small group to take a turn and come up with one article for the rest of the class to guess.

Information Gap

For this type of activity, students are paired and given the task of completing something together: a chart, a grid, a schedule, a list, etc. One student has information that the other does not, and they have to work together to complete the task. Usually students are seated back-to-back so they can't peek at each other's paper and so are forced to rely only on oral information.

Information Gap Example 1

Do You Want to Do Something Together?

Secret agenda: To practice vocabulary for courses in college, days of the week, telling time, and the future.

Materials: Provide an empty grid with times in the column and days of the week in the row. Provide a sample dialogue, such as:

Student 1: Do you want to go to the movies?
Student 2: Sure, at what time?
Student 1: Monday at 7:00 p.m.
Student 2: I can't. I am going to play tennis with a friend. How about Wednesday at 3:00?

And so forth. After several attempts, students decide when to meet.

> **Students 1 and 2:** Great. Let's go to the movies, Thursday at 8:00 p.m.

Procedure:
1. Review the sample dialogue and suggest more possibilities of activities.
2. Give the students time to fill out the schedule. Remind them to do it in the target language.
3. Direct the students to stand up and ask some classmates for a date.

Directions to students: Fill out the grid with your activities for the week. Include class times, study times, times for doing homework, dates with friends, exercise plans, when you plan to take a nap or go to sleep, etc. Talk to your classmates and schedule three dates to do something fun where you both have an empty space.

Follow-up: Share small: In pairs have the students ask each other where they are going, at what time, and the name of the movie. Share big: Ask them to do the same in groups of four. Share bigger: Have a whole-class check and see where some students have decided to go. Ask for the name of the movie, the location, who else is going, etc. Make sure their answers produce the verbs in your secret agenda.

Variation: Students are checking schedules to study together, to go to a new restaurant, to go on vacation together for spring break, etc.

Information Gap Example 2

What Is the Name of That Building?

Secret agenda: To practice location adverbs such as: in front, to the right, in between, near, far, etc.

Materials: Provide a map of two interesting towns or cities from Google maps. One copy has buildings labeled, the other one doesn't. Provide a sample dialogue, such as:

Student 1: What is the name of the building to the right of
_____?
Student 2: That is Mercy Hospital. And to the left is a Taco Bell.
Student 1: And what is next to the Taco Bell?

And so forth.

Students 1 and 2: Which city do you like best? Why?

Procedure:
1. Review the sample dialogue and model the questions using a different map.
2. Pair up the students, ideally back-to-back so they don't see each other's papers. Remind them to use the target language.

Directions to students: Ask your classmate for the names of the buildings you see in the map provided. Your classmate will do the same with a different town for which you have information. Decide which town is more appealing to visit (or has the greater variety of restaurants, or is more spacious and green, or has the most entertainment, etc.).

Follow-up: Share small: In pairs have the students ask each other which is the better city and why. Share big: Have the

students do the same but in groups of four. Share bigger: Have
a whole-class check and ask which is the better city or town and
why. Make sure their answers produce the verbs in your secret
agenda.

Variation: Have a map of your campus or your city.

Role Play

These are scripted situations you give the students to perform in small
groups, or you can ask the students to prepare a skit following your guidelines. This type of activity is very useful because it makes students act out a
practical situation, thus simulating real life. There are two pitfalls with role
plays: shy students won't like them, and role plays can take a lot of class
time. For the sake of shy students, instead of having them perform in front
of the whole class (stage fright can be debilitating), have them go on "tour"
by having them perform in front of each of the other small groups. Make all
groups take turns performing for each other. This also solves the excessive
class time issue. Don't ask every group to perform at the end as a whole-
class check, but only ask for one or two volunteers. It's OK that not all groups
perform the skit in front of the whole class because they have already gone
through it a couple of times on a smaller scale.

Role Play Example

You See a Friend at a Bookstore

Secret agenda: To practice, in a general way, vocabulary such as
numbers, greetings, and simple verbs.

Procedure: Pair up the students and have them rehearse the
dialogue first. Remind them to always use the target language.
Provide a sample dialogue, such as:

- Say hi, and ask how each is doing.
- Ask where each is living.
- Ask what classes each is taking.
- Ask what times each other's classes are.
- Mention how many books each has to buy for which classes.
- Say how much the books cost.
- Ask each other's phone numbers.
- Say goodbye.

Directions to students: Rehearse the role play in pairs, then go on "tour" and act it for other small groups.

Follow-up: Share small: Rehearse in pairs. Share big: Perform for another group. Share bigger: Have volunteers perform in front of the class.

Variations: Here are two other role plays:

1. You are at a party and strike up a conversation with someone:
   - Introduce yourselves.
   - Ask each other about classes, times, finals, likes and dislikes about foods or activities.
   - Comment on the party.
   - Describe and criticize what people are wearing and doing.
   - Gossip about some of the people at the party.
   - Agree to see each other again at another party.
2. You two are looking forward to graduation day and beyond. Ask each other:
   - When will you graduate?
   - Will you have a party?
   - What do you think will happen at graduation?
   - Will you look for a job or continue studying?
   - What kind of a job will you look for?
   - Will you get married?

Mixers

⏺🎞 This type of task requires the student to stand up and search for infor-mation from other classmates. There are advantages to having mixers: they break the monotony of the class, the students get to stand up and stretch, and they get to talk to different classmates. Following are some of the many types of activities under this category.

Signature Grid Activities

Here students ask many classmates the same question, searching for an affirmative answer. When the desired answer is found, the student gets the other student to sign on the square, and so on, until the whole grid is filled. I use this type of activity, but it is not my favorite because it does not mimic reality; in real life, nobody walks around aimlessly asking people questions out of the blue (unless they work for Gallup surveys). However, signature grids can be useful because they make students practice the vocabulary or grammar point you are presenting, but if they feel there is no purpose other than to fill out the grid, it becomes meaningless and will fall into the dreaded category of "busywork." Ways to spice it up are: (1) Have un-usual or funny questions. Instead of having a question like "Do you read every day?," include one that says "Do you read while in the bathroom?" Instead of "Are you looking for your book?," have a question that will elicit a chuckle, like "Are you looking for a spouse with money?" This makes stu-dents use the new structure to find out something new and interesting about their classmates. (2) Make the grid activity into a competitive game. I tell the class that the first three students to complete the grid will receive "fabulous prizes." Your students will be asking the questions, practicing the vocabulary you want, and now their aim is to win the game. The pace will pick up and their enthusiasm will be more evident. The prizes are not fabu-lous, really, just a chocolate drop, a mint, things like that; but you will be amazed by how hard they will work for a piece of candy or just to be able to say "I won!"

Signature Grid Example

What Do You Do?

Secret agenda: To practice reflexive verbs. **Note: The verbs in the examples below may not be reflexive in your target language.**

Materials: A grid with prompts to ask questions and space to write a name underneath. For example:

- Do you shave your legs?
- Do you comb your hair several times a day?
- Do you bathe every other day?
- Are you in love with a movie star?
- Do you wash your hands after going to the bathroom? [*For a complete list see Appendix A, Worksheet 3.1.*]

Procedure:
1. Go over any new words the students may need to complete the task.
2. Ask students to stand up and ask the questions in the grid. They are to write down only the names of students with affirmative answers. Remind them to use the target language.
3. Tell students that the first three to finish the task will win "fabulous prizes."

Directions to students: Stand up and ask the questions in the grid. Write the name of the student who gives you an affirmative response. Fill out two (or three, depending on time) vertical or horizontal columns.

Follow-up: Have a whole-class check and ask students to confirm responses. "Is it true you don't bathe every day?"

Make sure their answers produce the verbs in your secret agenda.

Variation: You can generate questions designed to produce any verb in the tense or mood you want: present tense, past tense, present or past subjunctive, future tense, conditional, etc.

Cocktail Party Searches

As the name suggests, students have to roam around the class, chit-chat with each other, and search for something that matches the information they are given. They may search for a long-lost relative among their classmates, a person that fits the description for the ideal person in a card given by the instructor, or a person with specific likes or dislikes, etc.

Cocktail Party Searches Example 1

Who Is This Person?

Secret agenda: To practice adjectives and number and gender agreement.

Materials: Index cards with the name of a famous person on each; matching index cards with three adjectives that describe each of these people. *[For sample cards see Appendix A, Worksheet 3.2.]*

Procedure:
1. Review any tricky or hard-to-remember adjectives the students may need to complete the task.
2. Ask students to stand up and find their match. Remind them to use the target language.

3. When someone finds their match, don't let them sit down, but ask them to help others find their match.
4. Some students may not find their match in a reasonable time. Ask them to come up to the front and read their name or their description. Have the class as a whole find the match.

Directions to the students: Stand up and look for the person that matches the description given to you. Or the opposite: look for the description of the person whose name is on your card.

Follow-up: Do a whole-class check, asking the class if they know the person on the card and if they can add a few more adjectives to describe him/her.

Cocktail Party Searches Example 2

Family Reunion

Secret agenda: To practice family vocabulary, possessive adjectives, professions, and activities.

Materials: Index cards with the name of a person, his/her profession, and a few other details. [*For contents of cards see Appendix A, Worksheet 3.3.*]

Procedure:
1. Review any vocabulary the students may need to complete the task.
2. Provide sample questions to find their relatives:
   - What is your name?
   - Where do you live?

- What do you like to do?
- What is your profession?
- What is your spouse's profession?

3. Ask students to stand up and ask questions using the information provided on the index cards to find their relatives. Remind them to use the target language.
4. When all three families have been created, ask them to remain together so you can ask them questions.

Directions to students: You are at a family reunion. Using a description given to you on an index card, you have to stand up and look for all your relatives and form a family. There are three different families. Be sure you know all your family ties so you can explain how each person in your family is related to you.

Follow-up: Ask each group to describe their family ties. Ask if they get along. Ask what their relatives' likes or dislikes are. Ask the class if they look alike. Show amazement at some of the relations!

You can use a somewhat different version of the Cocktail Party Search as a warm-up activity at the beginning of the class. Just like with the signature grid, students will be circulating and asking random questions of several classmates. Students usually come in and plop themselves down at their desks and have a hard time getting started. This activity gets them going by standing up and asking interesting questions. I always remind them to add conversational reactions or back-channeling phrases: "Really?" "You don't say!," etc. It is important to do a whole-class check to give the activity purpose, which in this case is to learn something new from the other classmates.

Cocktail Party Searches Example 3

Warm-up Questions

Secret agenda: To practice the imperfect tense (but this can also be modified for the preterit tense, the present tense, reflexive verbs, the future tense, present perfect, etc.).

Materials: Slips of paper with a question written on each, enough for everyone in the class. [*For a list of questions see Appendix A, Worksheet 3.4.*]

Procedure:
1. Review any vocabulary the students may need to complete the task.
2. Remind students to react to the classmate's response with "Really?," "How interesting!" etc.

Directions to students: Stand up and ask a classmate the question on your piece of paper. Your classmate answers your question and asks you his/her question in return. When you have asked the question and given a response, exchange the pieces of paper before moving on to ask another classmate.

Follow-up: Share small: In pairs, ask students what interesting fact they found out about several classmates. Share big: Do the same but in groups of four. Share bigger: Do a whole-class check and be amazed or horrified at the new revelations. Ask the class to react to it also with "You don't say," "How boring!" etc.

Variation: These warm-up questions can be modified for the present and future tenses too.

Whole-Class Searches

In this type of activity, students will be talking to many of their classmates to complete an individual task.

Whole-Class Searches Example 1

Speed Dating

Secret agenda: To practice formulating questions.

Materials: Provide a list of questions for the interviewer. *[For a list of questions see Appendix A, Worksheet 3.5.]*

Procedure:
1. Decide which option you prefer: ideal roommate, potential spouse, or friend. Tell your students they can make up a new invented name and personality, so it is not too personal and feelings don't get hurt.
2. Arrange the class in two concentric circles.
3. Give two minutes for the exchange of questions and answers, and call time.
4. Ask students in the outer circle to move two spaces to the right.
5. Repeat five times or more, depending on the size of the group and the time available.

Directions to students: Ask the classmate in front of you the given questions. Your classmate will do the same. When the teacher calls "time," switch to the next person and repeat. At the end decide which person is your potential or ideal roommate/ friend/spouse.

Follow-up: Ask who they found that was most compatible and why. This can be done in small groups first and then report to class. (Share small, share big, share bigger.) Find out who was the most popular person.

Whole-Class Searches Example 2

Bargaining

Secret agenda: To practice clothing vocabulary, numbers, and indirect object pronouns.

Materials:
1. Play money (such as euros) in various denominations: 100, 50, 20, 10, and 5.
2. Printed images of the articles to be sold at the market.

Procedure:
1. Review dialogue between sellers and buyers. [*For sample dialogue see Appendix A, Worksheet 3.6.*]
2. Divide the class in half: one half are sellers, the other, buyers.
3. Place the sellers seated in front of the class and facing the others in a straight line. Give them the images of the merchandise (they should all have the same thing) and an idea of the retail price; give each seller 150 euros (one 50, two 20s, four 10s, and four 5s).
4. Give the clients 500 euros (two 100s, three 50s, five 20s, four 10s, and two 5s).
5. As soon as three-quarters of the class is done, stop the activity and ask everybody to count their money.

Directions to students: Buyers, you have to negotiate and buy five different items, spending the least money possible. Sellers, you have to sell all your items and get as much money for them as possible.

Follow-up: The seller with the most money and all the merchandise sold wins. The buyer with all items bought and the most money left wins.

Using TPR (Total Physical Response)

This is a method developed by Dr. James Asher in the 1960s, and it is still very popular with teachers. Asher's idea is to teach the language by linking words to a physical activity. The more intense and the more frequent the connection between word and action, the more probable it is that the student will remember it. Using TPR may not seem like something communicative, but it is, if it is led by a student. You can direct a single student or a small group of students to give commands to others. "Simon Says" is an example of TPR, but there are other activity situations where one person has to give commands to another: parent–child, counselor–student, nonsighted person–friend, person–pet, sergeant–soldier, teacher–student, etc.

TPR Example 1

Do This, Do That

Secret agenda: To practice narrating in the present or past tenses.

Procedure:

1. Ask the class to form groups of three and come up with a simple skit. Here is an example:

   There is a big party at the house. John is dancing. Jane is drinking. Jim is saying hi to everybody. Someone is at the door. S(he) is not happy. S(he) is very upset. S(he) knocks on the door very hard. John stops dancing and opens the door. Jane goes to the door too and offers the neighbor a drink. Jim comes over and says "hi." The neighbor at the door says s(he) can't sleep and that s(he) called the police. Jane puts a drink in the neighbor's hand. John starts dancing with the neighbor. Jim is still saying "hi" to everybody. The neighbor is happy now and drinks and drinks and sings loudly. The police arrive and take the neighbor away. The End.

2. When finished, they choose another group to perform it.

Directions to students: In groups, create a skit and ask another group to perform it.

Follow-up: The class can vote for the best skit and the best performers. They can't vote for themselves.

Variation: Students can create their own skit and perform it themselves. One person in the group could be the narrator.

TPR Example 2

Lead Me

Secret agenda: Giving commands.

Procedure:
1. Review the commands students will need: turn left, turn right, stop, go back, continue forward, crouch, touch, extend your arms.
2. Ask the students to pair up. One student blindfolds the other and hides her/his backpack.
3. The sighted student will use verbal commands to lead the blindfolded student through the classroom aisles, taking a long way around to finding the backpack.
4. Because this will be done by all at the same time, traffic will make it tricky to navigate.

Directions to students: In pairs, give commands to lead your blindfolded classmate to find her/his backpack hidden somewhere in the classroom.

Follow-up: There will be one or two students still lost at the end, so the whole class can give commands to help the person find her/his way.

Debates

Debates are more appropriate for advanced students not only because they require good control of the language, but because students also have to create arguments to persuade the opposition, which is a tall order. It is best to pick interesting and current topics in the news, such as gay marriage, the death penalty, or the qualities of a current political candidate. As with role plays, it is more effective to have debates in small groups consisting of four or six students: two or three in favor, two or three against. The instructor assigns who is going to be in favor or against regardless of their true position in the matter. This is a relief for students because many don't want to share what they really think about the given topic, so they can debate confident that their privacy is respected.

Debate Example

Defend Your Side

Secret agenda: Using subjunctive to give opinions and persuade.

Procedure:
1. Form groups of four or six students.
2. Assign a pro or con position randomly to each of the group members.
3. Provide useful vocabulary they will need in order to agree or disagree. *[See Appendix A, Worksheet 3.7.]*
4. Provide starter arguments.
5. Have the students take turns debating the controversial topic.

Directions to students: You will be assigned a topic to debate and the side you will defend. Study the pros and cons provided to you and add a few of your own. Listen to the argument and provide a counterargument.

Follow-up: Ask each group who they think won the debate, who had the last word.

Dictation

With dictation, communication is somewhat one-sided: one student dictates to another what to do or what to draw, but the follow-up is communicative. Students could create a family tree based on the information given by a classmate. They could describe a person or a creature to be drawn. They could tell a story or a piece of gossip and have the classmate retell it.

Dictation Example

Family Tree

Secret agenda: To review family relations vocabulary and possessive adjectives.

Procedure:
1. Review family vocabulary.
2. Provide the questions the students will need to obtain information. [*See Appendix A, Worksheet 3.8 for questions needed.*]

Directions to students: In pairs, ask your classmate for information so you can draw his/her family tree / ideal home / bedroom, etc.

Follow-up: Share big: In groups of four (two couples), one student shows the most interesting family tree. Share bigger: Ask for volunteers to show their family trees in a (digital) projector and explain them to the class. Also ask general questions such as: "Who has a very large family? Who has a small family? Are there any twins or triplets? Is your partner's family similar to yours?"

Variation: If you sense some students are private about their families, ask them to "predict" their own family in 20 years. Make up names of parents, spouses, and children. They can also "marry" a famous person and invent a family.

Managed Competition

Games fit my personality well, so I can sell them to my class easily with my enthusiasm. Games transform any job into something fun, or at least tolerable for the sourpuss. Remember Tom Sawyer painting the fence, or Mary Poppins saying "In every job that must be done, there is an element of fun," or Snow White singing "Whistle while you work." Games and managed competitions break the normally passive nature of a class and make students spring into action and do their bit for their group in order to win that point for the glory of receiving the ultimate prize—a piece of candy, applause, or a trinket. And the best part is that if the game is well designed, the students learn at the same time. Some games require more preparation than other activities, but the response and energy generated make it all worth it. There are several elements in managed competition:

- Give clear instructions and don't change the rules midstream.

- Ask each group to pick a team name (they'll usually think up silly names).

- Don't lose sight of your linguistic hidden agenda; quietly focus on it.

- All group negotiation must be in the target language.

- Be fair; don't favor any particular group.

- Be energetic and enthusiastic.

- Avoid embarrassing students if they don't know the answer; encourage them by saying something like "that one was difficult" or "just unlucky."

- Plan a time limit; don't let the game drag.

- Require the structure you are practicing in the students' responses—don't accept "yes" or "no" answers in the follow-up.

- Follow up, checking their answers, discussing them, and being amazed by them.

- Deliver the promised prize.

Managed Competition Example

Is It True?

Secret agenda: To practice the preterit (or present perfect tense).

Procedure:
1. Divide the class in half facing each other.
2. Ask students to discreetly write something that they did or did not do. They must write a "T" for true or an "F" for false at the end of the sentence for you to see.
3. Ask one student to read the statement, and ask someone from the opposing group to guess whether the statement is true or false. For the answer to count, it must be in a complete sentence and include the desired verb. For example: "Yes, it is true, *you slept* for 16 hours yesterday."
4. The group scores a point if they guess correctly or if the opposing team guesses incorrectly.
5. The group with the most points wins the prize.

Directions to students: Write down something that you did or did not do on a piece of paper. The other group has to guess whether you are telling the truth or not.

Follow-up: Besides the prize, ask what was the most outrageous statement they heard.

WRITING TASKS

Cooperative Writing

Cooperative writing is a good first step to tackle the challenging task of writing in a new language. Positive aspects from group writing are:

- There is strength in numbers and so the task is less intimidating.

- Students help each other come up with words; remember, three heads are better than one!

- Students get feedback from their partners when they make a mistake (or at least the partners question the wisdom of the choice of one word over another).

- Group members brainstorm and negotiate meaning among themselves.

Some elements of cooperative writing are:

- Groups should not be larger than four students. If a group is larger, shy or weak students will let others do the work. The smaller the group, the more each of the members is obligated to contribute.

- As in oral communicative activities, roles must be determined: Who is writing the story? Who is the leader keeping the task moving? Who will be the spokesperson reporting to class?

- After the task is completed, students must be allowed time to edit the work.

- The finished text should be read in class. After the reading, focus and comment on the content first; be amazed, be saddened, laugh, or question what was read. Only then should you focus on form: spelling, accents, mechanics, etc.

Cooperative Writing Example 1

Who Is This Person?

Secret agenda: To practice adjectives, agreement, likes and dislikes in writing.

Procedure:
1. Ask the students to form groups of three or four, secretly choose a famous person, and write a description of her/him.

2. Ask them to use the following questions as a guide: What is her/his name? How old is this person? Where is this person from? What is the person like physically? What is her/his personality like? What does this person like to do? What does she/he usually wear?
3. All descriptions are read out loud and the class tries to guess who it is.

Directions to students: In groups of three or four, secretly choose a famous person and write a description without mentioning her/his name. The class will guess who that person is.

Follow-up: After the class guesses, ask the students to expand on some of the descriptions on the board.

Variation: Other possible topics: A weather report (guess the city), a typical day in the life of . . . (guess the celebrity), a classmate's childhood (guess whose), what someone did last week (guess who), what a classmate's future will be in 20 years (guess who), food menu (guess for what type of person—vegetarian, rich, poor, on a diet).

Cooperative Writing Example 2

Chain Stories

Secret agenda: To practice narrating in the past tense.

Procedure:
1. Ask the students to form circles of five students. A larger group is fine here because they are all participating.
2. Ask each student to write the beginning of their story with the sentence "Something terrible happened to me yesterday" or "Something fabulous happened to me yesterday."

3. Give them two to three minutes to get their story started, then signal "stop." Tell them to pass their unfinished story to the person on their right.
4. Repeat this four more times, but make sure to give the students enough time because they have to read and understand what the previous authors have written in order to continue the story.
5. When the story reaches the original owner, he/she must finish by writing a closing sentence.
6. Have students read the stories out loud within the group. The group will decide which is the best story of the five.
7. This chosen story is then edited by all in the group and given to the teacher.
8. The teacher may read the stories out loud to the class right there, or take them home and type them for better clarity and read them to the class the next day.
9. Project the story in a transparency or a digital projector for everyone to see.
10. React to content, then to form.

Directions to students: On a piece of paper, write the sentence "Something terrible happened to me yesterday" or "Something fabulous happened to me yesterday." I will tell you to start writing and you must stop when I give the signal. Then pass your paper to the student on your right. A paper will also be passed on to you. You must read it and keep writing, adding to that story until I tell you to stop and pass it to your right again.

Follow up: After all five stories have been read (assuming a class of 25 students), the class must vote for the best one. Students can't vote for their own. The winning group gets a prize or a standing ovation.

Variation: Other interesting topics are: 1. It was an ordinary day until . . . 2. It was an honest mistake . . . 3. When I became rich and famous . . . 4. I was walking home one day . . .

Cooperative Writing Example 3

Class Newspaper

Secret agenda: To practice the preterit tense.

Procedure:
1. Divide the class in groups of four.
2. Ask students to invent news stories on the given topics.
3. When time is up, project the story in a transparency or a digital projector for everyone to see.
4. React to content, then to form.

Directions to students: In groups of four, choose the name of your newspaper, write the date, and come up with invented news stories covering several topics: National, Local, Campus, Sports, Entertainment, Personal.

Follow-up: After all newspapers have been read (probably about five), the class must vote for the most creative news. Students can't vote for their own. The winning group gets a prize or a standing ovation.

Cooperative Writing Example 4

Fabulous Vacation

Secret agenda: To practice narrating in the past.

Procedure:
1. Ask the students to form groups of four, go to the board, and write about the most fantastic vacation they can invent.
2. Ask them to use the following questions as a guide: Where did you go? How long were you there? What did each of you do? Who did you meet? What did you tell him/her? What did they say? What did you like best?

3. The teacher reads all stories out loud, reacting to content first, then to form.
4. The group will vote on which is the best/most creative story of the whole class.

Directions to students: Form groups of four. Writing directly on the board, your group will come up with the most amazing vacations anyone could imagine.

Follow-up: After all stories have been read, the class must vote for the best or most creative vacation. Students should not vote for their own. The winning group gets a prize or a standing ovation.

Variation: Other interesting topics could be: 1. The meanest thing we ever did. 2. The best thing we ever did. 3. The biggest lie we ever told. 4. A famous person we met and what we did together. 5. An embarrassing moment.

Individual Writing Used for Communicative Activities

When time is limited, writing can be assigned as homework and then used in class for a communicative activity. Here are some examples:

Individual Writing Example 1

Mini-Biography

Secret agenda: To practice description, dates, numbers, and activities in writing.

Procedure:
1. Using yourself or a student as an example, write a mini-biography on the board using the guide questions. *[See Appendix A, Worksheet 3.9, for guide questions.]*

2. Assign for homework the writing of a mini-biography using the questions given as a guide.
3. Collect and redistribute all papers.
4. Arrange the class in groups of four, and ask each student to read the text out loud; the group will guess who the writer was.
5. Ask each group to read their most interesting mini-bio out loud and say who they think is the author.

Directions to students: Write a mini-biography using the given questions as a guide. Do not include your name.

Follow-up: After a number of biographies have been read, ask the class who they think is the most interesting person, the most athletic, the busiest, the laziest, the most studious, etc., and have them tell why.

Variation: In this mini-biography we are including adjectives, likes, and dislikes in the present tense, but the mini-biography can be used to practice the preterit or predict the future by changing the guide questions.

Individual Writing Example 2

What Happened in the Video?

Secret agenda: To practice the past tense.

Procedure:

1. Ask half the class to go outside the classroom. Give them a conversational task so they are not idle.
2. The other half in the room will watch a silent video. It could be part of a movie or a cartoon from YouTube.

3. Have the students pair up, and the ones who watched the video will tell their partner what they saw.
4. The listeners will write down the story and read it to the class.

Directions to students: Watch a silent video in class and tell a classmate, who has been outside waiting, what you saw. Your classmate will write it down and share with the class.

Follow-up: Watch the video again together and ask the class to vote for the most accurate account.

READING TASKS

If reading is a one-person job, how then can we make it communicative? While we may normally read alone, in our daily lives we often talk to others about what we're about to read or what we've just read. The same can happen in the classroom; the "pre-reading" and "post-reading" stages can give us opportunities to make reading more communicative.

Pre-reading activities familiarize students with what they are about to read so they can better understand it. This may include talking about the title, the topic itself, cultural nuances, new vocabulary, the genre, the author, the illustrations, etc. You could ask students to list what they know about the topic before reading or to predict what the text will be about. Or you may whet their appetite testing their knowledge of the subject by answering true/false questions about information they will only know when they finish reading. If the text is a story, you may provide an interesting fragment from the text and have the students complete the phrase or continue the story. They will then read and find out. If the vocabulary is challenging, you may consider having a "matching word and meaning" exercise, so your students can guess the meaning. This awareness before reading is best achieved collaboratively.

Post-reading activities include comprehension questions, discussions about the message of the text, and/or activities that focus on specific grammatical constructions or vocabulary. If it is a story, you may ask the students to write a summary in thirty words. This exercise makes the students consider carefully which words to use.

Reading Activity Example 1

What Do We Know?

Secret agenda: To raise awareness of the topic of the reading, to learn about the information of the text, and to practice the desired grammatical construction.

Procedure:
1. Create a quiz with interesting and little-known facts about the text the students are going to read. It could be multiple choice, true or false, agree or disagree.
2. Have the students take the quiz in pairs.
3. Take an informal poll about the answers. See what most students think/agree/believe, but don't give the real answers.
4. Read the text in class (teacher and/or students could take turns reading).
5. Throughout the reading, pose questions to point out the information that was in the quiz.
6. Generate discussion questions and have the students answer them in pairs. Or, have students write a different ending to the story if it is a narration.
7. With a different partner, have the students underline, circle, or modify whatever grammar construction you are focusing on that week. (You may ask them to change the tense, write questions, change the point of view of the narration, give advice, etc.)

Directions to students: Take the quiz with a partner and discuss it together. Read the text and answer the discussion questions provided.

Follow-up: Ask the students what information or sentence was the most interesting, most helpful, most amazing, most horrifying, etc.

Reading Activity Example 2

Strip Story

Secret agenda: To read an interesting text which also contains cultural information.

Procedure:
1. Select an interesting text.
2. Do a pre-reading activity.
3. Ask the class to pair up.
4. Make copies of the text for each pair.
5. Cut the text with scissors into six or eight parts and give all parts to each pair of students.
6. Ask them to read out loud all the sentences and together put the story back in order.

Directions to students: Read out loud all the pieces of paper given to you and, with the help of your classmate, put the story back in order.

Follow-up: Ask students which sentence is first, which is next, etc. Add comprehension questions and a post-reading activity.

This chapter covering communicative activities provides you with enough variety to get you started. The exciting thing to remember is, it is just a start! Keep your eyes open and you'll soon discover that almost any linguistic activity—speaking, reading, writing—can be turned into an info gap exercise, a role play, a TPR activity or competition. All you need to remember is to fit your new idea into the structure of secret agenda, materials, procedure, directions, follow-up, and variations. Do this and I guarantee that over the years you will never be at a loss for what to do in the classroom, your teaching will remain fresh, and you'll open your students' eyes to the wonders of a new language, a new way of perceiving the world.

Summary Questions

1. Why use communicative activities?

_____

_____

2. What are the elements of a communicative activity?

_____

_____

3. List several kinds of communicative activities.

_____

_____

4. Describe a bad communicative activity.

_____

_____

Scenarios

Scenario 1

A first-year instructor, Ms. Kerry Savala, talked about the layout of her house to introduce the vocabulary on furniture and parts of the house for the first time. She presented it thoroughly and had the students repeat the various words several times. When she was confident the students knew the vocabulary, she came up with a communicative activity: "Class, in pairs, interview each other so you can draw the layout of your partner's house, just like I did here. You have 10 minutes." As she circulated around the room, she saw that the students were all over the place with this activity. They were asking, "What house? Should we draw his parents' house or where he's living now? What if she lives in the dorms? How do you say 'Which room?' How do you say 'How big?'" She answered all of these questions individually, but saw that they were all asking the same things. She ended up writing all these questions on the board as they came up. Still, not everything they needed was up on the board, and the students had to spend time looking words up in the dictionary. The activity was nowhere near done in 10 minutes.

What happened here? What did she do right? What did she do wrong?

_____

_____

Scenario 2

Mr. Potter's students had been asking him for extra help with accent rules. It pained him as a linguist to see so many mistakes in this area, and he realized that the students needed help. He knew he should follow a communicative approach, so he tried to reconcile the two aspects—form and communication. He wrote a list of the most common accent errors, asked the students to form pairs, and told them to first divide all the words on the list into syllables and then add the accent marks. His follow-up was a little long because there were questions as to why this word needed an accent and others didn't. He spent 25 minutes of class time on this.

1. Was he able to reconcile form and communication?

_____

_____

2. What would you have done differently?

_____

_____

4 · Teaching Culture

NORMA LÓPEZ-BURTON

Teaching culture has always been part of the language curriculum one way or another. Teachers know they should include culture, but often don't know when or how to go about it. Back in my TA days, teaching culture meant setting aside one or two days out of the term to show some slides, bring exotic foods to class, or listen to music and ask the students to sing along. I used to pick the day before a holiday or a three-day weekend because half the class was not there and the remaining half was not mentally there either, so nothing important could be accomplished anyway. In my mind, that made it a perfect culture day.

Some of my colleagues didn't even bother with culture because of the time crunch. Teaching to the test, they didn't want to sacrifice reviewing the grammar and the vocabulary that were going to appear on the all-important exam. Presenting culture was just a fun activity that did not contribute to learning the language anyway, or so the thinking went. Other teachers wanted to include culture but felt they didn't know enough to teach it, or felt that students with lower proficiency levels were not linguistically capable of discussing the finer points of some cultural differences.

The textbooks of the time were not very helpful either. Many attempted to include culture in each chapter with author-generated readings about history or famous people or places. They also included sidebars or boxes pointing out an interesting or bizarre culture fact, usually a stereotype. These boxes had titles like *¿Sabías qué . . . ?* (Did you know that . . . ?) or, my favorite, *¡Increíble, pero cierto!* (Incredible, but true!). These "culture boxes" lacked

pre- or post-reading questions, nor did they include annotations for the instructor with suggestions on how to present information to the students. Culture was almost always seen as something secondary, just an extra.

WHY TEACH CULTURE?

If oral and written language are the meat and potatoes of communication, why bother with culture? It will not affect the students' grades, really, because it isn't usually included in exams. Maybe it should be.

But here's the problem: communication and language are not just listening, reading, and writing. Social scientists tell us face-to-face communication is comprised of just 20 percent words and a whopping 80 percent body language, tone, and cultural understanding. So here is the linguistic reason to learn culture in the language classroom: even the best laid out sentence is susceptible to misunderstanding if there is no basic knowledge of the culture.

An example: My seventy-five-year-old mother came from Puerto Rico to visit me in California, and I took her to the Spanish department where I worked and introduced her to the staff. I popped my head into one of the offices and said, "Hello everybody, this is my mother." She waved to them and said, *"Hola, ¿cómo están?"* (Hi, how are you?). One of the staff, who was just learning the language and wanted to reach out to her, said, *"Muy bien, gracias, ¿y tú?"* (Fine, thank you, and you?). This is perfectly correct Spanish, except that she used the informal form of "you." It is almost like saying, "Hey there, buddy!" One should not be so chummy with a seventy-five-year-old lady, especially my mother. Her hand froze in midair and she stood there as if tased. When I saw this, I ushered her into the hallway, returned to say good-bye to all, and quickly got back to my mother. Standing there in the hallway, her hand was still up. True story. I told her that the lady was just learning Spanish and didn't mean any disrespect. This person, bless her heart, meant well, but ignorance of this cultural point had the opposite effect from what she intended: a "dis" instead of a "hello."

This cultural point—the difference between the use of *tú* and *usted*, *tu* and *vous*, *mister* and *hey dude*—is easy to explain and memorize, but other concepts are more subtle and will take more skill to introduce, like concepts of time, family, personal space, social hierarchy, and almost any aspect of daily life. They are subtle, but important to know.

Recently I saw a commercial for a luxury automobile. An adult son enters his parents' house for the holidays and calls out to them, "Mom? . . . Dad? . . . Guys?" Through the large living room window we see the parents sneaking away down the driveway in their luxury car. Dad tells Mom, "He'll be fine." They both smile, and the large sedan speeds off. Because we in this society see ourselves *primarily* as individuals, rather than *primarily* as family members, that commercial is funny and it works. But knowing how important family connections are in other countries, would a culturally sophisticated company run an ad like this one, say, in a Spanish-speaking country? No way. A commercial like that would be met with appalled disbelief. The son is arriving and the parents are fleeing?! What a horrible thing to do!

This recently increased appreciation for the teaching of culture has been incorporated into the profession, as seen in the Standards for Foreign Language Learning developed by the American Council on the Teaching of

Foreign Languages (ACTFL). The organization's statement in support of the teaching of culture reads: "Cultural understanding is an important part of world languages education. Experiencing other cultures develops a better understanding and appreciation of the relationship between languages and other cultures, as well as the students' native culture. Students become better able to understand other people's points of view, ways of life, and contributions to the world." Gives you goose bumps, doesn't it?

CULTURAL KNOWLEDGE VS. CULTURAL PROFICIENCY

Cultural knowledge, or "objective culture," includes simple facts: knowing the location of all the countries where the language is spoken; knowing some important geographical facts; knowing the names of important people like politicians or artists; knowing important dates; knowing facts about their economic systems, institutions, family relationships, religions, and so forth. Facts are easy to teach and easy to test. There is not that much to understand—just have the student memorize, and voilà!

On the other hand, the teaching of "subjective culture" is a subtle thing and requires more thought and care to present in class. To be culturally proficient, students have to know what to say and when to say it, and they must also understand cultural behaviors and different points of view. If cultural understanding is the goal, teachers have to go beyond the simple textbook sidebars—*Nuestros amigos hispanos* (Our Hispanic friends), *Les francophones sur le vif* (French speakers on the spot), *Brennpunkt Kultur* (Hot topic)—and get past the boring slide presentations or shocking bits of behavior meant to spice up the class. If teachers present information without teaching the skill to understand, students will react with amusement, disbelief, or disgust: "They do what?!" "That is so bizarre!" "That's just wrong." "I would never do that!" "I would never eat that!" We have to remember these are young people who most likely have very limited international exposure. Many are ethnocentric. They believe that America is Number One!; everyone wants to be like us; we don't eat weird things; we have a blessed way of life; anybody in their right mind would rather live here, is dreaming of living here, or is trying desperately to live here. Given this consistent indoctrination, it is only logical for a young person to say "That's just weird!" when presented with unfamiliar customs without being adequately prepared to receive the new information.

Years ago, when I was a young TA and didn't know any better, I brought *morcillas* (blood sausages) to my class. I knew it was something they had never seen, and I knew it to be pretty tasty. The *morcillas* were not cheap, and so I thought introducing them to the students was pretty generous of me. It was the food chapter, and so I thought that was background enough.

Full of the expectation of providing a window to my culture, I told my students I had a surprise for them, uncovered the dish, and of course, when I told them the ingredients—blood, rice, and spices stuffed in pig intestines—they were utterly disgusted. Some laughed, some got religion and started evoking God's mercy, some rolled their eyes; at last a few dared to try my tasty morsels, and when they did, they reacted as if they had been pepper-sprayed.

What in reality had I accomplished? I reinforced the idea that they, Americans, don't eat repulsive things and other cultures—including their poor teacher's—have to. In a few short minutes, with the best of intentions and following what I thought was the best way to present culture, I just created an even taller cultural barrier. My students did not understand, accept, or see a different point of view, as I wanted them to, and as they are encouraged to do by the Standards.

How could I have done better? How could I have presented this cultural point and have the students accept its validity, not find it weird, not have them feel culturally superior, or not laugh? Unfortunately for that class, it was only later that I learned how to accomplish this by using a cross-cultural approach. I present it here to you so that you don't have to experience students laughing at your sausages.

CROSS-CULTURAL APPROACH

With this approach, we preempt students' complaints, comments, or arguments, and we address those objections first, slyly and artfully, before presenting our culture point. I recommend, especially at the beginning levels, starting with mild dissimilarities and working your way up from there. In the above example, if I could time travel, I might have told that young teacher not to bring *morcillas* to class at all, because it is a little shocking. But let's say that she really wanted to (she could be stubborn), and see how we could have helped her out.

First step, we would tell her to predict her students' comments or complaints: "That looks disgusting!" "What's in it?" "I would never eat that!"

Once she guessed what they might say, it's on to step two in the classroom: prepping students by asking, "Is there anything in our diet that would be objectionable in other countries?" The usual lofty response is "No! What? We are Americans. We don't eat disgusting things." Now in for the kill: bring up something similar to what they will be objecting to. In this case our young teacher asks: "What are the ingredients in a hot dog?" Half the class will know what is in a hot dog and will get pensive and look a little sheepish (I've seen this happen time and time again). The other half still don't see the ambush coming. Our young instructor lists the ingredients, using the target language, of course: carcasses from old or diseased cattle and swine, cheeks, jowls, hearts, tongues, lips, eyelids, gums, intestines, ears, nostrils, tails, snouts, tendons, windpipes, livers, kidneys, bones, blood, and preservatives. Some students don't want to hear about this reality, some make faces, but all have to accept the fact that that is what they eat. She asks, "Do you eat hot dogs?" Over half the class admits to it. Now, resistance is futile, and on to step three: introduce the cultural point, in this case the *morcillas*. Our young teacher then mentions the ingredients, and students are surprised, but because they no longer cling to a holier-than-thou position, they are less expressive in their comments and clearly more accepting.

This three-step presentation can be done with any fact or behavior you want to introduce: bargaining over prices in Mexico, Carnaval in Brazil, Three Kings Day in Puerto Rico, Oktoberfest in Germany, escargot in France . . . Here are a few examples:

La corrida in Spain (bullfighting)

1. Predict the complaint (cruelty to animals).

2. Ask if we are cruel to animals in this country. ("No. We are Americans, we have laws against that!")

> a. Then bring up, in a diplomatic and gentle way, a similar behavior (the treatment of calves for veal meat or the cruel use of animals for entertainment in rodeos).

> b. When they accept and understand that this is what happens in their own culture, they are ready for the new one.

3. Introduce *la corrida*.

The Tour de France

1. Predict a comment or complaint. ("Interesting, but they are racing across France on a bicycle, a child's toy. It is not very manly. It's boring because there are no teams or scores. The cyclists are not real athletes because they are so small and thin.")

2. Ask if there is a sport in this country that would look strange or silly to the rest of world. Then bring up the fact that a human pile of big football players may look very childish. Their protective equipment makes them look like giants. Or that the physique of some baseball players is not too athletic, and they are spitting and pulling on their crotches all the time.

3. Introduce the Tour de France as a team sport and endurance event.

Expressing emotion in Japan

1. Predict comments or complaints. ("The Japanese don't raise their voices or get emotional in arguments, and so they are a cold and calculating people.")

2. Ask if there is a time when Americans don't show strong emotion. Then bring up the fact that it is not generally customary to cry out loud or make a scene at funerals.

3. Introduce the even-keel behavior of the Japanese.

BREAKING STEREOTYPES

One trap we must avoid when presenting culture is explaining a celebration or behavior without specifying an area or a country where this happens. Students will tend to stereotype and think that this particular cultural attitude is common to all the speakers of that language. The attitudes and actions observed in Paris are not necessarily applicable to the rest of France, nor are they in other countries where French is spoken. People from Portugal and Brazil have different accents, different expressions, and different celebrations. This is true in English, too. George Bernard Shaw, speaking about the United States and England, is purported to have said that these are two countries separated by a common language. Just as we know that we cannot lump all English speakers (England, United States, Jamaica, Bahamas, Australia, and the other seventy countries where English is the official language) into one single tight cultural package, so we have to make sure we don't say things like "Our Hispanic friends" and generalize some aspect of culture across ethnic or regional lines, for example, eating "tortillas," which in Mexico are a flat bread and in Spain a heavy potato-and-egg dish.

Speaking of Mexico, when I first came to this country I was amazed and somewhat annoyed by how many people thought I was Mexican. I have studied and admire Mexican culture and history; it is just that I am not Mexican. I am from Puerto Rico. Without knowing where I was from, people would assume I ate spicy foods, listened to mariachi music, and made tortillas at home. Some would ask me out of the blue how I got my green card (Puerto Rico is a U.S. territory and so all Puerto Ricans are born U.S. citizens). It was somewhat bothersome, but understandable, since Mexico is our closest non-English-speaking neighbor. Schools usually do not cover other cultures that are not directly related to the United States, and when they do, they simplify by stereotyping.

It's not only the educational system that is failing us in cultural proficiency; I also blame the media for not understanding or caring about culture differences. I was watching an old movie, *Butch Cassidy and Sundance Kid*, the other day. At the end, the robbers escape to Bolivia. The Bolivians in the movie had overwhelming Mexican accents. Ouch! It is like having the extras in the movie *The Godfather* speak with an Australian accent. Seriously! Really?!

It is part of our job as educators to break stereotypes and be specific about a country or region. If students don't understand that each and every country or region has its own rich and unique culture, they are missing out.

An effective way to break stereotypes is by having the students discover them on their own. This is a much more powerful experience than just taking in information from the teacher. I would like to call it "setting up a trap for the unsuspecting," but in the profession it is actually called "guided discovery."

As an example, I could teach students about the racial variety in all the Spanish-speaking countries until I am blue in the face, but it wouldn't mean much to them. We, "Our Hispanic friends," despite the stereotype, do not all look alike. Unfortunately, I, with my olive skin, dark brown hair, and brown eyes, can't help but reinforce the perception. So, to unbalance the students' perceptions, I prepared a PowerPoint file with photographs of people of different ethnicities and asked them to note those they thought came from Spanish-speaking countries. I went through one quick cycle of the photos asking: "For image #1, raise your hand if you think he is from a Spanish-speaking country. How about #2? . . ." and so forth. Of course, they labeled as Hispanic the ones that followed their usual stereotype: dark hair, brown eyes, and olive skin. After we had a tally, I cycled through the photos again and revealed the subjects' names and where they were from: all of them—from the whitest, most blue-eyed to the gunmetal-blue darkest—were well-known artists or celebrities from various Spanish-speaking countries. The students discovered their errors themselves.

WHAT TOOLS CAN YOU USE TO TEACH CULTURE?

You have many tools—from no-tech to high-tech—at your disposal. Bring something to class such as food, musical instruments, objects, or just talk about a particular cultural difference (no-tech). Go over a reading from your textbook or photocopy an interesting article from a magazine that has an insight into a cultural behavior or fact (no-tech). Introduce a level-appropriate song from the target country: first focus on the cultural context, then focus on form by reviewing the lyrics (low-tech). Create a PowerPoint presentation about a particular event, festival, celebration, or custom (high-tech); or show a video segment on YouTube (high-tech).

No-Tech

Readings, especially authentic texts, are a good source of cultural information and a great way to integrate culture and grammar. And the nice thing is, readings are no-tech, so you can be sure nothing will fail (except maybe for the copy machine before class, so don't leave the photocopying for the last minute!). With any text, authentic or not, you will have to prep the students.

There are many things to consider aside from just cultural content: Does the reading have too many unknown words? Is it linguistically too complex? Does it have idiomatic expressions that will have to be explained beforehand? Does it have cultural nuances that will impede comprehension? It is best to choose a text that best matches the level so it is not too frustrating for the student. But still, all texts will have unknown words. Either write them on the board if there are only a few, or include them in a "guess what this means" multiple-choice exercise before they tackle the reading. Include cross-cultural inquiries to have the student reflect on their own culture and set the stage for the new information. Go through the text and ask comprehension questions along the way.

As an example, I once used a very simple, author-generated reading intended for the first-year level that featured Rigoberta Menchú, the Guatemalan political activist who won the 1992 Nobel Peace Prize for her efforts fighting for the civil rights of indigenous people. Since the reading was in the textbook and created by its authors, it was glossed and free of difficult expressions, and so for my class presentation I was able to concentrate on the cross-cultural component. I predicted that my students were going to be surprised that Spanish was not the first language of many Guatemalans and that there are over fifty different languages spoken in that country. I also suspected they were not aware of the difficulties the Mayans faced due to discrimination and political persecution. So I started by asking whether we had indigenous people in the United States. It seemed like an obvious question, but in many places in the U.S., if they are out of sight, they are out of mind. I also asked if English was, in some instances, their second language. I had the students guess how many different indigenous tribes we have here (565 per the U.S. Federal Register) and how many languages (about 150 Native American languages, with most on the edge of extinction). Then I asked if Indians were discriminated against (yes, historically and presently), and if their standard of living was lower (yes, with a $12,000 average per capita income, about one-third that of the general population). With these questions I increased the awareness of the students' own country's culture and avoided questions like "What?! They don't speak Spanish? What?! There are fifty-two different languages there? How can they communicate? Oh, that is terrible that they discriminate against their own people." Well, now they realized, we do too! Next, I asked students to read a couple of sentences each out loud and have comprehension checks along the way. After the content had been discussed, I focused on form. The grammar point in this case was interrogative words. I asked them to come up with questions that were answered in the text. So, one student could be the interviewer and the other, pretending to be Ms. Menchú, the interviewee.

Low-Tech

Songs are a fun, low-tech way to introduce new cultural information. Objectives vary and can include introducing new sounds and rhythms from your target country, highlighting a culture point that surfaces in the lyrics, or integrating culture and grammar by having the students fill in the blanks with the newly learned vocabulary or grammar. As with the reading, your students must be prepped before they hear the song. Predict their reaction to the artist's style, the rhythm, or the meaning of the lyrics. If you have found a level-appropriate, grammar- and vocabulary-perfect song, but you think the students will find it a little sappy or silly, point out popular sappy or silly songs in this country first. Ask, "Who listens to _____? Now be honest!" By addressing this first, your students will become less critical and concentrate on the business of learning a new song or music genre.

Songs also help with pronunciation and linking words. Usually, when I am done with the pre-listening, the listening, and the post-listening questions, I ask the students to sing along. Many are shy or feel it is not cool to sing, so I tell them it is a requirement, and that it counts as much as a homework assignment. (A little fib never hurt anyone!) If you put it in those terms, students will comply because even though it's not cool, it's the teacher who's making them sing (although, in truth, I find most of the time students really want to sing—they just feel a little awkward getting started).

High-Tech

Compared to low-tech presentations, a presentation run from a computer using something like PowerPoint might not seem that high-tech, but it has a better chance of failing than a CD player. Of course, there are advantages to using electronic-based presentations. For example, with PowerPoint you can get images from the Internet or pictures from your travels to show a celebration, a festival, or images that show a particular behavior, and when projected onto the screen, students see your message larger than life.

What a difference technology makes! As a young TA, I relied on magazine pictures—they had to be big so the whole class could see them— which I taped to posterboard. Sometimes I would rip them off from magazines at the doctor's office real quick (I hope the statute of limitations has passed). We used to call all those images "picture files," and we were always on the lookout for images to increase our stash. Now with PowerPoint combined with the Internet, you young whippersnappers don't have to carry all that posterboard or go around the classroom with the image in hand to make sure everyone can see it. Getting images from the Internet and putting them in PowerPoint is now a very easy and clear way to present a culture point.

Another more recent classroom high-tech device is YouTube. YouTube has been an amazing innovation with enormous potential for use (or abuse) in the language profession. You can find just about anything with that search window. Just type it in: how to cook a fricassee, how to celebrate La Tomatina, where to find cherry blossom festivals, what are the origins of secular or religious ceremonies . . . And of course you can access short movies, parts of movies, verbal essays, cultural commentaries, music videos, and so on. Naturally, some videos are better than others, and this will be discussed in Chapter 12 on technology. But bottom line: any video—whether from the publisher, your home collection, or YouTube—that you introduce as a window to culture has to receive the same careful preparation as anything else you present in class.

So . . . using the cross-cultural approach:

1. Preview and carefully select a short segment.
2. Predict the students' comments, tapping into their ignorance about their own culture, and address that first. This way you are setting the stage and getting the students ready to understand and accept a new and valid point of view.
3. Consider giving a pre-viewing quiz to pique their interest in the subject, or to point out a special moment in the clip that you want the students to pay special attention to.
4. View the segment.
5. Go over the quiz and answer any questions.
6. View the clip again.
7. Ask post-viewing questions.

Here is an example. I found a good video segment about a parade for the Three Kings Day celebration, an important celebration of Epiphany on January 6 in many Spanish-speaking countries. The parade is similar to Santa parades in the United States. For the Three Kings parade, there are floats, participants throw candy, children wear King's crowns, there are marching bands, and the Three Kings appear at the end of the procession. The next day, the children, much like with Santa Claus, await the arrival of the Three Kings. Depending on the country, the children either leave a shoe in the window (Spain), or grass near their beds for the hungry and tired camels (Puerto Rico). Then, just like what Santa Claus does, late at night, when everybody is fast asleep, the Kings sneak in with their camels and leave gifts for the kids. While similar to our Santa, the date of celebration and the participants are completely foreign to students in the U.S. Usually "the holidays" are over by New Year's Day, if not right after Christmas. They think that Santa is all there is. So, for a cross-cultural preparation, I ask, "When you were little, did you or any of your friends go to the Santa parade? Who and what was in the parade? What did children wear? Who was the main attraction at the end? On the 24th of December, did you or your friends leave milk and cookies for Santa? Are there any other dates where children around the world would receive gifts other than their birthdays? When?"

After conversing about this and before showing the clip, I give them a "what to look for" questionnaire: What are the children wearing? Describe the parade. Describe the Three Kings. What do the children do the day before the big day? Next, the students view the segment. Some take notes while watching, but I also allow time to do it right after. They view the segment a second time. I go over the questionnaire and answer any other questions they may have about the event. With this procedure, they get to recall a similar event in their country that helps them relate better to what is being presented. They see similarities and differences, but more importantly, they see that this new cultural window that was just opened to them is not weird, but it is simply a different version of a common human experience, in this case, a winter celebration.

INTEGRATING LANGUAGE AND CULTURE

Teaching culture does not always require a twenty- or thirty-minute presentation. Objective culture, as well as subjective culture, can be introduced in other ways if the syllabus does not allow time. If grammar and vocabulary take all the class time, then multitask: integrate language and culture. For example, if you are practicing verbs of location (near, far, to the right, in front . . .), instead of using your textbook's line drawings, provide students with a map of a real city from your target country: if Paris, show where the Eiffel Tower is located . . . if Rome, show where the Coliseum is. This works with almost any grammar point or vocabulary. If you are introducing colors or adjectives, do it with art pieces by famous painters from your target culture. Introduce Botero or Monet and describe the colors, and use newly learned adjectives to describe the figures.

To introduce verbs like "to be," describe the personality or physical traits of a known artist, politician, or historical figure from your target culture. Dictate a mini-biography, address the content (culture), and then focus on form (spelling, or troublesome conjugations). Have a complete-the-sentence or multiple-choice exercise about the luminary. As a written exercise, have students fill in the blank with the desired verb conjugation and then guess where your new person is from, or describe their personality. Even if they don't know the historical facts, they will get the answers later in the class and will have learned something new. Here is an example of what I am talking about:

Evita Perón _____ (to be) from:
  a) Spain
  b) Paraguay
  c) Argentina

Want to practice past tense? Recount an important day in history in detail, and even embellish it with personal anecdotes to increase students' interest: "Last year I went to France in July, and I landed right in the middle of a big celebration. There were so many people out on the streets, all kinds of music and children and young adults lighting fireworks, throwing them and running away. Children were doing this! Do you know what they were celebrating? Does that kind of celebration ring a bell for you? Yes, the 4th of July. Do you know what happened on the 14th of July in 1879? Well, there was this building in Paris called La Bastille . . ." Recall something that happened to you or to a friend, or an interesting, funny, or embarrassing cultural misunderstanding, to drill home a cultural behavior: "I was in Lisbon on vacation and one day stopped at a supermarket to buy a beer. When I took out my money to pay I also showed my ID, as I automatically do in the U.S., but the checker looked at me funny. Apparently they don't card people who look thirty . . ."

Presenting future tense? Talk about your plans to visit a particular city and say why. Say what you will be doing, the important people you might meet: "In Berlin I will meet Angela Merkel. She is the prime minister of Germany, but she and I are actually pen pals, did you know that? If you are good, I will Skype from class one day so you can meet her." It's OK to exaggerate sometimes to make it funny! To continue this story in the future, talk about the family you will be staying with, or the particular festival you are looking forward to seeing, and then take the opportunity to explain the celebration—all in terms of future events.

Practicing commands? Dictate to the students what to do or not to do in a given cultural predicament. Make it multiple choice, and have them guess what the right thing to do is: "When I (a female) was studying Spanish in Colombia, a classmate of mine (a male) wanted to come to my house to study. He knocked on the door, I let him in, and we both went into my room to study. The lady of the house was upset. What did I do wrong? Which of the following was the proper etiquette: a) don't invite males into the house, b) wait for the lady of the house to be out, or c) don't study in the bedroom but in the living room?"

Giving instructions on how to make a typical dish from the target culture is a great tool with which to teach commands. You can dictate a recipe, or have the students bring a new recipe from the country of study and tell their classmates how to make the dish, or have students explain how to eat or buy a particular food item.

If you want to practice formulating questions or reviewing question words, assume the personality of someone famous from your target culture, and have the students ask questions to guess who you are portraying. Your answers will provide insight on the life and personality of this celebrity. If you are looking for more participation from the students instead of something teacher-centered, assign each to do research on someone from the country of study for homework, then pair them up to formulate the questions.

Working on oral comprehension? Recount a funny cultural misunderstanding of something that happened to you or to a friend. Telling anecdotes is a great way to introduce behaviors and different points of view, especially if you embellish them with details. The questions following the oral input should give new insight on the cultural difference being featured.

Use the same tactics with new vocabulary. If numbers are the agenda, make a guessing game out of important historical events in your target culture. Even if the students guess wrong, when they hear the right answer, they will have discovered something new. Research on the Internet and then talk about what percentage of the population does this or owns that. Presenting dry numbers is not wise, but a guessing game spices things up.

For weather vocabulary, talk about the different weather patterns, not only in the mother country, but also in the other countries where they speak the same language. Students then get to remember all the places where the new language is spoken and review their geography while being reminded of weather and seasonal differences. For clothing vocabulary, compare and contrast clothing choices in different countries. You can also show images and describe the traditional native costumes of the target culture. For food, definitely talk about typical dishes and spice preferences.

Remember, any grammar point or vocabulary can be integrated with culture. Just follow the syllabus and integrate culture with the grammar and vocabulary of the chapter. I have to tell you, however, that having a culture-based textbook does help, so keep an eye out for textbooks that have culture integrated into every exercise. If you are in the business of teaching Spanish, I happen to know a pretty good culture-based first-year university textbook named *Pura vida* written by yours truly. Just sayin'...

Back to where we started: there is no need to have a special culture day if the syllabus does not allow for that. Using the techniques you've just learned here, students will learn new cultural information as a beneficial side effect while they are learning new vocabulary or practicing grammar.

Bottom line about teaching culture:

- Go beyond just giving information.

- Have students discover new concepts on their own.

- Remember the importance of subjective culture vs. objective culture.

- Use different media and methods to teach culture.

- Break stereotypes.

- Integrate culture and form whenever possible.

Summary Questions

1. What do the Standards for Foreign Language Learning say about the goal of teaching culture?

_____

_____

_____

2. What is the difference between cultural proficiency and cultural knowledge?

_____

_____

3. Explain the philosophy behind the cross-cultural approach.

_____

_____

4. What are the steps to follow with the cross-cultural approach?

_____

_____

5. What tools can you use to teach culture?

_____

_____

6. How can you integrate culture with the teaching of grammar and vocabulary?

_____

_____

Scenarios

Scenario 1

A teacher wants to talk to his ESL class about American football. The students come from countries where soccer is king. Using the cross-cultural approach, he tries to predict what they will think about it first. Maybe they think it is a silly game because all the tackling makes it look like mayhem. Because he wants his students to know it is a complicated and sophisticated game, he asks, "How many rules does soccer have?" The students guess—20? "Oh yeah?," he says. "No, it has 11 laws, while American football has 244 . . .""Oh," they say, in amazement. And then he springs it on them: ". . . PAGES. The 2011 NFL rule manual has *244 pages* of rules." His students are amazed, but not in a good way. He proceeds to explain in simple terms the game of football. They are shaking their heads in disbelief. Why were the students not receptive to this game? Did the teacher succeed in this cultural presentation? Explain.

_____

_____

Scenario 2

A French teacher is tired of Americans thinking of France being symbolized by a man riding a bike with groceries and a baguette sticking out from the basket. She avoids old stereotypes and describes everything as modern and very much like the United States. Because there is no time in the syllabus to have special culture presentations, she integrates culture and grammar in almost every activity. When talking about clothing, she describes what urban Frenchmen and women wear, which is the same as in New York. When covering the past tense, she describes the plot of some American movies that have French actors in them, instead of talking about French movies. Seeking acceptance from her students, she avoids talking about food items like escargot, horse meat, or rabbit, and instead emphasizes similarities. Her students are curious and ask about the consumption of wine in France. But sticking to her crusade of breaking stereotypes, she mentions that beer sales have increased every year steadily in France.

This teacher wants students to accept France as a "normal" country such as their own. How is she doing at teaching French culture? Have the students benefited from emphasizing only similarities? Do you think she should approach teaching culture differently?

_____

_____

Part II • Theory

5 · History of Second Language Acquisition

DENISE MINOR

The world began with Noam Chomsky. Not the physical world, of course, but rather the world of modern linguistics, the world from which this book and thousands of others are direct descendants in the theoretical sense. Before Chomsky, most people thought languages were learned the way a human learns history or biology. Furthermore, most teachers went about teaching those languages, particularly second languages, using techniques like grammar, translation, and repetition—methods that had been developed hundreds of years ago in an attempt to keep Latin and Classical Greek alive among the elite. (Picture British schoolboys standing in front of classmates reciting Latin noun declensions while a stern headmaster holding a ruler looks on from the back of the room.)

But with the emergence of his theories beginning in the late 1950s, Chomsky did not simply add to the body of research that had been done until that time on language; he moved the research into a new realm. Although it took years for it to become apparent, he completely changed the way we view language structure and acquisition. Chomsky is to linguistics what Isaac Newton was to physics and Celia Cruz was to salsa music: a genius and a revolutionary.

In this chapter I will lead you down a path containing some of the research that has emerged since the 1960s, research that has led us to develop what we believe are the most effective ways for teaching a second

language. This path will not include all the research that has been done, nor will it include all of the names of experts who have contributed to this field. (Please refer to the bibliography for more reading you can do about other researchers and other areas.) Instead, I will concentrate only upon what I believe to be the essential theories that hook together like the links of a chain: Universal Grammar, the mind's Language Acquisition Device (LAD); Acquisition vs. Learning; Input +1; Whole Language; Output; interaction and communication; investment in the second language (L2); and motivation. I will also touch on research focused on the role of grammar instruction in the second language classroom.

NOAM CHOMSKY, UNIVERSAL GRAMMAR, AND LAD

Noam Chomsky is a true Renaissance man. He is a linguist, a philosopher, a cognitive scientist, a historian, and an activist; moreover, he is highly respected in all these fields. Chomsky was born in Philadelphia in 1928 to a Hebrew linguistics professor father and a radical activist mother from Belorussia. Although Chomsky's majors at the University of Pennsylvania were linguistics and philosophy, he was very influenced by brilliant mathematicians there who were using mathematical theories to understand linguistic structure (Fox 2007).

Chomsky completed his PhD in linguistics in 1955 and then moved to Harvard for post-doctoral work. It was there in 1957 that he published a slim volume, *Syntactic Structures*, that would come to be considered a turning point for modern linguistics. What the young Chomsky began to see that the white-haired scholars around him failed to recognize was the incredible similarity among all human languages. Until that point, these similarities had mainly been attributed to the fact that all languages were members of "families" and had evolved from a common ancestor of those families. It makes perfect sense that, for instance, in both French and Italian indirect and direct object pronouns are usually placed before verbs because that is the way it was done in Latin. Some linguists believed that there was, in fact, one common ancestor for ALL human languages, and this would certainly explain the similarities among them.

But Chomsky proposed a new way to look at these similarities. He proposed that all languages are outward expressions of an innate system that all humans share, regardless of ethnicity or culture. Languages don't all contain verbs, nouns, adjectives, and adverbs because a group of people eons ago invented those concepts and the words to reflect them, and then passed them down. Languages contain these concepts because they are built into our brains. Chomsky called this idea the Innateness Hypothesis, and later linguists further developed this hypothesis into what is known as Universal Grammar (UG). According to these linguists, we are born with a pattern of grammar in our heads just as we are born with a heart and lungs.

Until that time, many linguists examined what appeared to them to be incredible differences between languages, such as the fact that some rely almost entirely on word order in a sentence to communicate meaning, while others rely on inflections such as prefixes and suffixes. Or they examined the wide range of phonemic and phonetic differences between languages. But what Chomsky maintained was that human languages are as similar to one another as human faces are similar to one another. Differences in word order, inflections, and phonemes are similar to differences in eye color, hair texture, and nose structure. They are, in essence, simply different shades and textures of the very same thing.

Our ability to use this system of Universal Grammar is triggered by being surrounded by language. Chomsky called this ability to assimilate the language we hear and begin using it systematically the Language Acquisition Device (LAD). In children, LAD is primed and ready to go from the moment they are born. They drink in the sounds emanating from the humans around them and watch carefully the facial expressions, the body language, and the results that occur when these sounds are spoken. Within two or three years they are employing language in constantly creative ways to produce sentences that they have never heard and that might never be heard again.

When I first learned of Universal Grammar, I imagined it as a map of the New York subway system. I pictured this system lying quietly, with no lights and no trains running, in the brains of every newborn. Then I imagined the tracks lighting up slowly and one or two trains at a time beginning to run on the rails as the LAD triggered construction along each line. I imagined that some lines would never be completed because some languages have no use for some forms that are built into Universal Grammar, such as gender for inanimate objects. These lines would fall into disrepair, only to be activated if the child were exposed to a new language that contained those forms. By the time the child has grown into an adolescent, most of the lines will be running efficiently with only occasional delays or problems—even the lines that take communication to the levels of abstraction that require verb forms such as the past subjunctive and the conditional.

But what happens to the Universal Grammar and the Language Acquisition Device if a child does not hear or otherwise experience language? There are many deaf children born in isolation from signing communities, and there have been very rare instances of children raised by animals or kept in isolation from humans during early childhood. These children have taught us that the LAD does not stay primed and waiting for input forever. It begins to deteriorate if it isn't used, and a child who does not acquire a first language at a very young age will never truly acquire a language. She might learn a few words and even be able to create some simple sentences, but she will never have full access to the intricate system of Universal Grammar (Lennenburg 1967; Rymer 1993). This train of thinking is called the Critical Period Hypothesis, and it theorizes not only that it is impossible to acquire a first language after early childhood, but also that it becomes more and more difficult (though not impossible) for a person to acquire a second language as she grows older.

Are there scholars who differ with Chomsky in any of his theories? Yes, there are many, particularly cognitivists and behaviorists. The latest challenge to Chomsky has come from academics in the field of Modern Computational Linguistics, also known as Natural Language Processing (NLP), whose statistical models of language are used to create translation tools such as Google Translate and Siri. Some of these experts maintain that deep-structure models of language such as Universal Grammar have not been corroborated by the massive amounts of data that they have gathered for their statistical analyses.

And are these theories in truth much more complicated than can be explained in a few paragraphs? They are, without a doubt. But I believe that the essentials I have provided here are a solid foundation. If you are interested in learning more, please consult the bibliography, especially Lantolf and Frawley (1988), McLaughlin (1987), MacWhinney (2008), Pienemann (1999, 2005), and Tarone (1982).

WHOLE LANGUAGE, STEPHEN KRASHEN, ACQUISITION VS. LEARNING, AND INPUT +1

The Chomsky revolution was followed by new approaches to language pedagogy, the most important of which were the Whole Language Approach and the Natural Approach. In the 1960s Ken Goodman began publishing his theories about the importance of employing Whole Language in teaching literacy. He maintained that children should acquire reading naturally, the way they acquired spoken language (Goodman 1967). A decade later Tracy Terrell employed a similar analysis to second language acquisition (Terrell 1977). He maintained that students should not be memorizing vocabulary lists or studying grammatical structures before they even get to hear, read, or try using the target language. They should be exposed to whole chunks of the language employed in context or with visual aids, and in that way they will naturally assimilate the language. In other words, teachers should not be doing things such as making students memorize past tense conjugations before allowing the students to hear stories about past events or try communicating about something that happened to them. The students should FIRST hear a story about something that happened, and by means of the context, begin processing how past events are communicated in the second language.

During the 1970s another linguist came on the scene and turned the field of second language acquisition on its head. His name is Stephen Krashen, and he is most famous for five interlocking theories about language acquisition, three of which will be described here. With his Acquisition vs. Learning Hypothesis (1982), Krashen proposed that we were going about our jobs as language instructors in the wrong way. He maintained that children naturally acquire their first languages without being taught anything, and that students of a second language can do the same thing. *Language acquisition*, he maintained, is a subconscious process that does not require tedious drills, memorization, or extensive and conscious use of grammatical rules. *Language learning*, according to Krashen, is a conscious process that requires memorization and learning rules but does not necessarily result in giving the learner any communicative abilities. As proof, he pointed to the numerous students who spend years studying a language, and possibly even get high grades, yet cannot carry on a conversation. On the other hand, he pointed to the numerous examples of children who have moved to a new country and, after six months playing with other children, were fluent in their new languages without having received any overt instruction.

When I first heard about this theory, the image of two kids with bicycles came to my mind. I imagined one child studying her bicycle carefully with the help of a tutor, memorizing all the names of the parts and how the mechanisms worked, studying the principles of how it is that a human being is capable of balancing on a bicycle and pedaling at the same time. None of this study would help her to ride her bicycle. The other child watches her siblings and other kids on the block ride their bicycles. She sits on the seat sometimes and balances herself up against a tree. One day, her mother holds her up on the bicycle and runs alongside her as she pedals. The mother lets go and the girl wobbles and then falls down and scrapes her knee. Once more they try, and this time when Mom lets go . . . she's off! The way that I interpret Krashen's Acquisition vs. Learning Hypothesis is that we as teachers need to be more like this mother than the tutor.

Another hypothesis developed by Krashen is known commonly as Input +1. In essence, Krashen maintained that everyone, children and adult students of a second language alike, acquires language almost entirely by being exposed to comprehensible "input." The key to making progress in the language is being exposed to language that is slightly beyond what we already understand, hence the term Input +1.

Allow me to give two examples. Imagine a baby that knows the word "doggy." He loves this word and uses it repeatedly every time he sees a dog. One day he is next to a dog that barks loudly, which causes both him and his father to jump. The father widens his eyes and says, "The doggy barked! Ruff ruff! Doggy barked." In that moment, if he is ready for it, the child acquires the word "barked," because he already knows the word "doggy," and this new word is clearly associated with the somewhat scary action by the dog.

The next example I'll give comes from my own experience acquiring Spanish. When I was twenty-four years old I quit my job as a newspaper reporter and moved to Spain, even though I'd never had a class in Spanish and could do nothing more with the language than order food in Mexican restaurants. Soon after arriving I made two friends, one of whom spoke no English. One evening we were at a café when one of my friends widened her eyes and said to the other woman, *"¡Qué tío más guapo!"* I followed her eyes to the front door, and there stood a stunning man with thick black hair. I understood the word *tío* and that, even though in most varieties of Spanish it meant "uncle," in Spain young people used it to mean "guy." I knew the word *más* (more) (*más vino, por favor*), although I wasn't quite sure what it meant in this context. But as I looked at the flirty smiles on the faces of my new friends, and then looked over at the male model who had just walked into the room, I was pretty certain that *guapo* meant "good-looking." Because I already knew the words *tío* and *más*, I was able to deduce the meaning of *guapo*.

The third Krashen theory I wish to touch upon is called the Affective Filter Hypothesis, and it has to do with stress. Krashen created the term to refer to a psychological barrier that goes up for many people when they are nervous, stressed out, or tired. This psychological barrier makes language acquisition and production much more difficult. This might be a difficult concept to relate to for those of you raised bilingually. But those of you who have acquired a second language, particularly if it was in school, can probably remember a moment when you were nervous and all of sudden the language coming at you made no sense whatsoever, even though you recognized many of the words. Or perhaps you found yourself blanking out during an exam or being totally tongue-tied in a conversation with people who made you nervous. Language acquisition and interaction take place most effectively, according to Krashen, when the affective filter of your students is low.

What does all this mean for you as language teachers? It means that it is YOUR responsibility to provide comprehensible input in a low-stress environment. Little by little, day after day, your students will acquire the target language because they will hear new forms embedded in utterances containing language that they already understand. Think of it as a type of scaffolding. They will hear language from each other and, if they are lucky, will also hear it from native speakers. But you are the expert who knows where they have been and where they are headed in terms of language, so it is up to you to provide them with comprehensible input that is slightly above their level. Learning to provide input in this way is hard work and, as you hone your skills, you might be tempted to make your life easier and teach in English. DON'T DO IT! Your students will be fine if they don't understand much of what you say in the beginning. They will start to understand, and you will get better at providing Input +1 the more you do it.

I imagine that at this point you are feeling somewhat skeptical about one aspect of this, as I did when I first started studying the field of second language acquisition. You are questioning Krashen's claim that all a person needs is Input +1 in order to acquire a language. If that is what you are thinking, your skepticism is valid. Even Krashen came to admit that the process of acquisition is far more complicated than that. Nonetheless, Krashen radically changed the way we think about learning, acquiring, and teaching languages, and he moved the field into a new realm, as did Chomsky. Because of Krashen and others working along the same lines, we know how important it is to teach IN the target language, not just about it.

MERRILL SWAIN AND THE OUTPUT HYPOTHESIS

In the 1980s linguists began to grapple with the perplexing issue of the low level of oral proficiency of some children in immersion elementary schools, despite having been surrounded by the language of instruction (in most cases French or Spanish) for many years. Merrill Swain spent years observing in French Canadian schools and came to the conclusion that, although

many children reached near-native levels of listening and reading comprehension, they were not producing enough oral language to become fluent
speakers. She formulated what became known as the Output Hypothesis
(Swain 1985).

I have a favorite quotation that comes from an article Swain published
in which she writes that "output may stimulate learners to move from the
semantic, open-ended, nondeterministic, strategic processing prevalent in
comprehension to the complete grammatical processing needed for accurate production. Output, thus, would seem to have a potentially significant
role in the development of syntax and morphology" (Swain 1995).

When I show or read this quote to students in my teaching methodology course, the first reaction by the majority is something along the lines of
"What in the heck does that mean?" But after they reread it slowly and we
discuss the issue, the meaning becomes clear. There is one kind of processing that goes on in a person's head when she mainly listens to a language
and is required to show comprehension. The act of creating speech to express thoughts in her head requires a higher level of ability, a more "complete grammatical processing." In other words, in order to learn to speak a
language, you have to speak it.

The logic of that statement sounds simple and natural. In fact, for children
surrounded by their first language, the process of learning to speak is simple
and natural. But in a classroom it is a very different story. You will come to
see that getting students to actually speak the language you teach requires
considerable knowledge and numerous strategies on your part because of
one simple fact: in the majority of classrooms, they speak another language
perfectly well that they can use for communication.

As I've contemplated the research by Swain and others, an image often comes to mind: the image of water turning into snowflakes. I imagine
the water as the fluid language ability that comes with understanding
words that are flowing past you. But as you begin to speak, connections
are made in your mind and abilities are solidified that resemble the connections that occur between individual crystals as water solidifies in tem-
peratures below 32 degrees Fahrenheit around particles of dust. We want
this "solidification"—the ability to use morphology and syntax in the new
language—to happen for our students.

In Chapter 3 we taught you a number of strategies to get your beginning
students speaking with each other in the target language. As you begin to

implement these strategies and you look out over the classroom, content-edly watching your students engage in interaction, please remember one thing: not all output is equal. Are your students using one-word answers that they've chosen from a list? Or producing multiple variations of the same type of verb conjugation? That is fine and, in fact, is all you will expect in the beginning. But as your students move on in this process, you will want to hear them creating with language to express original thoughts. In that way, they are moving beyond the abilities required for comprehension and into the realm of "complete grammatical processing."

SUSAN GASS AND INTERACTION

Gass and other linguists have looked closely at the role of output and how it impacts the development of a second language (Gass 1997). She maintains that output is a way to practice new abilities, a way to get richer output, and a way to move language structures to a point in which they are more automatic. But Gass's primary contribution to the study of second language acquisition is her analysis of what happens during interactions between hu-mans. She takes a step back to look at the intersections and connections be-tween input and output and at what is going on both between the speakers and inside each of their heads. When I shared her 1997 book *Input, Interac-tion, and the Second Language Learner* with a student, he flipped through the complicated diagrams inside and said, "Wow, looks like physics!"

In truth, what Gass has done in her research is very much like science. She thoroughly distilled the research (both hers and that of others) and created models of second language acquisition that are reminiscent of complex chemical reactions. I encourage you to read the book, but here I will provide you with a synopsis of what I consider her most important points.

First of all, Gass looks very closely at the "1" part of the Input +1 hypoth-esis. Quite logically, that extra bit of language beyond what the student comprehends is not all the same for every listener. A student (1) might be almost certain that she understands, (2) might get the gist, (3) might simply recognize it enough to guess at its meaning, or (4) might not understand at all. At this point in a conversation, numerous things could happen. If the student is quite certain she understands, she might try to check her under-standing with a question or might immediately integrate the new language into her reply. Also, she might simply put this new understanding into a type of "storage" to be used in another conversation.

If the student gets the gist of this new language or thinks she understands part of it, she might enter into a type of conversation that linguists call a *negotiation sequence*. She might negotiate the meaning ("A badger? Is it like a dog?"), or she might negotiate the form ("Not drinked? It's supposed to be drank?"). Of course, she might not come to any kind of an understanding, but next time she hears these words or similar words she will probably notice and enter into another negotiation sequence that leads her closer to comprehension.

Looking at them in this way, misunderstandings can be viewed as positive occurrences, as long as they result in continued conversation to try to resolve the misunderstandings. In fact, it is usually because of these little misunderstandings that two speakers enter into negotiations that result in one or both of them improving their comprehension or oral production. These moments are catalysts for change in language abilities.

Teresa Pica included an excellent example from a conversation between participants in research she conducted (NNS stands for Non-Native Speaker and NS stands for Native Speaker):

NNS: The windows are crozed.

NS: The windows are what?

NNS: Closed?

NS: Crossed? I'm not sure what you're saying here.

NNS: Windows are closed.

NS: Oh, the windows are closed, oh, OK, sorry. (Pica 1994).

Let's examine what all of this means for you in your classroom. If this type of negotiation occurs between your students, will you hear them produce the "correct" form immediately? If you don't, does that mean that this approach isn't working? No and no. Gass and Varonis have noted that incorporation of the target-like form heard in a conversation can take a long time to appear in the speech of a learner (Gass and Varonis 1989). I like to image the subconscious toying with this new understanding the way a child toys with Legos. "Should I connect it here or here?" she asks herself. "How about over here?" When the child is ready, she snaps the block into place and holds up her new creation. When a speaker is ready, she snaps her new phrase into place and opens her mouth to use it. Voilà! Acquisition has taken place.

LANGUAGE CHOICES, SPEAKER IDENTITIES, AND MOTIVATION

At the end of it all, after providing our students on a daily basis with comprehensible input, and after skillfully setting up interactive activities for them to produce sufficient output, they will naturally acquire these wonderful languages that we teach. Right?

Well, I hate to tell you this, but there is a complicating factor. You can get your students to class, you can choose excellent textbooks or materials, you can provide them with Input +1 at just the right level of difficulty, and you can design excellent communicative activities. But there is something you cannot do: MAKE your students speak the language you teach. They have choices. They can speak only English, they can speak the very minimal amount necessary in the second language to comply, they can speak a mixture of English and the second language, or they can speak the second language during the entire class time as much as they are capable of given their proficiency level. You can provide rewards and consequences, but it is ultimately their choice.

Despite the fact that almost all of your students have most likely chosen to be in your class (languages are usually elective courses), some will not really want to speak the language for a number of different reasons. One of those reasons is embarrassment or feelings of insecurity. Teenagers, in particular, don't want to sound like a baby. It is very important for them to be "cool." Another reason is simple lack of intrinsic motivation: they're fine with hearing and reading the language, but speaking it feels like too much of an effort. Another reason is the fact that some people do not like to comply with the wishes of authority figures. Their personality, their "identity," is closely tied to rebelling, and by not speaking the language they are exhibiting their rebellious tendencies (Minor 2009).

An increasing number of linguists are looking at the factors that impact language choices in the classroom, and they have developed a theory of investment to analyze and explain the factors. Bonny Norton proposed that learners invest in a language when they believe that they will receive in return symbolic and material resources, such as friendship, education, status, and money. There are at times conflicting investments at work, pulling a speaker in two different directions concerning language choices (Norton 2000).

Kim Potowski employed various paradigms, including investment, to examine the language choices of elementary students at a Spanish immersion school, a model of education in which children are taught content areas in the target language. She observed that many of the students chose not to use Spanish with one another a good deal of the time. Her data led her to believe that their reasons for speaking the target language were tied up in their investments in being perceived as well-behaved, popular, funny, or proficient Spanish speakers. She wrote, "No matter how well run a language program is, if students' identity investments compete with their investments in developing the target language, or if the classroom environment denies them opportunities to participate in ways that are acceptable to them, their target language growth will not be as great as educators might hope" (Potowski 2004, p. 95).

Whether you teach children, teenagers, or adults, I can guarantee you that there will be some students who resist speaking the target language. Since you will run an interactive classroom that on a regular basis places learners in situations in which they have to speak to each other, the language choices of the rebels will have an impact on the other students AND upon your authority in the classroom. What is a teacher to do? I strongly believe in positive motivational systems that have backup plans involving consequences. These techniques will be discussed in Chapter 9, which deals with classroom management.

But I also want to propose something: the Fun Hypothesis. (I'm going to have to come up with a fancier name if I want to do quantifiable research in this area.) If the activities you bring to class are fun and the students have to use the target language in order to participate, the level of second language output will be considerably higher. Except for a very few rebels or introverts, most students from the very beginning will want to participate in something fun. Plus, the holdouts will usually come aboard soon.

Crucial to the success of "fun" activities is the fact that the teacher is enjoying himself or herself as well. Watch the companion videos for this book of us teaching beginning language courses. You might even want to mute the sound and simply watch the eyes, the expressions, and the body language of everyone involved. Are we having fun? Without a doubt, we are enjoying ourselves, and enjoyment is contagious. Are the students having fun? They certainly appear to be enjoying themselves. Is having fun the goal of your class? Nope. Your goal is for the students to acquire the language you teach. But one of the best ways to reach that goal is for you to design fun communicative activities.

TEACHING GRAMMAR

After guiding you through a half century of research on second language acquisition, after teaching you about the importance of Whole Language, comprehensible input in the target language, communication, interaction, identities, and motivations, I'm going to do a full circle and tell you something that might be unexpected: you probably still have to teach grammar. There are two important reasons for this. First, research over the past twenty years has shown that explicit instruction about grammatical forms can benefit the acquisition process. And second, most language textbooks contain grammar as a central feature of every chapter. At first glance, a chapter might appear to mostly be about communication regarding activities, subjects, or cultures, but as you begin to work with the text you will see that one or more grammatical functions are embedded in everything.

There are numerous explanations for how and why focusing on a grammatical function can help a student, but I am only going to tell you about two: automatization, and the recognition of the fact that the brain functions differently for children than it does for teens and adults. Automatization is the process through which humans learn a new skill. In the beginning they are very conscious of every step involved in using that skill. But with practice, the skill passes into being processed by a different part of the brain and is activated subconsciously. Barry McLaughlin has written that in order for a language learner to become proficient, sub-skills involved in communicating must be practiced, automatized, and integrated (McLaughlin 1987). This approach, which incorporates cognitive and behavioral therapy, has often been held up as the antithesis of Universal Grammar and the Chomsky approach. However, I believe that they are not mutually exclusive and that, in fact, good teaching practice incorporates both.

When I first read about automatization, it made me remember learning to type during my sophomore year in high school. In the beginning, I very consciously searched for each letter on the keyboard and then willed the "correct" finger to strike that letter. Now, typing is automatic for me. I type as fluently as I speak, albeit somewhat more slowly.

So what does that mean for your students? That every time they open their mouths in your classroom they will be consciously and deliberately practicing the target grammar or vocabulary you have set out for them? No. It means that you will explain to them the target grammar (in the language you teach!) and then, *within the communicative activities*, there will be moments when they pause and consciously choose a word or some words based upon what they have been learning. With time and practice, that language that they sometimes had to focus upon and "choose" will become automatic. Will they sometimes choose the wrong word or words? Of course. But with corrective feedback from you and other speakers, and with continued input and interaction, they will gradually begin choosing the correct forms. Then they will gradually begin using those correct forms automatically.

Secondly, it is important to remember that you are not teachers of two-year-olds, but rather of maturing humans ranging in age from twelve years to adult who are already fluent in at least one language. Explicitly studying the grammar of their new language keys into conscious cognitive functions that are part and parcel of what can be expected of an education. In this way, they are learning metalinguistic concepts that will help them analyze all languages, including their own. According to cognitive psychologists, this use of cognitive functions *to support* the second language acquisition that is going on in your classroom is very beneficial. Brian MacWhinney wrote that students who receive explicit instruction as well as implicit exposure to the language have the "best of both worlds" (MacWhinney 1997).

You might be asking yourself at this moment, "How does this work? How and when in my classroom am I going to teach my students about grammar?" There is no magic formula, although the lesson plans we provide with this book might be of some help to you. However, I can give you some guidelines:

1. DO NOT start with grammar. First, give your students input and the chance to show comprehension of the target grammar of vocabulary. Let them get a feel for it before they begin to analyze.
2. Keep your explanations as simple as possible in the target language, and use examples as you go along. Research has shown

that instruction of very complex rules or instruction employing complex language is counterproductive.

3. Expect your students to do much of the "learning" outside of class. They must study and do homework employing the target language.

4. As much as possible, use your class time to interact and practice what they have studied outside of class.

Should you ever use English (or the dominant language of the group) to explain grammar or clear up confusions? We recommend that you do this outside of class. Make yourself available during office hours, or even in the hallway, to go over their questions in English. For some, this check-in time in English can go a long way toward lowering their affective filters.

◊   ◊   ◊

Input, output, interaction, Universal Grammar, the Language Acquisition Device, psychological investments, motivation, and the overt teaching of grammar—how can a new teacher remember all of these theories and concepts? I will summarize by dividing this chapter into four overarching points:

1. *All humans without damage to the language centers of the brain have a subconscious ability to acquire language.* Most of us have observed the amazing ability of children to soak in language and begin producing astute and original observations before they even enter kindergarten. Chomsky has named this ability the Language Acquisition Device (LAD). This ability diminishes with time, but it does not disappear. We as teachers must key into our students' natural, innate capacity to acquire the language.

2. *It is important to teach in the target language and to expect your students to speak in the target language.* It is your job to provide regular comprehensive oral language that is just slightly above the level of the average student. Only by regularly hearing this natural language will your students key into LAD. It is also your job to design and implement communicative activities that provide students with regular opportunities to speak and interact.

3. *Language exists for communication, and this fact must be central to your classes.* Instructors who teach language with the primary focus of their classes being on grammar, vocabulary, and translation

have missed the boat. The primary focus of a language class must be upon communication, and all the other things such as grammar and vocabulary should be taught to support that communication. What good does it do a person to perfectly conjugate a verb in all persons and all tenses if he or she can't have a basic conversation?

4. *You should create an environment that is low-stress and supportive for students to begin to "identify" themselves as speakers of this language.* If the affective filter of students goes up, acquisition will go down. Try to keep the focus on interaction and away from perfection. If they are having fun and feeling successful as speakers, they are much more likely to begin thinking of themselves as someone who can acquire this language.

Doing all of this well is difficult, but you will get better with practice. If you have days when your students don't seem to understand anything you say, they are reluctant to speak in the second language, or the activities you painstakingly planned fall through, try to keep some perspective. Give yourself the same kind of compassion and understanding that you give your students as they make mistakes in their interactions. Just as they will gradually acquire the language you teach, you will gradually become better and better at teaching.

Summary Questions

1. How did Noam Chomsky revolutionize the field of modern linguistics? What is LAD, and how is an understanding of LAD applicable to the teaching of a second language?

_____

_____

2. What is the connection between LAD and Krashen's distinction between language learning and language acquisition? What is Input +1? Does the "+1" part of Input +1 mean the same thing for all students? Explain.

_____

_____

3. Is Input +1 enough to move students forward in their process of acquiring a second language? If not, why not and what else is necessary?

_____

_____

4. Explain the positive impact that miscommunication during a conversation can have on two L2 learners in a language classroom.

_____

_____

Scenarios

Scenario 1

You and another new language teacher just got hired at a high school. You have different preparation periods and decide that once a week you will observe each other's classes in order to give each other helpful feedback. This new colleague is a very energetic and funny guy. You like him and so do his students. On your first day of observation, to your great dismay, you see that he uses English almost all of the time and organizes his class almost entirely around teaching grammar. Students are only expected to speak the target language when they respond to questions from the teacher based upon the questions in the book. You know that it would probably damage your relationship and would not likely do much good if you criticized everything he did. But you resolve to encourage him to make one change in the way he teaches. What will you recommend? Why did you choose this one issue?

_____

_____

Scenario 2

Imagine yourself at the end of your first year of teaching. Which of the following issues has proved to be the biggest challenge for you and why? (1) Staying in the target language. (2) Providing input to the students that is just slightly above their level. (3) Keeping the affective filter low for your students. (4) Creating fun communicative activities. (5) Getting the students to stay in the target language.

_____

_____

6 · Standards of Foreign Language Teaching
The Five C's

DENISE MINOR

During the 1980s there were major shifts in attitudes about education, and a movement began to introduce national standards for all subjects. As part of that movement, the U.S. Department of Education and the National Endowment for the Humanities funded the enormous task of examining the state of K–16 language instruction in this country to see how it aligned with the latest research in second language acquisition (SLA) and pedagogy. This endeavor was a collaborative project, and instrumental to its work was the participation of the American Council of Teachers of Foreign Languages (ACTFL).

THE FIVE C'S

The National Standards Collaborative Board found that, as might be expected, there were many amazing teachers employing whole language and effective communicative techniques in their classrooms. But there were still plenty of teachers who more closely resembled the stern British headmaster portrayed in Chapter 5, who rarely spoke to his students in the target language and who relied on grammatical drills and translation. There was also a wide range of approaches being employed in the university programs that trained future teachers. The Board decided to develop standards for language instruction at the national level. What they unveiled in 1996 is

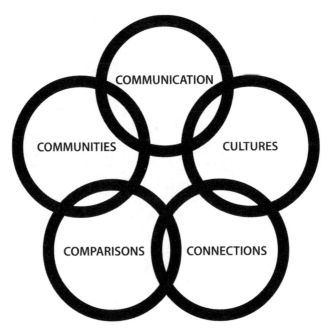

called the Five C's, which stand for Communication, Cultures, Connections, Comparisons, and Communities.

I have to admit that when I first heard about the Five C's I was skeptical. How could a paradigm boil down the incredibly complex research on second language acquisition and effective teaching methodology into five words that coincidentally all start with the same letter? Well, after just one year as an instructor in a language-teaching methodology course, I understood.

First of all, the designers of the Five C's have captured most of what appears to be the essence of all the research on acquisition, communication, culture, and the use of language to express critical thinking. Secondly, by doing so using five terms that start with "C," they have divided these concepts into categories that teachers-in-training are able to recall more easily. I have watched my own students wade with good intentions (but in a slight fog) through readings about the theories of Chomsky, Krashen, Swain, Gass, Potowski, Martinez, and Colombi, only to have a lightbulb come on in their heads when they got to the Five C's. All that they had studied before suddenly made more sense to them, and they began to discuss second language acquisition with greater confidence. The first evening that we were studying the Standards in my seminar, I remember looking over my students' shoulders to see that some of them had written in small letters or in the margins of their handout on the Five C's because they had so many reflections and ideas that they wanted to put down in writing. I have come to realize that this approach works for them, and I am now a big fan of the ACTFL Standards.

Let's look at the standards individually and compare them to the research that had gone before.

Communication

Communication is the most important of the five standards. In fact, it is as important as the other four standards combined, for the reason you studied in Chapter 5: language exists to communicate. This standard captures all of the research done by linguists such as Michael Long and Susan Gass. Through communicative activities teachers learn to stress the use of language in situations that are as close to real life as possible. They learn to emphasize what students can do with language, written and oral, as opposed to what they know about language.

There are three categories within the standard of Communication: Interpersonal, Interpretive, and Presentational. Interpersonal communication is the heart of the standard and focuses on creating situations for the exchange of ideas and information and for the negotiation of meaning between two or more people. Interpretive expression requires that students process and evaluate information or visual input and arrive at conclusions. For instance, students might interpret the images of a painting or might create a new ending for a short story they have read. The presentational mode involves public speaking and the use of formal oral and written language. The importance of formal language has not been explored in this book, but if you are interested in learning more, please refer to the bibliography.

Cultures

Cultural understanding is essential to language education—so essential (in our opinion) that we have dedicated a whole chapter to the issue. Likewise, ACTFL has made cultural education a pillar of the Standards. Instead of confining cultural information to a separate section of a chapter or an occasional lesson, teachers are taught how to incorporate culture into all of their lesson plans. For instance, they learn that when the pedagogical goal is to learn vocabulary to discuss daily routines, their students can learn about daily routines in Japan or Senegal and how those routines differ from their own. By studying culture through language, students also come to better understand the history, customs, and points of view of other people.

Connections

The Connections standard refers to linking language instruction to the other subject areas that students are learning in school. By connecting to the topics being studied in other classes, students not only have an opportunity to reinforce other material from subjects such as science and history, but they also have a greater amount of material for authentic interactions. For instance, if all ninth graders in a high school must take a class on health, a beginning Japanese class could connect the textbook chapter on food and restaurants to the health curriculum. Students could discuss categories of food such as vegetables, carbohydrates, and proteins in Japanese. Then, as a communicative activity, they could plan a Japanese meal (seaweed? sushi?) and an American meal. They could present their menus to the entire class, or to small groups, and other students could vote for categories such as the healthiest, the unhealthiest, and the tastiest meals.

If sixth graders all must learn to play volleyball in physical education class, their German class could learn terms for discussing and playing the game, and then go play it. Before leaving the classroom they could learn essential terms like "Pass it!," "Mine!," and "Ah, I blew it!" If all tenth graders in a high school must study U.S. history, then a Spanish teacher could have students read and discuss in the target language the history of the Spanish presence in Florida or the period in which a vast expanse of the United States belonged to Mexico. There are numerous ways that language teachers can enliven a classroom by connecting with other subject areas. These methods require work, imagination, and communication with the other teachers in a school.

If employed properly, the Connections standard can greatly increase the variety of input and output in the target language by providing material for interaction that is beyond the normal scope of human conversation but is being discussed in other classes. For instance, a group of fifteen-year-olds hanging out together at lunch probably would not employ a wide-ranging vocabulary to describe the food they are eating or what they had for dinner the previous night. Everything is probably good, bad, gross, or OK. However, if they are learning about numerous concepts in their health class including nutrition, food groups, muscle development, and heart rate, those concepts can be fodder for lots of language. The trick, of course, is getting them to really interact about those concepts in the language you teach.

Comparisons

When teachers encourage their students to compare and contrast languages and cultures, they are using the Comparisons standard. Obviously, this standard overlaps with the Cultures standard. But it also goes beyond that standard by expecting students to recognize patterns, make predictions, and analyze similarities and differences, thereby placing them in a situation in which they must use more complex language forms, particularly in their writing. When this standard is employed effectively, a teacher creates situations in which students must use a variety of verb tenses, particularly in the more advanced classes. Also through this standard, students learn to analyze grammatical structures and begin to see how some languages express concepts such as time very differently. For instance, some languages employ the present tense to express something happening in this moment. English, in contrast, uses the present tense mainly to describe habits and uses the present progressive to describe something happening NOW. ("I walk to class with my roommate" vs. "I'm walking to class with my roommate.")

The Comparison standard embodies SLA research in that it includes the importance of cultures and requires students to focus on and analyze grammatical forms in both English and the target language.

Communities

The Communities standard refers to teachers learning about the importance of creating venues for students to use their new language outside the classroom. By nature, the act of going outside the classroom to interact is probably going to create natural, communicative opportunities. It is highly unlikely that a French teacher would take his or her class to a French restaurant only to have the waitress say to a student, "Now, conjugate your verb correctly. I won't bring your food unless you request it properly in the second person formal singular." If she understood him, she will bring the food.

This standard connects closely with a number of the theories stemming from SLA research. For one thing, by getting out of the class and interacting with fluent speakers other than their teacher, students receive varied and authentic *input*, something essential to oral comprehension. Secondly, depending on the type of outing or activity, students might have the chance to interact with fluent speakers. And thirdly, this type of activity Is usually very motivating to students and can increase the likelihood that they will continue trying to interact in the classroom.

This standard is much easier to implement well for teachers who work in a community in which their target language is spoken. If you teach Spanish in Florida, you can easily take your students on field trips to places where they will hear and probably speak Spanish. There are most certainly numerous people you could invite to come speak or (better yet) teach an activity such as cooking or art in Spanish. The same is true if you teach Chinese in San Francisco and Hmong in some areas of Minnesota. But if you teach Greek in Boise or Arabic in Des Moines, you will have to get creative. You could connect your students with pen pals in a country where the language you teach is spoken, and the communication could be done through e-mail or snail mail. You could search out a speaker of the language to visit your class. If you have Internet in you classroom, a projector, and a screen, you could arrange for an interview with a native speaker via Skype. If you live in a city with a movie theater that screens independent and foreign films, you could keep your eye on their billboard to see if a movie in the language you teach is presented. Whatever the case, do your best to help students realize the connection between this language they are learning and humans out in the "real" world. One of the goals of the Communities standard is to encourage students to come to think of themselves as lifelong learners who go out of their way to interact with people from different backgrounds.

IMPACT ON TEACHING

In 2011, ACTFL published the findings of an assessment it had conducted on the impact the Five C's have had in the areas of research, assessment, and teaching. The document is called *A Decade of Foreign Language Standards: Influence, Impact, and Future Directions* (Phillips and Abbott 2011). In essence, the council found that the Standards have had an enormous impact on research. Investigators found that, in the ten years after the introduction of the Standards, there were 591 references to them in scholarly literature, with the Standards being the principal focus of 167 of the published articles. At the state administration level, ACTFL found that the Standards have had a significant impact. In the education department websites of forty states, the Five C's were clearly prioritized.

At the district level, the university level, and in the classrooms, the impact of the Standards was harder to ascertain. However, they did find that most teacher credential/license/certificate programs they examined taught the Five C's, and that numerous districts funded training for teachers at conferences focused on the Standards. But they also found challenges. For instance, some districts have been unwilling to provide funding and education for language teachers to become better educated about the Standards. They also found considerable evidence that many teachers "are unwilling to abandon a primarily grammatical syllabus, focus on textbook coverage, consider the Standards a waste of time [and] want classroom autonomy, not collaboration." Among those teachers who had embraced the Standards, the majority wholeheartedly focused on Communication and Cultures. Many found the standards of Connections, Comparisons, and Communities to be less essential.

What do I take away from these findings? I happen to agree with the majority of the teachers who have embraced the Standards: Communication and Cultures are at the heart of what we are doing in the classroom. Those who create classroom activities where they constantly employ communicative activities and where culture is a centerpiece for much of the communication are likely doing a very good job. In fact, if they are truly employing those two standards, it is likely that they are reaching many of the goals of Comparisons and Communities.

I also imagine that creating significant change in the way languages are taught in this country is something that will take more than one decade. The catalyst for change will most likely be in the places where future teachers are trained: teacher credential/license/certificate programs and beginning language training programs at universities. As more departments of education and graduate programs in language begin incorporating the Five C's or other approaches that focus on communication and culture into their curriculum, more and more teachers and professors will move into the workplace trained in this philosophy and methodology. It will simply be a matter of time.

◊ ◊ ◊

In some fields there is a disconnect between research and practice when it comes to pedagogy. But through the implementation of the Five C's, the

American Council of Teachers of Foreign Languages and other educational organizations have launched a drive to help bridge the gap between what research has shown to be best practice when it comes to language instruction and what is actually happening in the classroom.

At the heart of the Five C's is the standard of Communication, which includes the Interpersonal, Interpretive, and Presentational categories. In the Interpersonal mode, students will interact with one another in conversations, games, debates, and projects. In the Interpretive mode, they will employ the target language to analyze and interpret art, literature, music, and other cultural practices. In the Presentational mode, students will use formal or academic language to present things such as plays, skits they have written, or research they have done.

The other four C's are: Cultures, Connections, Comparisons, and Communities. Through the Cultures standard, students gain knowledge and understanding of the practices, perspectives, and creations of cultures other than their own. Through the Connections standard, they reinforce their knowledge of other disciplines. Through the Comparisons standard, they develop metalinguistic insight to help them better understand not only the language they are studying but also their first language. They also learn to more objectively compare their own culture to the cultures they are studying. And through the Communities standard, they learn to better participate in bilingual and multilingual communities both in their own regions and in other parts of the world.

How will you as a new teacher incorporate the Five C's into your teaching? That will depend on many factors, including the education you receive in your training program, the expectations of your supervisor, and the resources your school has both to support your professional development by sending you to conferences and to support activities such as field trips. I have heard new teachers say that they tried to focus on improving their abilities in one standard at a time, at first focusing (for example) on Communication, then on Cultures, and then on reaching out to teachers of other disciplines in their school to incorporate Connections. In our book we hope we have given you some guidance that will help you develop your abilities to meet all the standards, particularly those of Communication and Cultures. Please consult our webpage for resources for learning more about all Five C's and links to other sites such as the American Council of Teachers of Foreign Languages.

Summary Questions

1. What are the Five C's? How do the Standards connect to research during the past fifty years in second language acquisition?

_____

_____

2. What was the impetus for the development of the Five C's?

_____

_____

3. Why do you think teachers have been much more likely to embrace the Communication and Cultures standards than the other three? What is your reaction?

_____

_____

Scenarios

Scenario 1

You teach German 2 in a high school and many of your students are juniors. Most juniors are also taking world history, physical education, and biology. You want to incorporate the Connections standard in your practice by including other disciplines in your teaching. What will you do?

_____

_____

Scenario 2

You are teaching first semester Chinese (Cantonese) in a private university in San Francisco, a city with a large neighborhood called Chinatown where there are thousands of residents and business owners who speak Cantonese. What kind of event or outing can you plan that would meet the Communities standard? What are the concrete benefits that your students would get from participating in that event?

_____

_____

7 • Factors Impacting Second Language Acquisition

DENISE MINOR

In your beginning language class there are two students who sit near each other. Both come to class regularly and do all of their homework. Both seem to be paying attention and interacting with others. From chatting with them after class, you know that neither has had much contact with the language you teach before taking this class. At the end of the semester, the first student gets an A on the final exam and can carry on a simple conversation. The second student gets a C on the test and during the oral exam stares blankly at you as if she has never heard this language in her life. What happened?

Decades ago most teachers would have said, "The second student didn't study." But we know now that the situation is often more complicated. There are numerous differences between individuals that significantly impact their ability to acquire a language. Some of the differences are age, aptitude, personality, attitude, anxiety levels, and motivation (Dörnyei 2005; Ellis 1985; Galloway and Labarca 1990; Larson-Freeman and Long 1991; Omaggio Hadley 2000; Rymer 1993). Most of these factors, with the exception of motivation, are out of your control (Minor 2009). You can, however, have some influence upon or work with the other factors. In the first part of this chapter, I will briefly review the characteristics most commonly researched by linguists in order to understand the differences among language learners. The second part of the chapter will be dedicated to understanding various motivations and how you can work with those motivations to improve student learning and to better create a community in your classroom. If you

are interested in learning more about any of these characteristics, consult the bibliography.

AGE

Nobody will argue that age does not matter when it comes to acquiring a language. We see the reality of this difference everywhere, as in the children who move to the United States from non-English-speaking countries and, within two years, are fluent. As they animatedly recount in great detail the story of their summer vacation or negotiate complicated interactions on the playground in English, their parents are still struggling to make a doctor's appointment on the phone. Quite likely, their grandparents can communicate very little.

Most research in this area starts from the premise of the Critical Period Hypothesis, a hypothesis that postulates that the ability to acquire a second language begins to deteriorate at a certain age during childhood. The debate lies in the discussion of *when* that deterioration begins to take place, with the majority agreeing that acquisition gets harder after puberty. There is considerable evidence that phonemic coding ability declines very early, possibly as early as infancy. What that means is that with each passing year it becomes harder to achieve a "native" accent.

The majority of you will be teaching at a high school, college, or adult school, so you will be teaching people who have passed the critical period. But most of your students are still young enough to become fluent, and it will simply take more time than it would have if they were five years old. Also, remember this: there are outliers. I know from having taught adults in night school for years that there are many older students who have an uncanny aptitude for language and are highly motivated. I'll never forget the best student in my Spanish 2 night class at a community college, a sixty-five-year-old retired engineer. In the beginning, he seemed to be somewhat shy and did not appear confident sitting in the middle of a large group of twenty-year-olds. But as the semester wore on there were constantly situations in which he stood out, because his homework was well done or he knew the answers to difficult questions. The younger people started gravitating toward him for group work. On the last two exams he got the highest grades. After the final exam we all went out to a restaurant and he was the center of attention.

On a final note about age, I must add that I didn't begin to learn Spanish until I was twenty-five years old, and now I am a Spanish linguistics professor.

APTITUDE AND COGNITIVE STYLE

Some people are gifted when it comes to language acquisition, although few of those are gifted in every single attribute that impacts the process. For instance, some students have an uncanny knack for capturing native-like pronunciation. It may be a coincidence, but I have found that many of my students who are also musicians are attuned to the differences they hear in phonemes and are able to repeat them.

Some people are very analytical and can look at a conjugation paradigm (the pattern for conjugating verbs in a tense) and understand it immediately. They often score very high on the sections of exams that require verb conjugations. Some people have excellent memories for vocabulary. I have been stunned by beginning students who, at just the right moment in a communicative activity, come up with words we had studied months earlier, such as *butaca* (easy chair) or *yuntas* (cuff links). Sometimes they seem surprised themselves and shrug their shoulders as if to say, "It just popped into my head."

Then there are the students who are simply strong in communicative competence. It's not that they can always conjugate verbs correctly or that their accent is particularly good. It's simply that, when you put them in a situation in which they need to communicate, they are excellent at pulling everything together to make that communication happen. They might use gestures or paraphrasing or lexicon that isn't quite right, but they manage to get their point across.

Whenever you notice the strengths of your students, say something to them. You can simply point out the fact that their pronunciation is very good or that they have a great memory. However, be careful not to give this encouragement when there are only one or two students standing nearby unless you have some encouraging words for them as well. It might be taken as a sign to them that their pronunciation is not very good or that they don't have good memory.

PERSONALITY

Some researchers have studied the correlation between personality type and language acquisition. These studies are numerous and often complex, but the bottom line seems to be that extroverts learn more quickly than introverts. This is simply because they interact more, and there are myriad benefits that come from interacting in the target language. For instance, by interacting more, extroverts produce more spoken language. The act of speaking a language out loud in real communication appears to improve the syntactic structures of the language learner. Also, by talking more, the extrovert elicits more input from her conversation partner and therefore is hearing more language. This back-and-forth of conversation gives the learner opportunities to test new language structure, to self-correct, and to negotiate meaning.

When I started teaching I assumed that it would be best to pair extroverts with introverts for communicative activities. I reasoned that the extrovert would draw the introvert out into more communication. But I've learned that is not always the case. Sometimes an extrovert ends up dominating the conversation so much that nobody gets a word in edgewise. Try different pair and group combinations, and then watch carefully. Sometimes, if the communicative activity is truly interesting, two introverts will end up sharing the "talking time" (instead of just sitting there listening), and both will get the benefits of speaking the second language out loud.

ATTITUDE

If you have a positive attitude about the culture in which the target language is spoken, you will be more successful in the process than you would be otherwise. At least, that is what research has shown, and it certainly makes sense. If you are fascinated by Japanese history, love Japanese food, and plan to travel to Japan, you will probably do much better in your Japanese class than the person who is learning the language because it is a work requirement.

Hopefully, most of your students have a positive attitude about the cultures that speak the language you teach. But you can help that along by incorporating culture into your class as much as possible. Music, movies, and Internet pen pals are some of the ways you can impact your students' attitudes.

ANXIETY LEVELS

If you are following the recommendations in this book, you are probably creating classroom environments that are low-anxiety. In that way, you make it much easier for your students to acquire the language. But even if you do everything right, you still might have a few students who are very anxious about speaking. When anxiety kicks in, it is not only their ability to speak that decreases but also their ability to comprehend. Some linguists, such as Stephen Krashen, call this the affective filter. When the affective filter goes up, understanding and the ability to communicate go down. To promote understanding of what this phenomenon feels like, I tell teachers-in-training to imagine driving through a mountain range while listening to a radio station. At times the reception is clear, but then suddenly you turn a corner and it fades and becomes fuzzy with static. Then, around the bend, it might become clear again. That is the way it feels for some students as they listen in your class.

If you have a student who appears to suffer from anxiety or tells you that he does, there are a few ways you can help. The main thing to remember is that by reducing stress, you reduce anxiety. During class, give him some questions with English cognates to see if that helps. If he says anything at all, smile and nod your head. Take whatever he has said and give some type of positive feedback. If the student has come to your office for an oral exam and appears to be fighting off an anxiety attack, ask him to chat for awhile in English. Slowly switch to some very simple questions in the target language, and then ease into the oral exam. The main thing you can do is to let him know that you are on his side.

MOTIVATION

Human motivation is the most complex and (in my opinion) most interesting factor impacting acquisition of a second language. In fact, there are multiple motivating factors that intersect and affect each other—motivations that change depending upon the circumstances. I divide these motivations into three categories: internal, academic, and social. As teachers, you have significant control over the academic and social factors, but you can also key into the internal motivations of your students.

One of the most important things to remember is to respect the motivations of an individual or a group. Don't think of them in terms of "should," as in "They *should* be more motivated by grades" or "They *should* have more internal motivation to learn this language." Think in terms of what *is*, and create environments in which they learn the language because of things they care about.

Internal Motivation

Teachers and linguists both say that the internal motivation a student brings to the endeavor of learning a language is paramount. If the student arrives at class every day really wanting to learn, he or she will learn regardless of other factors such as age or aptitude. These people are a joy to teach. Some of the reasons for high internal motivation are: the student comes from a family or culture in which the target language is spoken; the student plans to travel to a place where the target language is spoken; the student wants to communicate better with people who speak the language, such as clients, patients, or new friends; or the student identifies himself or herself as the kind of person who speaks the target language (for instance, some young people in states like California, Texas, and Florida like to think of themselves as bilinguals who fit well in their bicultural/bilingual region).

How will you work with the internal motivations of students? It is very hard to look at every single student and try to nurture his or her desires to learn (especially if you have three or four classes), but you can look at your students in terms of groups. For example, if some students in your Chinese classes are third generation in families that emigrated from China, give the entire class assignments through which they can become more connected to their families. For Chinese 1, you might assign all students to create a family tree and encourage them to interview their parents and grandparents. For Chinese 2, you might assign them to interview an older person (such as a grandparent) in the target language about his or her childhood. For those who don't have Chinese grandparents, you might have to help them connect with somebody. Strengthening ties of heritage can be very motivating for language learners.

If you teach at a university with a study abroad program, invite somebody from that office to speak to your class about the campuses located in countries where the language you teach is spoken. There are few things that will light a fire under a language student in quite the same way as picturing herself in a beautiful foreign city talking to the people who live there.

Academic Motivation

Grades matter to most people. After going through a considerable amount of behavioral training in the last ten years, I have come to look at grades in a very different way from the way I did as a beginning teacher. Now I am amazed that we are socialized to work hard in order to receive a letter or a number on a piece of paper. Sometimes I wonder what this system must look like to people from cultures where education takes place only for the intrinsic rewards of getting better at something or learning more. Be that as it may, grades significantly impact the behavior of most students in our country. However, if you are a high school teacher you will undoubtedly have some students who truly don't care about grades. They are in your class because they have to be in school. If you teach at an elite university, you will probably have some students who care about nothing else except their grades. Whatever the case, recognize and respect the situation and then work with it. If you create a grading system that is consistent and fair, you will be able to get most students to buy into it, at least to a degree.

Assessing and grading students will undoubtedly take up a big chunk of your time, and it is an important part of your job. But beyond this job requirement, I have found that grades can be used to help develop other kinds of motivations. For instance, during the first quarter that I taught at a competitive research university, I was frustrated by the fact that most of the students seemed to be what I called "grade chasers." I had come to that institution from an urban medical center where I taught night classes to health care professionals, a group that refused to do homework but brought heart and soul to every interactive moment in class. Now that I have more understanding and respect for human behaviors and motivations, I no longer use the term "grade chasers," but instead prefer "high achievers."

From the first week at the elite university, I had the feeling that my students were sizing me up and asking themselves, "How do I get an A out of her?" When I would introduce fun activities for interacting in pairs or groups, some would undoubtedly ask, "Are we being graded on this?" I tried to tell them to just "let go" and have fun with the language. Some of them would smile and nod politely, but I could see that there was no way I was going to change the fact that this was how they operated. This characteristic was one of the reasons they got into that university in the first place.

So, I made extra credit index cards with their names on them and started recording points on the cards for particularly good Spanish interaction. I would watch them talk animatedly with other people, then immediately look over to see if I was scribbling down points. It amazed me. But over the course of the quarter, as they began enjoying these interactions more and more, I would "accidentally" leave the cards in my office. I was happy to see that they stopped caring about the points and got caught up in the enjoyment of speaking Spanish.

On the other end of the spectrum are students who really don't care about grades. Look at their situation and ask yourself why they should care. Maybe they have no intention of going to college, and getting an A is no different from barely passing a class when it comes to earning a high school degree. And maybe they don't even intend to graduate from high school, but instead will drop out and get a job as soon as they can. For these students, you will probably have to link grades to something that *is* meaningful to them. In order to do that you will have to get to know them. Considerable research has shown that high school students are very motivated by money and getting paid for good grades works wonders. (They had to do research to figure that one out?)

But there are things other than money that you can use. For instance, one high school teacher I know constantly carries around little tickets she calls "Bravos." She hands them out for various reasons, including good grades. Students cash them in at the end of the week for things such as time on the computer, glow ink pens, chocolate bars, or a "freebie" on a homework assignment, meaning that they don't have to turn in that assignment. How did she come up with the rewards for the Bravo system? She simply asked them. One of the many future teachers she has mentored reported to me that this system helped some lower-achieving students become more invested in their grades. In turn, they started speaking more in class. Additionally, an improvement in grades is usually an indication that the student is learning the language, which is your ultimate goal.

In the middle of the spectrum are plenty of students who care somewhat about grades but are just as invested in other reasons for learning the language, such as connecting with their heritage or having fun interacting in class. Some of these students are perfectly satisfied with a B or a C. Some are working hard and still getting a B or a C. I respect that, but I also like to boost their confidence by praising them when they do get an excellent grade. Sometimes I say something to them after class, and sometimes I share with the entire class the short essay they wrote that scored an A+. For students who usually get Bs and Cs, those moments of getting to shine because of a high grade can be incredibly motivating.

Social Motivation

Just as we have an instinct to acquire language, we also have the instinct to interact with other humans. In fact, these two instincts are intimately intertwined. By the time your students arrive in your high school, college, or adult school classroom, they have grown used to fulfilling their social instincts through their first language. Your job is to channel that desire to interact *through* the language you teach. It seems like it would be easy, right? On the one hand you have humans who are motivated to socialize, and on the other you have this language, right? But it is not easy.

You can (to a great degree) control their input by speaking to them only in the target language, but you cannot control their output. In other words, you cannot force anyone to speak a language. However, you can increase their motivation to speak the second language in a variety of ways. In this section I'm going to address the ways you can use two kinds of social motivation to increase the amount of second language interaction in your classroom: first, the motivation to interact in pairs or small groups, and second, the motivation to form a community or a "team."

Small Group Interaction

Your students are going to get to know each other. They are going to tell each other about their habits, families, and dreams. They are going to learn about each other's childhoods, including who used to go camping and who stole candy from the store. They are going to find out from each other about the best places in town to hang out, to get Mexican food, and to listen to music. If you do a good job setting up interesting interactive activities, it is very likely that some of your students will become friends, and a few of them might even fall in love. And they will do all of this through the language you teach.

By creating pair and small-group activities you will dramatically increase the amount of oral language they produce in comparison to the old-fashioned teacher-centered approach to instruction. A natural by-product of this is that they will start to feel connected to one another, and will even start to like each other. This kind of bond is the perfect psychological situation for language development.

Classroom Community

Just as students in your class will begin to form friendship bonds, they will also come to feel connected to the class as a whole. Part of this will be because you will ask them to move around for interactions so that they get to know people other than those they usually sit by. Part of this will also be because they come to see themselves as an important member of the class. In order for this to happen, you cannot put too much emphasis on the grade hierarchy. Show that you value other skills, such as their acting ability in skits or their creative writing in poetry. I call this "the butcher, the baker, the candlestick-maker" approach in that every member of a village is valued for his or her skill. They are not all trying to be the winners in the grade game.

With the butcher, the baker, the candlestick-maker approach, almost everyone gets positive feedback. At first you will have to make a concerted effort to watch for their talents, but with time it will become second nature. As most students come to see that they are valued in your classroom without regard to their test grades, they will bring more and more psychological energy to your classroom. They will make more concerted efforts to interact.

When I try to teach this approach to students in my methodology class, some raise concerns that my students will become quite happy with no longer trying for good grades. But I assure them that is not the case. Grades are such an intrinsic part of our educational system that the high achievers will continue to shoot for them. I simply want all the B and C students to feel as good about learning the language as the A students.

You can take this community or "team" feeling one step further and use it to create more output in the target language with some type of group motivational system. If the team achieves the goal you propose, they win some type of award. The following is an example of how I use this method in a first- or second-semester Spanish class at a university. I adapted it from a similar method I saw employed in a second-grade Spanish immersion classroom. Take it and make it your own depending on your circumstances and what things motivate your students.

As you've learned in previous chapters, it is essential that you speak with your students in the target language. You will ask them to interact in the language as well, but you will often hear English. For the first couple of weeks, until students take their first exam, I simply ignore the English. On the day that I return their exams there are inevitably some happy expressions and some long faces. I find that this is a particularly opportune moment to propose a method of improving everyone's final grade. Here's what I tell them:

> Every day I will write two boxes in the corner of the board. One contains the word *Inglés* and the other the word *Español*. Every time I hear English I'll put a mark in the English box. Every time I hear very good Spanish or Spanish that isn't required (for example, chatting about the weekend) I'll put a mark in the Spanish box. At the end of class I will subtract the English marks from the Spanish marks, and that is the number I'll record in my roll book. The running toll will be written

above the boxes. By semester's end, if the class reaches 100 points, everyone's final grades will go up by 1 percent and there will be a semester-end party. Everyone is permitted to ask for a translation once a day, and English is permitted for clarification during the final five minutes of class.

After explaining the system, I allow the students to vote and, until now, their support has always been unanimous. This system has never failed to increase the amount of Spanish spoken in my classes. It works for many reasons. Almost everyone is motivated by grades and therefore each person has an individual reason to work for success. But there is also the social "team" motivating factor in that the group enjoys watching the number on the board inch further each day towards 100. They censor one another for speaking English, and that peer pressure increases the amount of output in the second language.

I have used other rewards besides grades, and they have been almost as effective. For instance, one semester I had a very sleepy 8:00 a.m. class. I told them that if they reached 100 points, during the last week I would take them all out for coffee and a bagel or pastry. About a month into the system, I overheard one young man say to another (in English!), "I hate coffee and I hate bagels, but I love to win." I pretended like I didn't hear that comment because I didn't want to take away points. He was saying this to a person who hadn't quite bought into the system, and I was hoping peer pressure would move his commitment along.

Another aspect that I like about this system is that I don't have to cajole or chastise students for speaking English. I simply put a mark in the English box and shrug my shoulders as if to say, "Sorry, it's the rule." However, I am usually very generous in that if a student loses a point for the class, she then has the chance to explain herself in Spanish and gain a point in the Spanish box.

Will this always work for every student? No. Will it always work perfectly for the group? No again. But it almost always works well. I have found that by keying into the multiple motivations of your students—individual, academic, and social—you can create an environment where MOST of the students will engage in stimulating interactions in the target language and truly enjoy learning.

However, I guarantee you that there will be rebels. You will need to develop behavioral intervention strategies to bring those rebels aboard, and you will need to do that not just for their benefit or so that you don't have to put up with disrespect. You will need to develop those strategies in order to prevent them from taking away from the dynamic learning environment that you have worked so hard to create. Those strategies will be the subject of a later chapter.

Summary Questions

1. What is the Critical Period Hypothesis? Have you seen a difference in the way age has impacted people you know who are trying to learn a language?

_____

_____

2. In what ways are some people better at learning a language than others? What does "communicative competence" mean?

_____

_____

3. How do attitudes and anxiety affect the ability of a person to learn a second language?

_____

_____

4. What kinds of motivating factors exist that affect learning a language in a classroom? In your opinion, is one kind of motivation more important than another?

_____

_____

Scenarios

Scenario 1

You have a student who sits in the back of the room and always keeps her eyes down. At first you thought she was not motivated and was looking down because she was texting with her cell phone. When you called on her the first couple of times she simply shook her head and looked away. The next time you called on her she answered, but you could hear her voice tremble. When you put her in a group and each student had to describe a drawing, you could see that her forehead was shiny with perspiration. It occurs to you that she might suffer from anxiety. Will you talk to her about it?

What can you do to reduce her anxiety but still give her opportunities to interact with the language?

Scenario 2

You teach a language class in which about half of your students are heritage speakers (it is their home language). Most of the heritage speakers seem to be very motivated by activities that involve creating short skits or responding to video clips or short readings. However, they seem bored by the interactive activities that are designed to practice skills such as talking about the past. The other students appear to be more motivated by the simple interactive activities. They seem to enjoy simply practicing this new language.

What ideas do you have for activities that will motivate everyone? Do you have any ideas for pairing heritage speakers with second language learners?

Part III • Beyond the Basics

8 • Types of Teachers; Dos and Don'ts

NORMA LÓPEZ-BURTON

TYPES OF TEACHERS

Part of my job at the University of California, Davis, is to train and mentor new teachers. To that effect, I teach a methodology class and also visit each teacher once a quarter (three visits for new teachers), followed by a meeting to give feedback.

Although I have seen some amazing individuals who seem to have been born teachers, most of us mortals learn on the job, modifying what we do based on the supervisor's comments, reading sometimes unpleasantly accurate student evaluations, or learning from unsuccessful or embarrassing moments in the classroom that are quickly followed by "Note to self . . ."

When visiting teachers, I go through many emotions. Sometimes the classes I observe are very good. Some are so good, I have to tell them at the end, "That activity was superb, do you mind if I share it with others?" or, "You know, I am going to use that line. That was very funny." It is thrilling to observe a natural. It is like sitting down and eating a fine meal. It is very satisfying, even if I didn't have anything to do with the cooking. The comments to those teachers are easy: "You have very good control of the class," "The students responded well to that last exercise," "You are so well organized." My compliments to the chef!

On the other extreme are the classes that are a challenge to sit through and to improve, but I strongly believe there is always hope; I am the perfect example!

Knowing when and how to give feedback as I critique these classes is a little tricky. The long list of dos and don'ts that I come up with in a short fifty minutes can be overwhelming to a new teacher and render the whole process counterproductive. It can be overwhelming for me too, so to help me better understand the teachers, pinpoint problems, find solutions, and keep my sanity all at the same time, over the years I have classified teaching assistants (TAs) into different types of teachers. Some have characteristics from one or several types, and I see a little bit of each in my early teaching life. Look at where I and others have failed, and learn from our stories of the good, the bad, and the funny ways we used to teach.

The Guardian Angel

This teacher feels he is the protector of his children from the evil educational system. He doesn't want the students in his care to have a bad time, stress out, or hate him in any way. He will side with the students and empathize when they are suffering due to some oppressive departmental policy, like prohibiting the use of dictionaries during an in-class composition. If he must comply with this, he will then help the students by being a human dictionary, translating any word the students don't know but need in order to complete the task. Students, far from hating him, love him! He will speak slowly, veeerry sloooowly, to make sure they understand eeeeevery woooord. Phrases are said word by word, even syllable by syllable to ... make ... sure ... they ... com ... pre ... hend. He also tends to use gestures (a truly essential part of language teaching) way too much. "*Yo*," (I) the teacher says, urgently pointing at himself to students already in the fourth week of class, "*Yo hablo mucho*" (I speak a lot). This is accompanied by the "blah, blah, blah" hand gesture near the mouth, and *mucho* is acted out with arms wide open. "*Yo hablo mucho*," he repeats, and gestures again. "*Mucho*," more gestures.

Gestures are very necessary to get the message across the first couple of times you introduce a new word (maybe three times, four tops). After that, the students generally get it. Drop the gesture and use the word in context. To keep using a basic gesture for a word like *hablo* for four weeks is phenomenally unnecessary. Your students are not idiots; they got it a few weeks ago.

Speaking unnaturally slowly is a disservice to the student. Students will never encounter that kind of speech anywhere in the real world. Additionally, it can come across as patronizing. If your only goal is that they just pass the next test, then don't change a thing. But if you want your students to eventually communicate with people other than their fellow students or language teachers, you must start speaking at a more normal speed. I don't mean fast, I am just saying normal. If the new structure is *Vas a hacer* (You are going to do), you could say, for example:

"¿*Quévasahacer?*" (Whatareyougoingtodo?)

They stare at you and wonder what you just said. You break it down:

¿Qué – vas – a – hacer? (What – are – you – going – to- do?)

Write it on the board.

Repeat it slowly, then faster until you reach normal speed.

Say it at a normal speed again: "¿*Quévasahacer?*"

Say it several times.

Have the students repeat it at the normal speed several times.

After that, don't go back to slow! Maybe the next day if some students don't remember, write it on the board so they see it, but don't revert to unnaturally slow speech. They will get used to the normal speed and will understand. Have a little faith in yourself and your students.

I have visited teachers who seem to speak twice as fast in class as I do. I am thinking, "What? There is no way the students will understand," but to my amazement, they do! They understand and respond well to Mr. Speedy

González. They get used to the speed, just like they'll also get used to your accent. It is a natural human process. Just like our eyes adjust to light or the dark, our stamina improves with increased exercise, or our bodies get used to high altitude, so do our ears adjust to faster language. We may struggle at the beginning, but we get used to decoding the faster speech.

The Guardian Angel also makes sure he doesn't incorporate in his speech any word at all that he has not introduced before, so his expressions come out a little funny: "Yesterday I go to the store and buy a pencil." The teacher wants to describe something that *happened*, but because he has not introduced the past tense, he doesn't go anywhere near it. Even if it isn't correct, he feels that at least the students will understand every word he is saying. They may understand every word, but they won't be exposed to the normal whole language, and down the road they won't be able to say, "Oh, that sounds familiar." It's like never saying "What's happening?" because you have not gone over the progressive, and instead saying "What happen?" If the teacher uses whole language and says "What's happening?" in context, the student will get the idea of what is being said even if the gerund has not been formally presented, and he will get a feel for what sounds right later on.

It is the teacher's job to provide normal-sounding speech and to show confidence in the belief that the students will get it. If your face shows doubt, the students will also doubt and ask for clarification in English, and that's when the floodgates will open.

This is not a matter of using the language to talk about difficult concepts. You should not be talking about the meaning of life, or explaining political opinions and hypothetical situations at an elementary level. You should use mostly the vocabulary the students know and the tenses that have been introduced. What you say should be comprehensible, but if what you say has a few words and tenses your students don't know, as long as they are not essential to understanding the story, please leave them in. If the unknown words are surrounded with words the students know, they'll figure it out. It's similar to when we read; we don't know *every* single word. The words we don't know we skip and figure out what they mean through context. It's the same with spoken language.

If the Guardian Angel does not feel the students will understand every word, he will switch to English—"only temporarily though . . . not too much," he says, "only 2 percent of the time . . . maybe 3 percent at the most." Which gradually becomes a lot more. I have seen it so many times. After a class visit,

I ask the teacher to tell me what percentage of the class he felt he spoke in English. The answer is between 2 and 5 percent, when the reality I have observed is something like 40 to 50 percent. The teacher simply does not realize it. It is very interesting. With that much English spoken in the classroom, the target language input is greatly diminished. One thing I have learned while visiting classes of languages other than Spanish is that I really wanted and needed to hear the target language. The teacher would go on and on in English about a particular grammar point, but I still had not heard the new language used in a larger context. As a student I needed more language input and less explanation in English.

This Guardian Angel means well. He wants to be fair to the students, and in return he wants their love and appreciation. He gets a heartfelt thanks from the students for briefly going into English to clarify a point or two, or three, or ten. The students are grateful for this nice teacher and his kindness as he lightens the burden of having to concentrate and having to figure out things on their own. Learning takes a lot of energy and focus, and it can be terribly frustrating when you don't get what is being said. But is the teacher really doing them a favor? How are they going to fare when they go on to Spanish 2 with a normal-speaking teacher, or worse, with other teachers who naturally speak at warp speed? Just imagine how frustrated they are going to be! The Guardian Angel probably got good student evaluations, but has he really done his job?

The Clueless

This teacher is not mean-spirited; she is just simply unaware of her audience. In a beginner class she will tell something funny that happened to her, using completely unknown vocabulary, with grammar way above the students' level, laugh at her own joke, and then be puzzled, truly wondering why the students are just staring back. "Come on, you guys, that was funny!" Some teachers recover and explain again in simpler terms, use the board or gestures, to get the message across, but the truly clueless will tell the story again louder, as if the students had all of a sudden developed some kind of mass-induced hearing problem. Or she will say the joke again slower because maybe her students have missed a vital piece of information or may have misunderstood the punch line. She thinks she only has to say it again. She is clueless. She might as well have spoken in Greek.

To make what we say comprehensible, we have to keep a mental score-board at all times of the words and the tenses the students already know. Not only should we do this so they understand us, but also to reinforce and repeat the structures that have been introduced. But remember, what we say does not have to be 100 percent known words. Many, many new words could be included in the story as long as you use gestures or use the board. Other unknown words can also be included if they are not terribly essential to the overall understanding of the story.

If we have a story to share, we must go through it in our minds first. Will it be too complicated to explain? Does it require unknown tenses necessary to understand? Could the students understand this or that key word if we drew it? If it requires too many gestures, too many drawings, and too many unknown words, it is best not to share the story. Let's save it for a boyfriend, or our mothers, but let's forget about our students, because to tell it to them we'll have to go into English, and that will benefit only us by getting the laugh we want. It will not benefit our students.

Using too many gestures and drawings to explain something detracts from the point of the story itself. This is what we affectionately call at our institution "The Ceviche Syndrome." This label came about because of an in-cident that occurred in a Spanish 1 class during one of my visits. The teach-ing assistant was telling an input story about what he was doing before and after a big World Cup soccer game. He was introducing verbs like "to eat," "to watch," "to buy," "to walk," "to play," "to talk" . . . all centered around his ex-citement about the big game. In the story, with the purpose of introducing the verb "to eat," he said he was eating *ceviche* (a Peruvian seafood dish). He could just as easily have said Doritos or tacos, but he stuck to the truth and said *ceviche*. He was about to continue with the story when a student raised his hand and asked, *"¿Qué es ceviche?"* (What is ceviche?) The TA stopped for a moment and I saw panic in his eyes. He was probably thinking, "How in the world will I be able to explain that and stick to only Spanish?" But he took the challenge with vigor and plunged in:

TA: *"Ceviche es pescado."* He sees the blank stares and realizes they don't know the word *pescado*, so he gestures the swimming mo-tion of a fish.

Student: "To swim?"

TA: *"No, pescado."* He gestures a better fish-swimming motion accompanied by sunken cheeks and puckered lips gesture. That was funny.

Student: "A fish?"

TA: *"¡Sí! ¡NO! ¡Más o menos! Es un pez pero muerto."* (Yes! NO! More or less. It is a fish, but dead.) He gestures "dead" with a hand across his neck. *"¡Pescado!"*

Students: "Dead fish?!"

TA: *"¡Sí!"* He agrees, not realizing how strange that sounds. *"¡Sí! Y cebolla."* (And onion.) The students don't know that word either, so he gestures crying.

Students: "You are crying about a dead fish." The students are giving him the business now.

TA: *"¡No, cebolla!"* He gestures something round.

Student: "A ball?"

TA: *"No, no, cebolla."* He gestures bad breath.

Student: "You ate something dead that smelled bad?!"

He went on and on, sinking deeper into this unforgiving quicksand, for I don't know how long, trying to describe all the ingredients in *ceviche*. He was exhausted at the end, but managed to get back to the story, which turned out to be anticlimactic because of the *ceviche* detour. Talking to me at the end of the class, he laughed at himself and realized, without help, what he should have done. The whole thing could have been avoided by simply saying, *"Ceviche es un delicioso plato típico del Perú"* (Ceviche is a delicious Peruvian dish), and moving on with the story. Being a good sport, he reenacted the whole thing for us at the practicum. His fellow TAs were on the floor laughing. Thanks to him the word *ceviche* has a new meaning for us: "Move on, don't go there."

Think to yourself if explaining a point is essential to the story or not. I have heard some people tell funny anecdotes, and instead of following a clear path that is interesting and relevant to the listener, they get stuck on unimportant details:

So I was going to Phoenix one day when this guy walks up to me and says, or wait, was I going to Phoenix or Flagstaff? No, no, it was Phoenix, yeah, yeah, because I was going there to visit my aunt, and she had been insisting I visit, like, forever, so anyway, I was going to Phoenix, stopped at a gas station, and this guy walks up to me and says, he says, or his buddy says to me, well, let's see, no, it was the clerk at the store of the gas station who says, "How do you say 'basketball' in Spanish?" And I said I didn't speak Spanish because three years of high school really don't count, but anyway he said, "Basketball in Spanish is 'Juan on Juan!'" Wasn't that funny?

He laughs out loud at his own little anecdote, but by the time he is done with the story the muscles in your face hurt from holding the frozen smile waiting for the punch line. We must focus on the structure or vocabulary we are presenting and avoid getting distracted by inconsequential bits of information that tire the listener.

Another sign of cluelessness is not understanding what the students are going through when they are learning a new language. If the new phrase is, for example, *¿Cómo te llamas?* (What is your name?), stick to that formula for a while so they hear it many times during class. It is second nature to you, but it is new and scary to your students. A teacher I visited introduced *"¿Cómo te llamas?,"* and two seconds later asked another student, *"¿Cuál es tu nombre?"* And to another, *"¿Y tu nombre es? ¿Cómo tú te llamas? ¿Cómo se llama usted?"* All these different variations of the same thing will overwhelm and confuse the student. Present a structure and use it for some time, and introduce other structures and exceptions later.

The Clueless is also unaware of the students' vulnerability when learning a new language. She, without malice, and just for the purpose of lightening up the class, will point out a silly mistake one of her students made. In her point of view, it is a perfect opportunity to point out this common mistake to the rest of the class and get a good laugh at the same time. I understand. I have done that too. But some students can take the teasing and others can't. The shy and sensitive student will not openly complain, but will send subtle signals that the Clueless is not getting. The student will turn red, look down, try to smile with the group, but not too convincingly, and get busy with something like a pencil or an eraser. Being picked on, even as an adult, is annoying, and it turns students off to the language. All of a sudden Urdu is more appealing than the language you are teaching. Thoughts turn negative: "I'll never learn this right . . . I can't pronounce this well . . . I hate this class."

Making light and laughing at mistakes students make is something we all do. It is hard to resist the classic *Estoy embarazado* (saying I am pregnant instead of embarrassed) or *Tengo tres dolores* (I have three pains instead of I have three dollars) and many others. Some students take it very well and actually laugh out loud at their own mistake. Make a mental note. You can joke with this type of student, but how do you know how they are going to react before you know them? When you point out and laugh at a mistake, you must look at the student and watch for the "please lay off" signals. As soon as you see this, *do* lay off.

This teacher is not malicious, but simply oblivious to her audience. It is important to put ourselves in the students' shoes since they are the reason we are in this profession. Ask yourself: Do they need to know this now? Am I making what I say comprehensible enough? Am I using the structures I introduced? Am I aware of the students' discomfort? Everything we do matters. Everything we do has an impact on others.

The Entertainer

This teacher just wants to be cool. He wants his students to above all have fun in his class. He wants the students to see him as a friend, a buddy, and a facilitator more than a highfalutin teacher. To gain their appreciation he tries to be antiestablishment—*for* the students, not against them. As a result, he will be lax about homework or deadlines:

"I forgot to bring my homework."

"Oh, was it due today? Right . . . that's OK, you can turn it in tomorrow, don't worry about it," he says, smiling.

"Cool!" is the expected reward.

To keep up with this image, the teacher acts young. No matter if he is twenty-three or forty-three years old, he wants the students to feel that he is one of them. For example, he'll either use foul language or come close to doing it by mouthing the words clearly but silently. He will try to dress like his students and slip into English to tell a joke or two. He talks about himself, his friends, and his family with a lot of detail his students do not necessarily want to hear; it's the proverbial TMI (too much information), but he's got the bully pulpit and the students have to put up with it.

The Entertainer wants the students to think of his class as being fun. Actually, we all do, but we also have to remember we have a linguistic goal. The Entertainer will have fun communicative activities with so much emphasis on the fun part that he forgets what the students should be practicing. I visited an Entertainer type recently. He had a fun communicative activity to practice numbers. The students had a blast. He divided the class in groups of four and gave each group a name. He came up with a list of items, and each group had to guess the price, à la "The Price is Right." The winning group would win a prize. The students were pumped. The linguistic goal was to have the students practice numbers as they negotiated and reached a consensus in Spanish. The beginning was promising; he reminded all to speak Spanish. But as the game got more and more heated, Spanish went out the window. Unchecked by the Entertainer, they were all enthusiastically arguing about the price of the item in English. When reporting the group's consensus, students attempted to say it in Spanish, but as the competition grew more intense, even the *teacher* switched to English. At the end, one of the groups won and got their prize. There was laughter, shouting, and applause all around. "Did you like the activity?" the Entertainer asked in English. "Yeah!" was the overwhelming response, again in English. What happened to practicing the numbers in Spanish?!

The Entertainer tends to forget to focus on the goal of the activity. He is having too much fun with the students; plus, their happiness is No. 1 to him. I often see this type of TA walking down the hall with bags of treats.

"What do you have there?"

"Ah, just some flan and Spanish tortilla I made for my students last night, and something to wash it down."

"What is the occasion? Food vocabulary?"

"No, I don't know. They are just nice students."

It is very generous of the Entertainer to spend the time, the effort, and the money on students, but I worry about the reason why. Many of us bring food and treats to the class when we deal with the chapter on food, if we are introducing a particular culture point that would be enhanced by a food item, if we have a game that requires prizes, or if it's the end of the quarter. But bringing elaborate treats for no particular reason seems to be outside the purpose of teaching. I see the Entertainer craving approval and good evaluations in any way possible. Buying the students' love this way is unnecessary. The Entertainer should concentrate on the business of teaching itself. If the teacher is fair, sure of himself, fun, and professional in the classroom, he will earn the respect and appreciation of the students.

Students usually prefer a teacher who is casual, kind, understanding, and lighthearted, because they are less intimidated asking questions or making mistakes, but they do not respect or take seriously a teacher who acts just like another peer. Students will not accept the teacher in that fashion; friendship with a teacher grows out of respect, which has to come first. A teacher, although kind and gentle, must also be firm and mean business. If you are lax about deadlines, and students realize that, missed homework deadlines eventually become missed exams, now defended by the thinnest of excuses.

"I'm going to say I can't make it to the test."

"Are you sure you can do that?"

"Oh yeah, he's cool." (Read: a pushover.)

Missed deadlines will open the floodgates for others to do the same, and for the ones who follow rules to complain bitterly. It doesn't seem fair that the lackadaisical student gets the same credit or chances as one who is really trying.

The Entertainer will realize mid semester that he is losing control of the class, and when he gets complaints from the other students and realizes his gradebook problems, he decides to enforce deadlines. This is met with resistance and resentment: "The dude is turning mean." Whereas if he had started with firm, reasonable, and fair rules, presented matter-of-factly and with a smile, just as the sun rises in the east and sets in the west, they would have accepted that that's the way it's going to be.

I think of a parent-child relationship; I would like my parents to be kind, to understand and to relate to me, but I wouldn't want them to be my buddies. I don't want to hear about the most intimate details in their lives—it would be embarrassing. Similarly, with a teacher, students would like to be understood, to have a relaxed and friendly atmosphere in the classroom, but that has to come from a leader or guide they look up to, not from an equal. If he does not establish a little bit of a distance, he will struggle to get a coherent class going.

The Finger-wagger

I am sitting in the back of the room observing a class. The teacher speaks from behind the lectern: "Yesterday we talked about Gaudí and his unusual architecture. He designed La Sagrada Familia, remember? Where is this church?" Silence. Then, louder: "What is the name of the city?" Students look at each other nervously. Then, visibly annoyed, she raises her voice again: "COME ON, WHAT IS THE NAME OF THAT CITY?" The students sink in their chairs. If this is happening while I am visiting, I can't imagine what she does when I am not there—threaten to beat them like a piñata if they don't answer correctly? It's the eighth grade for me all over again.

Although that type of teacher scared me as a child, as a young new teacher I became somewhat of a Finger-wagger myself. When I was in college I came prepared to class, did my homework, followed rules, and got good grades. Why can't these students do the same? It offended me that they did not study every day or care about what I was so enthusiastically teaching them. Not everybody thinks and reasons the same way, and yet I could not understand why the students could not get a particular grammar concept. It was so simple! Instead of understanding that not everybody thought like me, or had the same logic that I have, I became a scolding mother that turned the students off even more.

While it is certain that there are some all-American, corn-fed teachers who routinely act like they have not had their coffee yet, I find that most Finger-waggers are foreigners who grew up exposed to other teaching philosophies in their earlier school days. We've had teachers from many Spanish-speaking countries, as well as from Romania, Korea, Italy, Brazil, Canada, and Portugal, and they are floored by the way students behave in the United States. In their countries students show a lot more respect to the teacher. Foreign instructors believe institutions in this country are too permissive and their students are undisciplined. For example, students should not turn in homework on a piece of paper they got from a recycling pile with something else written on the other side. The paper, the Finger-wagger believes, should not have food stains, and it should be written in pen instead of pencil. It should not have arrows all over the place to guide the teacher through their mistakes, nor have scratched-out words. To do any of these things in the motherland would have been unthinkable, and the Finger-wagger is appalled. Students should take notes and come prepared to class or face her anger. In her view, students are not showing the respect she deserves, and she can't help but react harshly. She will tend to be a hard grader ("That will teach them!"), return exams without concern for privacy, or humiliate students by scolding them publicly or laughing at a mistake.

Being a foreigner myself, and being familiar with this kind of abrasive educational background, I can see how a new teacher would tend to do what seems more familiar. After a few years of living in the United States, I started to understand the students' point of view. Their side of the story is that they have many classes at one time. Some classes, depending on their major, are more important than others. They feel that it is their right to study or not for your class, to do the homework or not . . . to cram for a test the day before or study every day, to participate or not . . . to get a low grade or not: it is their choice. "This is 'Merica!" they say. Students don't do it to upset you. They do it because they have made the conscious decision of putting in more time on other classes over yours. If your class is Pass/Fail, and it is just a requirement, the law of the minimum effort kicks in. The student will do the least amount of work she or he can get away with and still pass.

The Finger-wagger feels that the fact that a student shoots for a C instead of for a better grade reflects badly on her personally. As she grades exams, she gets frustrated: "But I told them about this yesterday!" The fact that she explained something does not mean that the students got it or that they were paying attention when she was talking. Yes, she saw all eyes on her, but some may have been thinking about lunch or a friend they were planning to meet later that day. We wish all students were excited about what we are teaching, that they would ask questions, study daily, and show interest. However, we have to accept that a certain percentage of students simply don't care, no matter what we do—yell or not, care or not. It used to hurt me deeply that after the last day of class, when I would ask enthusiastically, "So, are you going on to Spanish 3?," some would answer, "No way, I'm done." I stopped asking that question after a while.

Some students don't care, but even the ones who do care can forget grammar rules. I consider myself a good language learner and yet, when I was beginning to learn French, I would say something like:

"Je ne danse."

Then my teacher would add *pas*.

"Oh yeah, *je ne danse pas."* (I don't dance.)

In Spanish we don't need the *pas* at the end, but I intellectually understood that it was needed in negative sentences in French. I *knew* that. She had told me many times! I just had to remember, but invariably a few minutes later, I would be so absorbed trying to communicate a thought that I would say:

"Elle ne l'a pris."

The teacher would look at me.

Did I say something wrong? Is the verb wrong? *Pris* is "took," no? *Elle* is "she," right?

Still staring at me and a little annoyed, she would add for the nth time: *"PAS!"*

Crap! Yes! *"Elle ne l'a pas pris."*

This is not an early sign of Alzheimer's; it happens often with all students. If their focus is communicating something, sometimes grammar goes out the window. It doesn't matter if you have gone over the rules many times. It is not a reflection on you.

The Finger-wagger shows her displeasure at one or several of these faults, but she has to consider that if the transgression is not directly relevant to learning the language, maybe it would be best to let it slide. Language teaching is not just teaching the language, it is also "marketing" the language. We want our students to fall in love with the language we teach. We want them to really like it so they continue learning later on. Marketing cannot have a negative approach, or it won't work. I have never seen a company use a negative commercial to sell their own product. Sure, our classes will always have some students who don't care or will do the minimal work, but our classes also have students who love to learn and are genuinely interested in the language and the culture. If we lose our patience, yell, scold, or have a sour attitude with the class, we are spoiling it for the ones who really care. So, if you are a Finger-wagger, pause a moment . . . in through the nose . . . out through the mouth.

The Space Cadet

The Space Cadet is similar to the Clueless in the sense that there is a disconnect in what the class needs and what the teacher provides. The difference is that the Space Cadet usually *knows* what he should be doing, but he doesn't focus and sometimes forgets office hours, some appointments, what he said the day before, what he promised to bring, forgets to record the grade before returning the exam, to take roll, to respond to an e-mail . . . In short, the Space Cadet is absentminded and covers by saying, "Oh, it's OK." He actually believes it's all OK. He doesn't pay attention sometimes, maybe because it is not his priority, maybe because he is overconfident about his memory and teaching abilities, or just because he knows the world will not come to an end if things are not done exactly by the book: "It's all good, no need to be anal about it. Relax, people!"

The Space Cadet is often late to class, which creates problems in the classroom, whether he is aware of it or not. Some students, following his example, will start arriving late to class too, and the ones that don't, resent that they are there on time and the Space Cadet is not. Sometimes the teacher will arrive on time and see that only half the class is there. He may start the class and repeat what he said to the latecomers, which is an annoyance to the ones who arrived on time, or simply wait for more students to arrive and teach fewer minutes than he is paid to teach. "It's OK, it's only a few minutes." It may not be a big deal for the Space Cadet, but in this society, being late is considered a character flaw. It does not look good.

One day I was watching Dr. Phil talking about the chronically late and summarizing them as people who simply don't care, period; otherwise they would change their behavior. Many may be like that, but I have my own layperson's only-based-on-observation-of-a-few-TAs-and-loved-ones theory. I am clearly not a psychologist, but here is my take on the Space Cadet. Some of them care and feel somewhat bad about being late, but when it comes time to calculate how long it takes to get from one place to another, the culprit is consistently too optimistic about his own abilities to calculate time accurately. He miscalculates, again optimistically, that it takes a normal person, let's say, twenty minutes to go from door to door. He is also convinced he can make it in even less time. Not only that, he does not allow for the keys or wallet he can't find right before leaving the house, for that quick trip to the bathroom; for the lesson plan he left behind and has to retrieve; for traffic and long lights; for a friend who stops him to talk; for a phone call from his mother . . . One or two of these things will happen every time, but for him it is always an exception, and his valid excuse to be running late. One quick call to the office to say he is running behind schedule will fix everything. But these calls are often expected and are met, unbeknownst to the Space Cadet, with rolling of eyes and an "of course." This reflects badly on the Space Cadet. He knows it in the back of his head, but prefers to think he doesn't do that too often, and it's not a big deal. He is not going to change his behavior and be ruled by the clock. And the roof is still standing. Unrealistic optimism—I think that's what's going on.

Maybe it is overconfidence. Some Space Cadets are so confident they don't see the need to prepare a lesson plan or to review a PowerPoint borrowed from a friend who said, "It covers food items; it's pretty good." The Space Cadet is so sure about what he will be doing in class that day that he won't need a lesson plan. Piece of cake, he thinks. If he forgets something or doesn't know something on the PowerPoint, he can ad-lib. He's done it before and things came out all right. But sometimes they don't. I have had some Space Cadets stare at the images they are showing and end up asking me, the visitor, about the image. He could normally make it up ("It's OK, I can correct it later"), but with me there, he can't pull a whopper. Other times a simple exercise is skipped and the teacher moves on to a difficult one that students can't do very well. The students struggle, they get frustrated, and the second exercise flops:

> "You should practice the structure first before doing the more difficult activity," I tell him afterwards.

> "Yes, I know, it would have been best to practice it first. I planned to."

> "So, why didn't you do it?"

> "Oh, I had it in mind, I just forgot to do it, but it's OK, no big deal. We can do it again tomorrow."

A simple lesson plan and a previewing of the PowerPoint or video would have avoided this whole scene—the students' frustration, the wasted time doing something the students were not prepared to do yet, my lackluster impression of him, and the impression left on students when their teacher does not know what he is showing them. Having a lesson plan does not mean you are a novice. I have been in the classroom for many moons and I still write a lesson plan for each class. It not only helps you remember, it makes you look organized. As a young teacher I used to "mentally plan" my class. It went well most of the time; I would forget a few things, of course, but not too many . . . after all, I am an anal-retentive Virgo. But I was surprised when in my evaluations I was labeled "disorganized" by quite a few students. After that, I always had a lesson plan, and even if I knew what to do next, I would look at my paper for a few seconds in plain view of my students and proceed to the next activity. I never got a "she is disorganized" comment again.

Having a lesson plan prevents accidental skipping of activities or de-railment from the original order of events. It can help you remember an-nouncements, collecting papers, taking roll, or returning exams. Remember, everything you do matters, even small things you think are unimportant. People around you notice and are making an image of the type of person you are according to your actions. What impression you leave on people is up to you.

The Grammarian

This teacher has the tendency to spend a little too much time explaining grammar. And she will not only explain the basics, she will go on and on in English with examples and all kinds of exceptions. Even if the tendency in language teaching is toward a student-centered classroom, this teacher be-lieves that she has to impart instruction on something. She feels that if she is not lecturing, she is not earning her keep as a teacher. Plus, she *knows* the rules. She can't teach students fluency, she can't teach how to acquire a lan-guage, but with grammar, she has something to offer, something concrete to teach. She will give extra handouts in efforts to "clarify" what is in the book already, and give more examples and mechanical fill-in-the-blank exercises so the students can practice the grammar rules at home.

I visited a Grammarian a few years ago. She was teaching Spanish ordinal numbers. The book only covered ordinal numbers from first to tenth. After that, it gets more complicated fast. It's not like in English, where you can add "st" for first, "nd" for second, "rd" for third, and "th" for the rest. The Spanish is not that simple. The forms are so complicated that I, as a native speaker, don't know half of them, nor are they used very often. Well, this TA gave a handout with all the ordinal numbers that the book neglected to provide. The flyer had ordinal numbers from one to a thousand. She had researched this, put it all neatly packed in one sheet, and happily distributed it to her students. She later added that that information was not going to be in the next test, and that it was only for their reference. I saw students' expressions change from panic when they took a look at the dense sheet, to relief at the sound of the word "reference." Many students glanced at it and quickly tucked it away. Chances are very good they will never, ever have the need to use those words. I haven't. Yet the Grammarian felt the need to do this, for reasons I cannot fathom. Was it to show off her command of the language? To show something she finds interesting? To be thorough? To scare the students? Does she truly believe the students need or will use those words in the future?

There are theories, different opinions, and plenty of controversy about the amount of explicit grammar taught in the classroom, but at least there is a general consensus on one thing: teaching grammar helps figure out the mechanics of the language, but it does not help much with speaking. Learning how to conjugate verbs in Spanish will not help a student order a meal at a restaurant, for example. I have heard countless stories of students who took two years of Spanish in high school, where they often learn to speak vertically—

yo hablo
tú hablas
él habla
nosotros hablamos
vosotros habláis
ellos hablan

—instead of sideways: *"Mis amigos hablan por teléfono con frecuencia."* These students are good at conjugating, but they don't feel they can speak Spanish and often want to start all over again in college.

The reality is that we have a limited amount of class time when the students are exposed to the language, and limited time to practice it. Therefore grammar, although helpful to organize the learners' thoughts, should not take too much of the class time. Input (listening and reading in the target language) and output (speaking and writing) are far more useful to developing communication skills. Lectures on grammar make students passive, and they get used to being spoon-fed. The students will know the grammar rules, but will they be able to use those rules effectively when communicating? The students will not be able to recall all the examples and exceptions you have presented them when they are trying to say something. When it comes time to communicate, rules will be forgotten, unless subconsciously acquired through listening or reading.

To better develop communication skills, the teacher has to allow the right conditions, activities, and opportunities for productive output to happen, as by creating activities and tasks that will mimic what happens in the real world, or by having students work in small groups so there are more opportunities to speak.

Grammar is a tool, not the goal. Instead of saying, "Today we are going to learn the difference between the preterit and the imperfect," try saying, "Today we are going to learn how to narrate past events." In construction, learning how to use a power hammer is not the goal, is it? Learning how to build a fence using a power hammer is. Building the fence is the goal. It is important to tell your students what the communicative goal is: "We are going to learn how to describe a person" (not learn about number and gender agreement); "Today we are going to learn how to talk about future events" (not learn about the verb *ir* + the pronoun *a* + a verb in the infinitive).

Grammarians love grammar. They are good at it. They find it interesting and useful, plus they are actively teaching something *they* know but their students don't. If you exhibit "grammarian" tendencies, try to curb your enthusiasm about grammar. Even if you think grammar is as sweet as sugar, sugar is still an ingredient in a dish. Let your students learn to cook the dish.

The Heir Apparent

The Heir Apparent is a graduate student whose aspiration is to teach literature, or linguistics, and/or to do academic research. But in order to make this happen, he accepts a teaching assistant job the university has offered him.

He is going to be teaching elementary Spanish; it is not what he wants to do, but it pays the bills.

The Heir Apparent has to put up with taking a methodology class where he will be trained to teach language at the elementary level. He doesn't care much for the class because teaching basic language is not in his future. The rest of his curriculum will be literature or linguistic courses that require his concentration; teaching elementary Spanish is just a job.

This kind of thinking is not entirely his fault. The main directive given by many graduate advisors is, "You're a student first; teaching comes second." This attitude is reinforced throughout the student's career. Indeed, many professors openly trivialize the work of teaching. And so, teaching is not viewed as a goal but as a step to get somewhere else, and TA-ships are viewed just as a form of financial aid, a handout given to all graduate students regardless of teaching abilities. Language and teaching are subordinate to literature and research: this is the reigning attitude in many research institutions, and this belief trickles down to graduate students.

Many graduate students feel the pressure of their studies, but they also feel the responsibility of teaching the undergraduates and try to do a good job. The Heir Apparent thinks that teaching elementary language is beneath him; he will be teaching upper division! He is doing great in his graduate courses, and these language classes will be a thing of the past in no time. He does not care to memorize students' names; he teaches from behind the desk; he just can't get himself to plan anything fun for the class. It takes too much time, and he can't get too excited about irregular verbs right now. His students are just not high on his priority list. Some days are better than others, but all in all, he doesn't see the point of putting effort into this.

Even if your passion is literature or linguistics, teaching literature is still teaching. Your training at the basic-language level will be a good learning experience because all the skills that you learn will be transferable to your future goals as an educator. You have to learn how to organize yourself, follow a syllabus, have a lesson plan, and learn insights as you interact with your students—how to deal with their different personalities, how to motivate them, how to correct them, how to cater to different learning styles, and how to evaluate their performance. And even in upper division classes you will still have to decipher what the students want to say. Their language skills are not perfect, and the experience teaching basic language will be very helpful. The elementary language teaching job is not just training for immediate duties; it is the foundation for a lifelong career in education.

When you get your first position at a university, you will not go directly into teaching upper division. Most junior faculty have to start their careers teaching language courses too. So an important component of an on-campus interview is your being observed teaching a language class. The hiring committee will ask you to teach a class to evaluate your teaching skills. They will also consider your students' evaluations. If you have not done a good job with the undergraduates, their evaluations will come back to haunt you. Comments like "The inanimate book had more personality than he did" will not help. You may have a very good dissertation and several publications, but in this competitive market, if the university can find somebody who has comparable qualifications AND is an inspiring teacher, that candidate will have an advantage over you.

THE NATURALS

There are two types of Naturals: the gifted ones who know exactly what to do and how to do it without formal instruction, and the ones who work hard at self-improvement and go on to become great teachers. The first one is very rare, but the world is full of the second type, myself included. The truth is, most great teachers are made, not born. Let's analyze what those effective teachers do day-to-day. Below I list thirty-one practices (aren't you glad there aren't sixty-three?!) that I have observed in many wonderful teachers over the years. I don't think there is one especially important or outstanding characteristic that is better than the others; rather, I find that it is a combination of many practices that makes these people Naturals.

Presence and Control

Practice no. 1: They are aware of their audience.

While in front of the class speaking, Naturals still pay attention to their students' body language. Staring out the window, yawning, or texting are clear signs that the students are not engaged. Naturals know better than to proceed with an activity that is not working. They can also spot students that get off track, get distracted, or start speaking in English about something unrelated to the class. Gently, and with humor, they bring them back into focus again:

"*¿Estás hablando inglés? Quizás es mi imaginación*" (Are you speaking English? Maybe it's my imagination), says the teacher, to give the student an out.

"*Sí, es su imaginación*" (Yes, it's your imagination), says the student, to save face.

"*Ah, bueno, porque yo sé que esta es tu clase favorita*" (Ah good, because I know this is your favorite class).

"*Sí, es mi clase favorita*" (Yes, it is my favorite class). The students will invariably answer this because they are grateful for not being seriously reprimanded and embarrassed in front of the class.

Practice no. 2: They praise and encourage.

When students struggle to learn something new, anything new, praise from the teacher is so encouraging. Praise is a confirmation that their hard work is paying off and that they are going in the right direction.

Naturals are not cheap with their praise. They hand it out in every class. Their praise is also specific and sincere. A general, unenthusiastic "You're doing OK" remark can have a discouraging effect. Naturals show with their eyes that they mean what they say: "*¡Bien dicho!*" (Well said!). Saying "*buena pregunta*" (good question), even after a predictable inquiry, encourages participation and affirms that all questions are welcome.

Practice no. 3: They respect the students.

Students are people too (or so they tell me). Naturals recognize their students' worlds and are sympathetic about what happens to them. They quickly memorize their names and pronounce them correctly. They ask permission to Latinize (Frenchify, Germanize, Japanize, etc.) their names, rather than doing it automatically:

"Harrison, Richard!"

"Aquí."

"Ricardo, ¿está bien?"

Naturals are careful not to play favorites and try to call on all students. They try to develop an atmosphere of mutual respect where students don't feel they are being picked on because they are weak. Naturals will still call on weaker students, but feed them easy questions or ask for a response that others have already volunteered so that there is a pattern the weaker student can follow.

Practice no. 4: They are helpful and attentive during activities.

While Naturals sometimes use the time during communicative activities to return papers or take roll, as soon as this is done they mingle and are watchful of problems, derailments from the activity at hand, or the need for encouragement to use the target language when students slip into English. Naturals also crouch down to get to the level of the seated student's eyes to answer questions. This makes them more "down to earth" and less lofty.

Practice no. 5: They have good control of the class.

Naturals don't allow students to use their bad behavior to seize control of the class. They quickly neutralize students who use foul language, utter inappropriate remarks, or openly challenge them. Naturals don't get upset or lose their temper, but look the student in the eyes and clearly and emphatically say in front of the class, "That is not appropriate." This sends the message to the student and the whole class that that behavior is not tolerated.

A True Story from the Front Lines: An Unedited E-mail Sent the Last Week of Class

Dear Professor XXXX:

I have noticed in SmartSite that my grade is averaging a C– probably due to some absences and a few missed homeworks. *(I checked his attendance record: That's an understatement . . .)* I understand this, but I had no idea my grade was so low. *(So NOW you check your grades even though they've been posted throughout the term?)* I understand this is the last week of class, however, the importance of this grade to my future in this university warrants every attempt I can make to raise it. *(Operative words: the last week of class.)* If I receive a C− my GPA will drop below 2.0. A C+ will give me a GPA of exactly 2.0 which will allow me to play sports. *(Your grades add up to a C− it is a mathematical fact, boy genius.)* I would not be asking this change if I did not think it was fair or reasonable. I have worked very hard throughout the term *(except when you were not in class . . .)* and truly feel my efforts are worthy of this request. If you are not able to raise my grade based on the merit of my work *(your work was a few sandwiches short of a picnic . . .),* is there any extra assignment I can do to raise my grade whatsoever? *(So, you do not show up to class, do not do the work, and now you want me to give you an extra assignment, that I will have to grade, making more work for me? Is that what you are proposing?)*

Please understand the importance of this grade to my future. *(I understand, did you?)*

Thank you,

xxxxxxxxx

Teaching and Learning

Practice no. 6: They have clear and simple explanations.

Naturals know beginners can get overwhelmed with complicated grammar rules, extensive explanations, and dozens of exceptions. Beginners want to get started and say something to feel a sense of accomplishment. Lengthy explanations only paralyze them. Students don't know where to begin and are afraid of falling into one of those dreadful exceptions. Naturals simplify rules and give contextualized simple and funny examples supporting them. The funnier, more useful, and interesting the example, the better. The same is true for direction lines on midterms: the instructions should be as short and as true to life as possible, mimicking the natural language the students may encounter in the real world.

Practice no. 7: They encourage learning outside the classroom.

Being in class for four or five hours a week is not enough exposure to eventually achieve fluency. Naturals not only tell the students to watch movies, read magazines, search the Internet, watch TV, listen to music, or search YouTube in the target language, but also direct them to what movies are appropriate for their level, what TV programs can be more beneficial, and what singers articulate better or have more interesting lyrics than others.

They also promote agency; they encourage students to get control of their own learning by suggesting they read about their own hobbies in the target language. If sports are what they like, then a magazine or a website that deals with their favorite sport is what the students should be seeking.

Practice no. 8: They don't shy away from the
challenge of teaching disabled students.

Having disabled students in the classroom can be a challenge. Some students may have vision or hearing impairments; others may have an autistic disorder, while others still may use a wheelchair or have other physical disabilities, such as not being able to write due to paralysis or injury to the dominant hand or arm. If a student is unable to move freely around the classroom, teachers will have to instruct the rest of the students to go to him or her; they will have to describe all visuals to a nonsighted person, and may have to modify other activities keeping a particular disability in mind.

Such conditions make teachers think outside the box and help develop a larger repertoire of teaching tools. Naturals understand that the presence of a disabled student in the classroom also provides teaching moments for the rest of the students; they get to witness a different kind of struggle and learn how to deal with it in pair or group activities.

Practice no. 9: They raise expectations.

Naturals care about their students, and that is exactly why they don't lower the bar by speaking unnaturally slowly or translating into English. Naturals make sure what they say is understandable using the board, cognates, and gestures, but they speak at a normal speed with all the linked words normal speech exhibits. Their goal is to prepare students to use the language in the real world, not just to function in the class or prepare them to pass a test.

*Practice no. 10: They are aware that students
have different learning styles.*

Naturals understand that not all students learn the same way, so they have a variety of class activities that appeal to several learning styles. A class could include (not all in the same day) dictation, writing directly on the board, PowerPoint images, songs, group writing, repeat after me, group or pair activities, role playing, reading out loud, human graphs, managed competition, signature activities, and many more.

A True Story from the Front Lines: True Postings on ratemyprofessor.com

10. You can't cheat in her class because no one knows the answers.

9. Evil teaching robot who crushes humans for pleasure.

8. I learned how to hate a language I already know.

7. He will destroy you like an academic ninja.

6. He hates you already.

5. His class was like milk. It was good for two weeks.

4. Boring! But I learned there are 137 tiles in the ceiling.

3. Instant amnesia walking into this class. I swear he breathes sleeping gas.

2. Bring a pillow.

1. Your pillow will need a pillow.

Class Mechanics

Practice no. 11: They are organized.

Naturals are good time managers. They make their photocopies early, not five minutes before class, risking a malfunctioning machine or long lines of Space Cadets. They arrive a little early so they can lay out handouts or other papers they will be using in class, hook up the laptop, and find the files they will be showing.

They don't let activities drag on and on or spend valuable class time taking roll or returning papers. They do this during an activity. They have a lesson plan and follow it. In it, they include extra activities in case the class comes out short.

Practice no. 12: They follow a logical instructional sequence.

Naturals don't jump from "Good morning" to "Open your books to page 242." They include a warm-up, not consisting necessarily of a review or what students have learned so far, but of small talk in the target language about their students' world. It could be about their activities on the weekend, classes, exams, mention of a pretty hat or shoes and where they bought them, etc.

A logical sequence could include contextualized presentation of new material through a personal or invented story with questions to check comprehension, followed by simple guided practice from the book, and ending with a pair or group communicative activity. Naturals are careful to have a student-centered class where they allow as much opportunity for individual output as possible.

Practice no. 13: They are patient.

Naturals wait for the students to respond. Silence does not necessarily mean the students don't know the answer. Many times they are thinking about what or how to respond. Just as we have the patience for a computer to "think" and finally connect us with the link we want, Naturals imagine the students' thoughts racing to find the answer. Naturals know when this is happening and don't quickly fill in the silence; they patiently give a reasonable amount of time for their students to come up with something.

Practice no. 14: They have meaningful activities.

Since the ultimate goal of learning a language is to be able to communicate our desires and thoughts in a given situation, the classroom communicative activities should mimic real life as much as possible. Naturals prefer authentic and meaningful communicative activities over mechanical drills. They collect and classify good materials over time and keep updating and perfecting them.

Practice no. 15: They return graded materials in a timely fashion.

Naturals understand that feedback is part of learning. Returning homework, essays, and exams within three days is best. They also post results right away on the course website so the students can keep track of their grades. Their written comments focus on grammar or translation errors, but they are sure to include comments on the content.

Practice no. 16: They have clear goals.

When designing and implementing a communicative activity, Naturals focus on the goal of the activity. If the goal in a Spanish class is to state a preference, they require the student to answer using the verbs *preferir*, *querer*, or *gustar* (to prefer, to want, or to like). They do not accept a "yes," "no,"

A True Story from the Front Lines: Actual Student Translation Errors

Warning: Translation errors of a language foreign to you may not be funny!

German:

5. *Nachtkeule* = nightclub (*keule* is actually a club that you hit with)

4. *Mangel an Lebensmittel* = mangled in the middle of life (*mangel* means lack, *leben* means life, and *mittel* means middle)

3. *Er spielte vor seinen ventilatoren* = He played in front of his fans (*ventilatoren* are fans that blow air)

2. *Zeltglockesuppe* = Campbell's soup (*zelt* means tent, *glocke* means bell)

1. *Bremsefeder* = spring break (*bremse* are brakes and *feder* is spring or a feather)

Spanish:

5. *No hay animales izquierda* = There are no animals left (*izquierda* means left, as in direction)

4. *Voy a ser espalda* = I'll be back (*espalda* is the back of a person)

3. *Anoche tiré arriba* = I threw up last night (*tirar* is to throw an object, *arriba* means up)

2. *Colgar afuera* = hang out (*colgar* means to hang something up, *afuera* means outside)

1. *La raza terminó en una corbata* = The race ended in a tie (*raza* means human race, *corbata* means a necktie)

French:

5. *Je suis fini* = I am done (*je suis fini* means I am finished, as in done for or ruined)

4. *Je suis plein* = I am full (*je suis plein* means you are filled with something, or are pregnant)

3. *J'attends l'université* = I attend university (*attendre* means to wait for)

2. *Je mange la Turquie* = I eat turkey (*Turquie* means Turkey, the country)

1. *Je te rate* = I miss you (*rater* means to miss, as in missing the bus)

"uh-huh," "yep," or "nope" answer, but require complete answers that contain the words they are studying. They make sure the students produce the desired structure many times during the activity as well as in the follow-up.

Everything that happens in the classroom has a goal. Naturals never show a video clip because they are tired, have a headache, or just for entertainment's sake. They show an interesting video clip because they want to enlighten or cover something specific. So, they will always focus on the linguistic purpose and have "pre" and "post" activities, and a follow-up to wrap it all up.

Practice no. 17: They integrate culture and grammar.

Naturals know that language and culture are inseparable and that cultural information should be included in every class, not just with an occasional or isolated cultural presentation. Naturals are good at integrating culture with the grammar and vocabulary assigned for the day. For example, while learning the preterit tense, students could learn about what a painter or writer did, thus learning culture at the same time.

Practice no. 18: They demonstrate an activity
before asking the students to do it.

Besides giving clear and simple instructions how to do a particular activity, they also demonstrate how to do it partnering with a student as an example. Students are then able to start without asking each other, "What are we supposed to do?"

Practice no. 19: They have "pre" and "post" activities.

Before doing a reading or showing a video, Naturals first prepare the students for what they are going to read or watch. They introduce new vocabulary the students will encounter. They point out a subtle cultural twist students may need to understand, or have a list of a few things for which to watch. After the reading or viewing, Naturals will not only have comprehension questions, but will also have a follow-up such as a communicative or writing activity to wrap it all up.

Practice no. 20: They stay professional in behavior.

Naturals know the fine line between being friendly and open (good) and being a buddy to the students (not so good). They gain students' respect by being consistent with rules and deadlines; by not losing their temper and raising their voice in anger; by waiting for silence before speaking and not talking over others; by not allowing disruptive behavior; by being humorous but not clowny; and lastly, because they are confident that they are fair, by not ever having to argue about discipline. They are calmly in charge.

Practice no. 21: They brainstorm for ideas on writing assignments.

Naturals don't just give a topic, tell the students the desired length, and say, "Go ahead, good luck." The vastness of the task is just too daunting for most students. Naturals announce the topic and proceed to brainstorm with the students about all the possible subtopics they can write about. Naturals empower the students by activating what they have learned so far and how they might use those forms on this assignment:

"The topic is *La familia*. What can we write about?"

"Siblings."

"Yes, what about siblings?"

"We can describe them."

"Yes, we can describe their personalities, their physical characteristics . . . what else?"

"We can say what they like to do."

"Exactly. We can write about their activities. What else?"

In five minutes the board will be covered with ideas, and now the writing assignment is no longer a scary thought. Students realize they can do this.

Practice no. 22: They have a student-centered class.

Naturals know they are good at what they do, but they don't have to be the center of attention. Using well-planned activities, Naturals provide plenty of opportunities for the students to practice speaking in pairs or small groups. They also vary the pairs or groups often so the students encounter different speakers. Students can be paired up by same color of T-shirt, same color of socks, similar shoes, same birth month, same length of hair, or simply signing off.

Practice no. 23: They use technology to enhance their teaching.

Naturals don't use technology for technology's sake, but rather when it truly enhances their teaching. They know that technology is a tool, not a fad or an end to please students or look hip. Used in a meaningful way and with a clear goal, the Internet, PowerPoint, YouTube, document cameras, iPods, Skype, etc., can be used to bring authenticity to the classroom. Naturals also have a low-tech or no-tech backup in case connections or equipment fail.

Delivery

Practice no. 24: They show enthusiasm and passion for the job of teaching.

Naturals are what they want their students to be: enthusiastic, active, and imaginative. Their attitude shows that they love their job. They act as if they can't imagine doing anything else. Their enthusiasm shows how tremendously important learning this language is. Enthusiasm is contagious.

Practice no. 25: They move around and engage the students.

Movement is the most powerful means of expression. Naturals don't drape themselves around the lectern, but are physical, using gestures and body language to hold students' attention. They move around the classroom and address the class from all sides, not just the front.

Practice no. 26: They are creative and funny.

Naturals understand the classroom is a stage, and just like performers, they must keep the students interested and alert throughout the whole class. Naturals are always in search of creative ways to present and practice the

A True Story from the Front Lines: Another Unedited E-mail

Hello Professor XXX:

I have missed a few lab sessions this semester *(this is the sixth week; he has missed five previous labs)* and when I attempted to go to today's session, there was nobody in the classroom listed. *(The lab is conducted across the hallway in RM 217. If he had just looked around, he'd have seen his classmates, 24 of them, in the other room—that is, if he had attended the lectures enough to know what his classmates looked like.)* I arrived there on time at 1:00 p.m. and waited till 1:10 p.m. before leaving, in hopes that everyone was late to show; however when nobody had arrived by then I left. Because of this I was wondering if there has been a permanent switch to a different classroom of which I was unaware of. *(No. We were really there. We're just wearing our invisible cloaks.)*

Regards, XXXXX

language without losing sight of the pedagogical purpose of the activity. Teachers who are normally shy and private become extroverted and funny in the classroom for the sake of the students. They learn to take on a different persona because if they are boring, students won't engage and get interested in learning.

Practice no. 27: They respond to content.

Naturals accept and exchange ideas and opinions in the target language without complete grammatical accuracy. They respond to what the students say, not how they say it. When grading essays, they not only comment on the grammar errors but also add comments related to the content: "You went to Australia! I would love to go there one day." Naturals acknowledge that the student is trying to communicate something, and it is a small triumph for the student if the teacher understands and reacts to that too.

Practice no. 28: They have a low-anxiety environment.

Naturals understand that some students will have a debilitating type of anxiety and will want to escape a new learning task, leading them to adopt avoidance behaviors. They resent the teacher for creating this poisonous atmosphere and feel learning the language is a chore. Sensitive students avoid participating for fear of ridicule by their classmates or the teacher. Naturals try to create a relaxed, fun, and safe class by not picking on students, gently using humor, not laughing at students, and being kind and understanding when they are struggling.

Practice no. 29: They are spontaneous.

Within a well-planned class, Naturals give the illusion of spontaneity. They greet predictable students' questions with surprise; they may, all of a sudden, change to Plan B if something is not working; they'd rather pick students randomly than ask questions following the line of students' desks; they may "change their minds" and instead have students stand up, or sit down, or write on the board. Any change to the order creates spontaneity and keeps the students guessing.

Practice no. 30: They are good storytellers.

When Naturals present new vocabulary or grammar through an interesting story, students automatically put down their pencils, smile, and lean forward in anticipation. Their stories, well-rehearsed at home, could be true or invented, funny, sad, or informative, but they are always interesting and well-told with suspense, pauses, sound effects, and the perfect rhythm for maximum effect. They make themselves understood with cognates, gestures, and simple drawings. Students tend to remember unusual and interesting stories, not the boring ones. Naturals collect good stories and anecdotes from their own lives and tell them when the time (grammar- and vocabulary-wise) is right.

Practice no. 31: They don't wear their medals.

Naturals are usually humble (at least in front of the class, although they may be legends in their own minds). They don't tell the students right off the bat the years of experience they have in the classroom or the degree and awards they have earned. Students find out eventually, and when that happens, their estimation of the teacher goes up. Boasting only puts the teacher on an unreachable pedestal and prevents the friendly atmosphere preferred for ease and enjoyment of learning.

Naturals don't ever say they know it all, or that they have nothing else to learn. They keep growing, reading their student evaluations, updating

---

A True Story from the Front Lines: Quotes from New Teachers at the End of Their First Year Teaching

1. I learned that I don't have to be the students' buddy. If they don't like me, it is not the end of the world. The most important thing is to be a good and fair teacher. *EL*

2. I learned that it is OK if teachers are not always right. It is better to admit that you don't know something rather than being shamed by the Internet. *KD*

3. I learned to enjoy preparing class. OWN IT! *GAG*

4. I learned that my role is to facilitate discussion. The classroom is not a forum for just my opinion. *AB*

5. I learned that it is best to enforce assignments instead of giving them voluntary options. If it is voluntary, nobody does them. *AS*

6. I learned not to give students too much guidance and reminders at the beginning. They expect me to hold their hand throughout the class! *RC*

7. I learned to curb my enthusiasm so people take me more seriously. *EF*

8. I learned to be consistent with rules. *TQ*

9. I realized that even though I am an auditory learner, many of my students were visual learners and I needed to give more visual input. *WW*

10. I learned to always have Plan B. *JD*

materials, attending conferences, and getting new ideas by visiting colleagues. They also generously share materials and mentor less-experienced teachers.

This section on Naturals contains a lot of information and numerous tips to remember about what to do and not to do. Most teachers don't get all thirty-one practices right on any given day ... we are not superheroes! But if you want to be an effective and respected teacher, reading and understanding these practices is half the battle. Awareness of your style of teaching, a willingness to practice, and a desire to be a good teacher make up the other half.

Summary Questions

1. What type(s) of teachers do you most identify yourself with? What should you do about it?

_____

_____

2. How were your favorite teachers in high school or college? What characteristics did they have that you admired?

_____

_____

3. How were your least favorite teachers? What characteristics did they have that you hated? Are you doing the same?

_____

_____

_____

4. Rank the top ten most important characteristics that Naturals have in your opinion.

_____

_____

Scenarios

Scenario 1

A teacher typically structures his classes to begin with approximately 30 minutes of grammar explanation, followed by practice exercises and ending with a communicative activity. After a month, due to illness, a substitute takes his place for a week. The new teacher tells the students to read the grammar and do the homework at home, and conducts a student-centered class. This new format is foreign to the students; it is not described on the syllabus, and the homework has no weight on the grade. When the grammarian comes back he sees that only half the students have done the homework, and the other half said they didn't understand anything at all. Frustrated, but vindicated, the teacher goes back to explaining grammar explicitly. A grateful class sings his praises.

What happened here? If the student-centered class is so good, why didn't it work?

_____

_____

Scenario 2

Karen, a Guardian Angel type of teacher, had a tough time in school when she was growing up and is determined not to have her students go through the same struggle. She remembers some teachers covering some material very fast because they thought it was easy: "Well, it was not easy for me!" she recalls. Now that she is in charge of this class, she takes great care in enunciating in a crisp and slow way so the students understand everything she says and don't get stressed out. She believes her way of doing things works because students are happy and they appreciate her. Her supervisor has noted several times in her evaluations that she should pick up the pace and speak at a more natural speed. Karen believes in her heart that she is right and her supervisor is too harsh. "That's not me. I cannot be mean to my students."

1. If students are happy, why should Karen change her style of teaching?

_____

_____

2. What should you do if you disagree with your supervisor?

_____

_____

9 • The Captain of the Ship
Classroom Management

DENISE MINOR

If you stop to think about it, having one person step in front of thirty other people and take charge of their activities, behavior, and learning for an hour is a remarkable feat. But teachers do it every day, sometimes five times a day, and some of them do that with adolescents, no less. To top it off, we language teachers do this remarkable feat in a language that for all or most of our students is one that they are in the process of learning.

How is this possible? For one thing, by the time they reach junior high school, most students have been socialized to comply with what is expected of them in a class. But beyond that, teachers learn classroom management skills, abilities that (in my opinion) are equally as important as the knowledge of the subject matter they teach.

Those of you who have gone through teacher credential programs will most likely have taken a class dedicated to classroom management. For language teachers, however, there is an additional skill set that is required, because we are not simply teaching an academic subject matter but must also convince this group of twenty, thirty, or forty to communicate in a new language. It is one thing to get fifteen pairs of students to stay focused enough to design the mansion of their future. It is another thing to get them to do it in Chinese, French, or Arabic. In addition to providing pointers in this chapter to keep students speaking in the target language, we are outlining a six-step intervention process for problem

behavior that is beyond what is taught in typical classroom management courses.

Thirty years of teaching language in a wide variety of circumstances have brought me into contact with many kinds of students. I have taught children in an academy in Spain, doctors and nurses at a medical school, middle-aged people in night classes at a community college, and the typical young-adult students of a university. I have also observed high school classes and spent hours interviewing secondary teachers. These experiences, combined with research in the field, have convinced me of one thing: the same principles work for all environments, although these principles have to be implemented somewhat differently to suit the different environments. These are the principles I believe to be most effective:

Establish rules and procedures: Students learn and behave better in classrooms with clearly established expectations and rules. At the junior high and high school level, this principle is even more important simply because these students are younger. But college students also benefit greatly when they know exactly what is expected of them in the classroom, on the tests, and in their assignments. (Thornberg 2008)

Foster a classroom community: Whenever students come together in a class, a community will establish itself. Allegiances will be made, habits will form, and people will start to take on roles. It is your job to establish a community in which everyone is respected and valued and in which you are the recognized leader. You are the "captain of the ship," a benevolent but firm and consistent captain. (Jackson Hardin 2011)

Have a behavior intervention plan: By creating a supportive and positive classroom environment, by assuming the role of firm and consistent leader, and by establishing classroom rules and procedures, you will minimize the number of behavior problems that you have to deal with in class. But I can promise you this: you will eventually have problems. Whether you teach at an elite Ivy League university, an adult night school, or a high school in a poor area, you will have students that disrupt the class and make your life difficult. The differences between school settings and the ages of your students will have an impact on the number of behavior problems and the degree of difficulty. But no matter what the situation, you need to have a plan.

I will deal with these principles individually, but first I want to establish some parameters for explaining my approach. First and foremost, I am a behaviorist. Although I certainly respect those who critique the behavioral approach, I believe most of them do so because they don't understand it. Their limited exposure to the theories underpinning behaviorism, or their experience with poor implementation of behavioral plans, has left them with the impression that it is mostly about giving candy to kids for being good. They maintain that students will only be successful if they operate on internal motivations and, further, that the external rewards will make them dependent on things that have nothing to do with the value of the educational goal. But I maintain that the behavioral approach is much more complicated than that.

For those of you unfamiliar with behaviorism, here is a brief description. The first recorded example of scientific study of behavioral response came from Ivan Pavlov (1849–1936), who trained his famous dogs to salivate every time he rang a bell or provided other stimuli (Windholz 1983). In the beginning, Pavlov provided the stimulus and then gave his dogs food. But very quickly he conditioned the dogs to salivate every time they heard the sound of the bell or experienced the stimulus. Decades later B. F. Skinner (1904–1990) became famous for the behavior modification experiments he employed on animals and humans (Bjork 1997). Skinnerian behaviorism fell out of favor beginning in the 1950s, but it had a resurgence in the 1990s, in part because of work done by Dr. O. Ivar Lovaas at the University of California, Los Angeles, in his development of Applied Behavior Analysis (ABA) for the treatment of children with autism. His success, and the successes of numerous other behaviorists in helping children with special needs, has spawned a movement to incorporate behavioral principles into regular education classrooms.

At its core, behaviorism involves reinforcing desired behavior when it occurs, and for most students the strongest reinforcement is social, such as verbal praise and a smile from someone the students like or respect. Many teachers have found that students are even more motivated if they receive some kind of material reward in addition to the social praise. That sounds basic, right? But, as any teacher with experience knows, the following problems can get in the way: a student could be more averse to the desired behavior than he or she is motivated by the social reinforcement; a student could be more motivated by negative attention or confrontation than by praise and smiles; a student might not like or respect the teacher. These are some of the issues I will deal with in the final section of this chapter.

In the meantime, I want to assure you that the judicious use of material rewards cannot only modify behavior, but can help to nurture intrinsic motivation to engage in the desired activity. In other words, our students have to come to see or feel the benefits of speaking the language we teach. Sometimes we have to convince them to do that for some time before they begin to realize those benefits. In research for my doctoral dissertation I observed second and third graders at a Spanish immersion elementary school for about three years. In one classroom the teacher employed a system that rewarded the entire class with points for speaking Spanish and, at the same time, gave consequences to the entire class when anyone spoke English. At the beginning of the year, I observed that the children would switch to English as soon as the teacher was out of earshot. By the end of the year, however, they were often speaking Spanish to each other even if she was nowhere near. In interviews with five case study participants, they all told me that they were proud to be Spanish speakers and that they liked to speak Spanish, especially with their teacher (Minor 2009). Over the course of the school year, the intrinsic rewards of being bilingual supplanted to some degree the extrinsic rewards.

Now let's move on to the three most important principles of classroom management.

ESTABLISH RULES AND PROCEDURES

Humans show it in the way we play games, use languages, create hierarchies, and structure businesses: we like rules. That doesn't mean that all of us will follow the rules, but in group settings such as classrooms, the majority of us thrive on fair and consistent rules and procedures. My observations over the last two decades have led me to believe that the most effective teachers are good at establishing these parameters for everything from how to turn in homework to how to interact with one another. These effective teachers can be widely divergent in terms of styles and philosophy, but they have this characteristic in common (Thornberg).

The kinds of things that a teacher will need to be specific about will be very different for the different age levels. For example, small children might not know what is expected of them in a classroom, so teachers often post rules such as "Use your indoor voices" and "Raise your hand if you want to speak." But a high school teacher would run into trouble if he or she put anything that sounded even remotely like elementary school rules in a syllabus (Thornberg). A high school teacher can, however, have rules such as "Participate in communicative activities in German" or "Treat everyone in the classroom with respect." High school students know very well what respect looks like. If you have a student who talks back, interrupts, or rolls her eyes at you, after class you can tell her that her behavior is not respectful and will hurt her participation grade. If by some strange series of events, this young woman arrived at the age of seventeen without knowing that those things were rude, it will be up to you to explain that to her and then hold her accountable for changing in the future. But you don't want to make the other twenty-nine students listen to a lecture on the first day that says "Don't roll your eyes at me" and "Don't interrupt me."

It is important to put your expectations in writing. For high school, it might look similar to the following:

Classroom Expectations

- Students will behave in a respectful manner in their interactions with the teacher and other students.

- During group and pair interactions, students will speak in German.

- Homework will be turned in at the beginning of each class and placed in the metal basket on the teacher's desk.

- During tests and quizzes there will be no talking.

- Please remove hats during class. There are pegs near the door for anyone with a hat to hang it.

- Cell phone use is not permitted during class. If one rings or buzzes OR the student is caught texting, the phone will be confiscated and turned over to the principal.

- Have fun!!!!!!!!

At the college level, you probably will want to step back even further from etiquette rules, although you should include something just in case you find yourself in Intervention Mode (see below). You could include something like the following in your syllabus:

Participation: 10 percent

- The participation grade is based on participation in communicative activities in French, contributions to group discussions, and positive interaction in the classroom and with the instructor. Cell phones must be turned off during class. (That means no texting!)

The vast majority of university students will get the picture, and most of them will be participating anyway because your class is so much fun and so interesting. Almost everyone in my classes gets an A for participation. But, for the few who are a negative drain on the class's energy, it is good to have a written policy from the very beginning that you can point to in order to get the attention of the problematic student.

As you reduce the specificity of your relational and etiquette rules with each advancing year in education, you can become more specific for what you expect in written work. I prefer short, to-the-point syllabi, but I can get a lot in a three-page syllabus. For instance, give the exact day of all the papers' due dates, what style is expected (MLA? double-spaced?), and a paradigm for what they will be graded on, such as expected length, communicative abilities, vocabulary, structure, and grammar. STICK TO THE SYLLABUS unless an unanticipated incident occurs. It not only gives the students stability in terms of learning how to organize their time to reach goals for written work, but it also shows them that you are a consistent person.

Last but not least, start off the year on the right foot. Considerable research has shown that establishing from the very beginning the rules and procedures for how your classroom runs is one of the most important factors affecting the outcome. Robert Marzano, Jana Marzano, and Debra Pickering found that "virtually all research points to the beginning of the year as the 'linchpin' for effective classroom management" (Marzano, Marzano, and Pickering 2003, p. 92). One of the ways you can get the year off to a good start is by establishing your class as a "zone" where the target language must be spoken.

FOSTER A CLASSROOM COMMUNITY

I remember clearly being educated in classrooms based on a hierarchical model. The teachers were in charge (for the most part) and their favorite students were always the "good" students, the ones that listened quietly, raised their hands to answer questions, and got good grades. Then there were the average students who clearly were in class just because they had to be there and did not want to draw any negative attention to themselves. And there was always a handful of "bad" kids who didn't work and were as disrespectful as they could get away with being. One of the more interesting dramas of each day was watching to see how far they would go. I considered myself a good student, but I was fascinated by the bad kids. They seemed so powerful!

What I have come to realize after three decades of teaching is that the hierarchical model is only good for the "good" students. Everyone else—the rebels, the kids with learning difficulties, the distracted artists, etc.—are on the second tier. But in a classroom that is more similar to a natural human community, where everyone gets to shine at the things he or she is best at doing, most students will be much more successful. As noted in Chapter 7,

I think of this as "the butcher, the baker, the candlestick-maker" model because it reminds me of the way each person in a village has an important role. The ideal is for each student in your classroom to believe that he or she has an important role.

What does this model look like in practice? Does everyone get an A for being good at *something*? No, we can't revolutionize the grade paradigm of public schools. But all or most of your students can come to feel important in your classroom, and this psychological feeling of belonging could have a positive impact on their grades. For instance, some students are good artists and they will thrive if you incorporate activities such as the game of "pictionary" or the creation of comic strips. There might be students who have good voices or play instruments. Let them shine by incorporating music into your classes. Some students are creative writers and will be able to write beautiful poetry. Have a poetry jam and ask a chosen few to read their masterpieces to the entire class.

When I started very intentionally about fifteen years ago to make sure every student was given a chance to shine, I kept track with a yellow highlighter. Each time a student won the "regional" championship of Spanish Jeopardy, had her poem voted the best in the class, or drew a remarkable dream house, I put a small yellow dot next to his or her name in the grade book. This helped me keep track of everyone who had gotten some share of positive attention. Within a short time, it became second nature and I no longer used the yellow dots.

One practice I use that might be only appropriate for college is giving a thumbs-up to the people with the highest test scores as I am handing them out, and mouthing *Buen trabajo* (Good job). I realized that about half of those who receive the top grades on any test in my classes are quiet and don't stand out socially. Some of them barely speak. By publicly recognizing how well they have done (which is usually a reflection of how much they studied), they gain some status within the community. Every single quarter, at least one of these quiet, excellent test-takers has talked to me for the first time after having been congratulated for doing so well. Also, I see other students gravitating toward them for group projects. I believe that this technique has worked well to draw out shy, hard-working students so that they engage with more confidence in communicative activities.

At the junior high or high school level, public recognition might backfire and end up causing the serious student some flack in the hallway. In that case, a teacher might call up the students who got the top exam scores after class to congratulate them individually. I firmly believe that doing well on an exam should be socially recognized in some way more than a letter grade or high number on the exam.

Once in a while you will get a student who doesn't need to be "allowed" to shine in your classroom because she will always try to grab the spotlight or tend to go on and on when she does take the floor. The fact that you only permit talking in the language you teach will reduce the frequency of this, but you still might need to keep the situation under control. To deal with students who feel the need to steal the limelight, I have developed some interrupting skills. Sometimes I simply say "very interesting" while they are still speaking and turn away to start another activity. Sometimes I grab one of the words in their monologue and use it to launch the next activity.

Only one student (as far as I know) has caught on to my "let everyone shine" methodology, and I only knew that because of the evaluation he wrote at the end of the semester. I can't be certain of who the author of the comment was, but the handwriting looked exactly like the writing of a young man who had significant physical impairments, used a wheelchair, and had difficulty holding a pencil. The evaluation read, "She figures out what each of us does best and makes us feel good about it."

The butcher, the baker, the candlestick-maker approach sounds great, right? Everyone is equally as good and as important as any other person, including the excellent students and the struggling students. But one of the important keys to making it work is that you, the teacher, be respected as the leader. You are not their friend, and it is not a democracy. Jackson Hardin put it very well when she wrote, "Teachers who want total control in the classroom will find that students rebel against that control. Teachers who are too lax will lose control of the classroom as students take over the running of the class. What students want is a benevolent dictatorship in which the teacher is in charge of the classroom" (p. 265). It doesn't mean that you aren't friendly and that you don't consider their opinions when making decisions. But you are ultimately the one in charge.

As you become more secure in your position as the "captain of the ship," you will know when and how to step back to allow students to take charge of some aspects of their own learning. Another benefit of a classroom community in which everyone feels like he or she is a valued member is that stronger bonds are formed between students. I greatly enjoy watching as some of my students form relationships that extend beyond the classroom.

HAVE A BEHAVIOR INTERVENTION PLAN

Everything I have recommended that you do until now—establishing clear rules and procedures, nurturing the formation of a community, assuming the uncontested role of group leader—all fall into what might be considered "preventative strategies" (Clunies-Ross, Little, and Kiehuis 2008). In other words, by employing these strategies you are reducing the likelihood that you will see problem behaviors emerge.

But despite all the work you do, there will be some students who disrupt learning, show you disrespect, or both. There can be many reasons for their behavior, and one of them is the fact that some people have rebellious temperaments. Another is the fact that some students haven't gotten enough attention for positive behavior, so they have long-entrenched patterns of acting out because that guarantees them some attention. Whatever the case, the earlier you intervene successfully, the better school year you will have.

When I returned to the classroom after taking a leave of absence from work in order to spend two years in the behavioral program for my autistic son, I began to approach the issue of problematic students differently. I clearly remember the second week in a Spanish 2 class when a student mumbled something to his neighbor and they both looked at me and laughed. I said to myself, "This guy is going to cause me trouble. I need to come up with a plan." You might be thinking, so what? They shared a joke? Nope. My original impulse was correct. That student ended up causing me serious problems, and his instructor for Spanish 1 told me he did the same to her.

Let me confess that in my first attempt to employ behaviorism in the classroom, things did not go perfectly. I started out ignoring him and, when that didn't work, asked to speak to him in the hallway. I will never forget the spark in his intelligent eyes and the tiny smile on his face when we stepped outside. I realized, "He LIKES this added attention. This is probably not going to work!" But I learned from that unfortunate situation, and the following autumn I developed a six-step plan that in ten years has never failed me. I am not telling you that I have changed sullen, rude freshmen into bright-eyed, high-performing students. But I will tell you that in every case the problem students started controlling themselves enough that they did not have a negative impact on my class.

I am well aware that there are fewer problem behaviors in college than in junior high or in high school, in part because all college students have decided that they want to be in class and (most of them) are paying for it. But no matter what level you teach, these techniques will help you reduce the degree and the quantity of behavior problems. The steps are:

1. Identify the problem early.
2. Decide if a path other than intervention is warranted.
3. Put the behaviors on extinction.
4. Invite the student by your actions (not words!) back into the community.
5. Call the student out for the behaviors.
6. Implement a consequence.

Before we go any further I must emphasize one thing: you need to know where you are headed in Step 6—and then do everything you can to NOT get there.

If you are in college, does that mean reporting the student to judicial affairs? Does that mean giving her "0" for participation and thereby reducing her final grade by a full letter grade? You must have the specifics of this kind of result spelled out in your syllabus. Don't dwell on it the first day, but rather go over it very quickly. If you spend too much time on it you are starting on a negative note, and the likelihood is that you will not have significant problems.

If you work at a high school, does this mean sending the student to the principal? To detention? Calling a parent-teacher conference? Very importantly, the consequence has to be something that the student truly cares about. For college students, that is often their grades. For high school students, it might be grades and it might be loss of free time in detention.

Now let's return to Step 1 to discuss strategies for handling situations in ways that significantly reduce the chances that you and your student will arrive at Step 6.

1. Identify the Problem Early

There was a time when I simply ignored the first sign of rudeness from a student. I did not want to deal with it, and I thought that maybe it would go away. Truth be told, sometimes the bad behavior did go away, at least enough times that it seemed a viable strategy. My classes are fun, and always have been. Some students just decide to get aboard so they can have fun with everyone else.

But there were enough times that it did not go away, and I wished I had done something sooner. Now when I see behavior that is rude, confrontational, or distracting to the other students, I move closer to that area of the classroom and I look the student in the eye. This serves two purposes. First of all, in the whirlwind of getting three classes of thirty students off the ground, it helps me to remember who had done something that was the first sign of possible trouble. I don't do anything about it yet, but I am now paying particular attention. Secondly, I believe most students know by a look that I am making a mental note. I am certain that I don't look menacing or angry, but I also don't look friendly, which is my main mode of interaction with students.

2. Decide If a Path Other Than Intervention Is Warranted

Sometimes behavior that appears to be disrespectful or disruptive can be eliminated with a little bit of empathy and positive attention. For one thing, sometimes there is a personal problem that is seriously impacting a student, and the best thing you can do is initiate a conversation. This step is most appropriate at the high school or junior high level. Over and over again I have had teachers tell me that when they have a student who has been causing trouble stay after class to talk, they often find out that something is going on such as a divorce, an illness, or financial hardship in the family. Some students have really difficult home lives, and they bring all their anger to school. One high school teacher told me that she had a parent-teacher conference with a disruptive student, and when she witnessed how aggressively and rudely the father treated the boy, she thought, "No wonder he acts like that in class! It's the way he is treated." It didn't solve her classroom management problem, but it made her more empathetic.

It is important to begin the conversation in the right way. For example, don't say, "Brittany, you have been really rude and I am sick of it. Either stop it or you are in big trouble." You might say, "Brittany, I've noticed that you can't seem to concentrate on work in my class. Is there anything going on that you want to talk about?" One of the most dynamic and respected junior high teachers I have ever known said that this moment of reaching out to her students is often all that is needed to change the behavior. She lets them know that she is on their side, and she even gives them a break or two on homework, or gives them extra help. When a kid is going through problems at home or out in the world, having a respected teacher in his or her corner can make a huge difference.

You might not use this second step much at the university level, in part because it could be seen as intrusive into the personal matters of someone who is legally an adult. But, believe me, there are some college students going through some very rough times. I have had freshmen cry in my office because they were very homesick, and others pour out their hearts to me because they felt inferior to their peers. At one university I came to realize that the doctor's notes for psychological services were a different color from the medical center's notes. Most of the doctor's notes I was getting from students were for psychological services. That quarter, I had two students confide in me that they were severely depressed. What an eye-opener!

Another situation in which a bit of understanding and positive attention might help is with students who have rebellious personalities. Remember that in the big picture rebels are wonderful. They launched our nation's revolutionary war and fought the good fight for women's and minority rights. Without rebels in our midst, societies would never change. But having them in our classroom can be a challenge. Do what you can to invite your rebels aboard, and try to figure out a way for them to show their rebellious identity in a way that benefits the community. One student wants to write about a famous person not on the list of possibilities for the essay? Meet with her and expect her to explain why she wants to write about that person. Let her write that essay, and if she does a good job, allow her to read her conclusion to the class.

I have also noticed that some ethnic communities foster a type of verbal interaction that can appear rebellious or even disrespectful to those not from that community. For instance, I've learned from some of my African American students that there is a style of teasing that is meant to be friendly and is meant to show off the speaker's proficiency in using that style. One young woman used to ask me tough questions, like what was the Spanish term for "doing that thing," by which she meant having sex. She flashed her ultra bright smile and the class erupted in laughter. I told her *hacer el amor* (to make love), asked her to repeat it, and then told her she could consult with me afterward for richer vocabulary. I had no intention of teaching her sexual terminology, but rather planned on sending her to a slang dictionary. But there was no need for the referral. After class she simply flashed that winning smile again, said *"Adiós,"* and left class. From that young woman and others I've learned to let them be themselves by using humor, only permitting *español*, and creating boundaries for this interpersonal style with social reinforcement or ignoring.

Last but not least, I must bring up the issue of extremely intelligent students who cause problems because they feel superior or are bored in general by our educational system. First of all, it is important to remember that they might be right on both accounts. But I've learned that it is best to bring them aboard by using humor, providing a class that is not boring, and showing respect for their intelligence. It doesn't matter how high the student's IQ is, you still know more about the language and can still teach him or her plenty.

One of the best examples I have in recent memory of this type of student was an English major that I'll call Marina. During the first week, Marina sat in the back and had what I would consider a skeptical look on her face. When I would initiate interactive activities that called for everyone to stand up and move around, she wouldn't get out of her seat without a very direct request. Sometimes she would look bored, but then out of the blue she would ask a very penetrating question about grammar. She was clearly the type of person who liked to analyze language.

One day we were reviewing the imperative and I called on a few people to stand up. I gave them some humorous "Simon Says" commands. Marina stood up, but when I told her to shake Kristen's hand, she looked me in the eyes for a moment and said, "No." I moved a little closer, smiled, and said, "I'll give you back the points you lost yesterday for not bringing your textbook to class." She thought for a moment, turned to Kristen, stuck out her hand, and said, *"Buenos días."* Everyone laughed.

That week, students handed in the first version of an essay. I went to town on Marina's, both by pointing out what she had done well and what could be improved, not just in her use of Spanish but also in her logic and structure. I wanted her to see in my comments feedback that would help her

English writing as well as her Spanish. The day after I handed back those essays, Marina started sitting in the second-to-front row and participating much better than she had before. By showing her that I had plenty to teach her and by using humor rather than confrontation, I was able to bring Marina psychologically into the community.

3. Put the Behaviors on Extinction

After having identified students that have shown problematic behavior, and first intervening in an empathetic and positive way in the situations where you think it might be warranted, it is time to move on to the next level: putting a behavior "on extinction." Jackson Hardin describes extinction in this way: "When reinforcement is no longer forthcoming, a response becomes less and less frequent. This process of ending undesired behaviors by withholding reinforcement is known as extinction" (p. 28).

It is true that sometimes ignoring a behavior is enough to make it go away, but I have found that simply ignoring rudeness or refusal to participate is usually not enough. I have bumped up this strategy to a level in which I intentionally ignore the person in every way that I can. My message is: This is a fun community and I am a competent leader. If you want to stay "aboard," you have to treat me with respect and you must participate.

What does that look like? The first thing I do is remove his or her name card from my pile of cards. (I create this pile of cards at the beginning of the semester and use them to call on people. It is a method that makes sure people are given equal chances to speak and it keeps people on their toes.) The next step involves providing more positive feedback to students around the problematic student to make the student feel a bit left out. I mostly use physical proximity, eye contact, and smiles. For instance, if Jonathon has been identified as displaying problem behavior and Andrew sits next to him, Andrew will start getting more attention. When I call on Andrew, I will step closer to him and draw out his answers. I will smile and invite comments from other students. I do these things anyway, so it does not look out of place. I will simply do them more intentionally to the students sitting around Jonathon. It is extremely important to NOT even glance at Jonathon because eye contact from the teacher is a form of attention. Even if it is not registered on a conscious level, a student knows that if the teacher looks him or her in the eyes, the teacher is paying attention.

The third step involves "forgetting" something. For instance, I will forget to return Jonathon's work or forget to assign him to a group when everyone is getting involved in a fun project. This usually obliges Jonathon to step forward and ask to be included or ask to get his work back.

4. Invite the Student Back into the Community

If the student asks to be included in a project or to have his work returned, this is a psychological step in the right direction, and the moment is extremely important. In essence, Jonathon is asking to be included, and you should welcome him back warmly. I usually pause just for a moment (silence is powerful), and then I smile broadly and apologize for having forgotten him. I speak to him briefly, using eye contact, and then either return his work to him or put him in a group. You might not feel like warmly welcoming back a wayward student, because you are still angry at his rudeness and the impact he has had on other students. But remember, your goal is to improve his behavior, and this is a strategy that works. So, put on your best smile.

If I did not return an assignment to him and he does not ask to get it back, I hold onto it until the next assignment goes back to students and return it then without saying a word. If I did not include him in a group project and he does not ask to be included, I will wait until students get going on their activity and ask him with as little eye contact as possible to please go find a group.

If "forgetting" the student doesn't work, I continue with the intentional ignoring for one more week. The following week I "invite" him back into the community by calling on him to answer a question, usually an interesting one. I move close and smile as I ask the question. I give him lots of positive feedback for any kind of appropriate response. I put his name card back in the pile.

If the problem behavior continues, I give it one more round of ignoring and forgetting. This whole procedure usually takes about two weeks, and it has worked in most of the cases in which I have identified a student early on as having problematic behaviors. The best part about this technique is that it works. The second-best part about it is that nobody even knows I am doing it, or at least nobody has brought it up. I am under the impression that it works on a subconscious level.

5. Call the Student Out for the Behaviors

In the past ten years, the strategies I have described up until this point have only failed me six times. In those six cases, the rudeness of the students left me feeling that I had no alternative but to speak to them directly about their behavior. I usually wait until about ten minutes before class ends, and always wait until everyone is involved in a pair activity so that my comment is only obvious to the student and his or her partner. I go up to the student in question and touch the desk with my finger. When he or she looks up, I say, "I need to speak with you after class." One time, a young woman got a look of panic on her face, a look that said, "Uh-oh. I'm in trouble." She responded with, "I can't. I have to get clear across campus to my other class." I said, "Then I will dismiss class five minutes early so we have time." Secondary teachers often cannot dismiss class early, but they can write a note for a student to arrive late to the next class.

When class ends, I don't look at the student or say anything until the room has cleared. The moment needs to be slightly uncomfortable. Then I say something like, "I have found your behavior in my class to be _____ (disrespectful, disruptive, etc.). For instance, you have _____ (spoken to me rudely, interrupted other students working, etc.). Do you have an explanation for your behavior?" You must be VERY specific about the behavior that you want to change. Don't demand that they change the way they feel or think because you don't have the right to do that and, in truth, you have no idea what is going on in their heads. Stick with behavior that is observable and measurable in some way.

It has been extremely surprising to me that at this point three students that I had judged to be disrespectful and unmotivated appeared to feel quite bad and apologized. I accepted their apologies, reminded them that participation is 10 percent of the grade, and told them that if the behavior continued they would get an F. Even though a student's apology can appear very sincere, I believe it is important to remain slightly distant and objective. The student will get back in your good graces by changing his or her behavior, not by apologizing profusely.

Calling a student out is as far as I have ever had to take my intervention strategy. I have only once seen a problematic student switch and become a hard-working and respectful student after having been called out. But in every incidence their rude or disruptive behaviors have diminished enough that they no longer took away from the quality of my class.

6. Implement a Consequence

If calling the student out for the behavior does nothing to change it, you will have to follow through with the consequence the very first time it appears again. I recommend that you put the infraction and the consequence in writing. For instance, if any of the students I had "called out" had continued with the problematic behavior, my plan was to inform them in writing that their 10 percent participation grade had been reduced by half. That would mean that a person ending a term with a final grade of 74 would instead get a 69. If they had continued, the final participation grade would have been reduced to zero, which would bring a 74 down to 64. That would mean that a C for the class would become a D. In both universities where I have worked, I have also investigated the process for reporting disruptive students to judicial affairs. If bringing down the participation grade did not work, I would have initiated the process of requesting that they be removed from my class. However, as I said, I've never had to go beyond the step of "calling out" a student.

At the high school and junior high level, you will have to design a consequence meaningful to your students. It is likely that some of your students will care about grades and others will not, so you might have two consequences—one of them the participation grade and the other a loss of time or privileges. This could mean spending time in detention or missing the class pizza party. Whatever the case, you must follow through or there is little chance that you will reduce the problem behavior.

MY SEMESTER FROM HELL

To provide you with some specific examples of how differently this approach can be implemented with different students, I will tell you the story of the worst semester of my life: four problem students in an 8:00 a.m. Spanish 1 university class.

First there was "Brian." Brian would often walk in late, hood pulled over his eyes, and bump desks as he made his way to the back of the room. He would drop his backpack loudly and lean over to say something in English to one of the two star female athletes who sat in the back. When pair- and group-work assignments were made, he would at first pretend to be doing the work but then quickly start telling stories in English. He would groan loudly when the class was given homework assignments. A few times he fell asleep with his head leaned against the back wall.

Second came the dynamic duo, "Evan" and "Justin." They had graduated from the same high school in a prosperous town two hours south of our university. Their Spanish was good enough that they should have been in Spanish 3, and I suggested that they transfer to a more advanced class, but they shrugged and did not do it. I was under the impression that they wanted an easy A and were "punching the clock" in my class. One of the things they both did (one more than the other) was always speak in an exaggerated "gringo" accent in Spanish, mostly by drawing out their vowels. For instance, Evan would often say, "Kay Ba-WAY-no" for *"¡Qué bueno!"* (How nice!). They would look each other in the eye and laugh, delighted with their performance. I very clearly remember considering, just for a moment, changing my syllabus that semester to eliminate my mandatory attendance policy. I thought that maybe, by doing that, 75 percent of my behavior problems would stay home in bed and I would enjoy teaching more. It was just a passing thought.

Finally, there was "Tony," who sat in the back left corner of the room. He gave the impression that he was angry and bored. Sometimes when I asked him a question he would glare at me for one or two seconds before answering.

By the second week I was fairly certain that these four were not just freshmen showing adjustment to college issues, and I decided that the empathetic conversation was not in order with any of these gentlemen. I moved straight to the isolation technique. All four name cards were put away and, because of that, Evan and Justin no longer got to display their exaggerated gringo accents to the class.

The isolation technique immediately started to work with Tony. I was lucky in that the student sitting next to him was a dynamic, hard-working student who seemed to genuinely want to learn Spanish. "John" was an Iraq war veteran who told me after class that he was thrilled to be going to college. One day when I walked up very close to hear John talk about his family, Tony immediately joined the conversation! It was a great moment, because he was inviting himself back into the community. In that conversation, I learned a little about his five brothers and sisters and his grandmother. That little bit of information was all I needed to strike up a conversation after class. I learned that Tony was indeed a heritage speaker, that he was the youngest in his family, and that his Spanish was the "worst" of the siblings. *Now* his behavior made sense. Tony was insecure about his Spanish! I told him that his pronunciation was fantastic and that I was really happy he was in the class because the other students would get to hear a native accent. He gave me the only smile I got out of him the entire semester. After that, Tony still had a somewhat angry look on his face, but I came to think that was simply his personality. From then on he always participated willingly and treated me with respect. I have no doubt that sitting next to John helped in that regard. One on board, three to go.

Evan and Justin did not seem to care that they were no longer called upon to answer questions. They slouched in their seats, acted bored, whispered things to each other, and laughed. I decided to move it up one notch. That day, students were learning vocabulary associated with household chores. I brought aprons, rags, a broom, and a bucket, and put them in groups of three to come up with skits that involved chores and some kind of conflict. I told Evan and Justin that they could work together without anyone else. While the students were coming up with the skits I walked from group to group to help with ideas and Spanish phrases for conveying their meaning. I stayed clear of Evan and Justin.

When it came time to put on the skits, I called up all the groups except for the dynamic duo, and then said, "Now, let's move on to the next section." One of them said out loud, *"Pero, nosotros no hemos presentado"* (But we haven't presented). I turned to look at them for a few seconds before saying, "Oh, you want to participate?" They looked at each other, and I felt certain that they knew what was going on. One of them said, *"Sí."* I looked down and stayed quiet for a few more seconds, and then said, *"Bien,"* moving out of the way.

I don't remember what their skit was about, but it was somewhat confusing and seemed to involve a drunken motel custodian. If I had helped them with their skit as I did the others, it probably would have been more understandable. But as it turned out, they were the only ones laughing because nobody else got it. Normally, when skits deteriorate, I rescue the students and clarify their stories or jokes. But I allowed Evan and Justin to flounder, and they received weak applause from the class. They were clearly embarrassed.

I said nothing for a few moments. Then I smiled broadly, thanked them, and moved close to chat a little about what they had just presented. One of them spoke to me, for the first time, without the exaggerated gringo accent. Maybe they realized that I did have some power to make their experience in my class better or worse. Maybe they had simply been humiliated. Whatever the case, neither of them became attentive and respectful students. But after that day, the bad accents and the smirks disappeared. I put their name cards back in the pile.

Finally, there was Brian. It appeared that he could not care less if he wasn't called upon or if he was ignored. In contrast, the young women sitting around him seemed to thrive on my additional attention. One morning, I smelled beer on him—at 8 a.m!—and he looked a little drunk. I couldn't even imagine how that could happen. Had he stayed out all night drinking, or had he started his day with beer and cereal? I had never had a drunken student in class before, and I didn't know what to do. Should I pull him out of class right then and there and ask him in the hallway if he was drunk? If he said no, then what? And if I didn't pull him out of class, who was going to get stuck with him for the communicative activity? I decided to make the interactive part of class a small group conversation to dilute his impact on any one person. But, as it turned out, I didn't have to worry about that for long because he fell asleep quickly with his head leaning back against the wall and his mouth open. He started to snore. I walked over and stood next to him. All twenty-nine pairs of eyes turned to follow me. Many started to snigger. One of the women sitting nearby poked Brian and he jerked awake. I said in English, "I need to speak with you after class." He slunk down in his chair and stayed that way the rest of class.

When we spoke, I tried to control my anger, but I could feel it seeping out as I told him to never come to my class drunk again, to never sleep in my class again, and, if he could not control his disruptive behavior, that he should sit on the far side of the room away from the other students. To my surprise, he kept his eyes down and kept saying over and over, "I'm sorry, I'm sorry. I'm really sorry." I told him that he was already getting a D for participation, and that if there were any more problems the grade would drop to zero. Given the fact that he was getting a C− thus far in the class, it would take his final grade down to a D.

When I turned to the door I saw that one of the students had returned, a straight-A young woman who worked very hard and always sat near the front. "I'm sorry you had to hear that," I said after Brian left. "No, no. I really liked that you told him," she said. Serious students truly do want teachers to keep disruptive students in line.

Brian wasn't in class the rest of the week. The following week, and every week after that, he was always on time. He didn't fall asleep again, and I never smelled alcohol on him. He kept his eyes down and only spoke as much as he had to in order to participate in the communicative activities. His final grade was a C–. Although I can't be certain, I imagine that the scathing evaluation I got from one student in that class was Brian's. It was a small price to pay.

◊ ◊ ◊

As you will soon learn, it is not enough to know our subject matter and be adept at methodology for teaching a second language. We must also learn classroom management techniques to motivate everyone and to deal with behavior problems. The three most important principles are: Establish clear expectations and rules, foster a positive community in your classroom, and develop an intervention plan for problem behavior. Your intervention plan will involve early identification of students with potentially problematic behavior, an empathetic response when it is warranted, and strategic ignoring of the student followed by a nonverbal invitation to return to the community. In difficult situations, you will have to resort to some kind of consequence. At first, this approach might feel burdensome with all of its steps, but with practice it can become second nature.

It could take anywhere from one to four weeks to firmly establish a classroom community and to deal with any behavior problems that you identify. One seasoned professor I know calls that moment when she can feel that everyone in the class is aboard "the click." "I wait for that day, that moment when I am certain that we are all together in this voyage, that they are MY class," she said. Once that happens, once you have concentrated on establishing yourself as the credible leader, have done everything in your power to bring the rebels aboard, and have begun using strategies to better include students with disabilities, don't forget to turn your attention to the others. Speak to the quiet ones and pay attention to the writing assignments of those who don't grab your attention for either good or bad reasons. They're all your students, and you need to reinforce their feeling of belonging and development of the target language.

Summary Questions

1. What are the differences in the rules and expectations that a teacher would make explicit for elementary school students in comparison with high school students? What are the differences in the rules and expectations that a teacher would make explicit for high school students in comparison with college students?

_____

_____

2. What are some of the ways that a teacher can foster a sense of community in a classroom?

_____

_____

3. Do you agree that a teacher should be a "benevolent dictator"? Do you remember excellent teachers that either proved or disproved this idea?

_____

_____

4. Name the steps involved in the author's behavior intervention plan for students that are disrespectful or disruptive to the class. As a teacher, would you change that plan for use in your class?

_____

_____

Scenarios

Scenario 1

For their final project, your students must interview a native speaker about cultural practices that are kept alive in his or her family, such as celebrations, ways of food preparation, or storytelling. On your syllabus the assignment is described in the following way:

FINAL PROJECT—20 percent

For your final project you must interview a French speaker about the traditional cultural practices that have been kept alive by his or her family. Then you must write a paper comparing or contrasting the ways people engage in this practice in her/his country of origin and the ways her/his family engages in this practice. The paper will be due at the end of the semester.

A month before the semester ends, you tell students that the paper is due in two weeks. The following week you receive so many complaints that you change the date to the last day of class. The papers you end up receiving are not nearly as good as you would expect given the students' level of French. Other problems include the fact that some of the students interviewed each other even though none of them come from families of French descent, and the fact that some of the students wrote their papers in English. A master teacher tells you that you need to break up the final project goals into small chunks that students can work on during the semester. She also tells you that you need to be much more specific about your expectations. Rewrite the Final Project description for your syllabus using a calendar of the current year.

Scenario 2

It is your first week of school, and you are both delighted and concerned about the strong personalities in your class. There is one student who sits in front, is full of energy, and constantly interrupts. She often looks around to see if the others are looking at her. One student shows up early and draws on the white board with your erasable markers. One student keeps his cap low over his eyes and is constantly texting. Two heritage speakers are animated in the beginning of class and like to answer your warm-up questions, but as soon as class gets going they seem to be bored and often start doing work for other classes. What are some strategies you might employ to pull this community together?

---

10 • Heritage Language Learners

DENISE MINOR

If you work in a region where the language you teach is spoken by a significant portion of the population, it is very likely that you will have students that are often referred to as "heritage speakers." The language has surrounded them since birth as the medium of adult conversations, the banter of cousins, and the words flowing from the radio and television. For many, their only means of communication during the first years of life was this heritage language.

Yet during childhood or adolescence, most of them went through a process in which English took over as the dominant code. In conversations with friends they found it very difficult to stay in the home language for longer than short bursts and, when they did stay in the language, they sprinkled their messages with English. "Heritage speakers are people raised in a home where one language is spoken who subsequently switch to another dominant language. The version of the home language that they have not completely acquired—heritage language—has only recently been given the attention it deserves from linguists and language instructors. Despite the appearance of a great variation among heritage speakers, they fall along a continuum based upon the speakers' distance from the baseline language" (Polinsky and Kagan 2007, p. 368).

This continuum is evident in most communities of heritage speakers in the United States. For instance, there are heritage speakers who can understand most of what is said in their homes but feel very limited in their ability to express themselves. On the other end, there are young people who,

through education and summers spent back home with relatives, have kept their heritage language sharp and native-like. For the most part, heritage speakers occupy a unique world linguistically, a bilingual world in which they flow from one system to another depending on the topic, the environment, and the people with whom they are speaking. Yet many of them say they feel that they have deficits in one or both languages. I will never forget the student who once said in class, "I know I speak English and Spanish really well. But somehow I don't feel like either one of them is my native language. I feel like my Spanish is inferior to my relatives' in Mexico and I feel like my English Is Inferior to people around me in the United States." A few heads in the class nodded. I was stunned that this fluently bilingual young man felt inferior about language, and that many of his classmates felt the same. His comment was a first step for me in coming to understand both the psychological complexities of bilingualism and the power it gives to a person to have a command of formal spoken and written registers of a language.

Numerous studies have shown that the best way to educate bilingual students in their home languages is in classes designed for heritage speakers (Valdés 1997; Webb and Miller 2000; Shen 2003; Lynch 2003; Potowski and Carreira 2004; Colombi 2009). Most of the studies published in the United States have focused on Spanish speakers, but Helen Shen documented the remarkable benefit for Chinese heritage learners at the University of Virginia in taking classes designed for students who came from Mandarin-speaking homes. She followed two groups of heritage Chinese speakers, one that took two years of beginning Chinese in a blended class with second language learners, and one that took one year of beginning Chinese in a class made up only of heritage speakers. In a quantitative analysis of their reading comprehension, their knowledge of grammatical structure, and their knowledge of Chinese writing characters, the students who took one year in the heritage speaker class performed significantly better than those who took two years of classes with the blended group. As Shen noted, "Homogenous grouping of heritage students provided a learning environment in which they could best take advantage of their existing linguistic knowledge in the task of learning written Chinese" (p. 265).

Well-run heritage classes are distinct from those designed for second language learners. These heritage classes are not only taught in the target language but are created with a high expectation of listening comprehension. At the same time, teachers know to respect the vernacular brought to class and to gradually teach the difference between its lexicon and morphology and that of the standard academic variety. The expectations for literacy are broad enough to accommodate those who are still struggling with the writing system and to challenge those who have had some formal education.

Unfortunately, classes for heritage speakers are rare in most states. Instead, these students are shoehorned into classes taught using a method-

ology and textbooks designed to teach non-native speakers. In these beginning language courses they quickly become bored, because most of the
language is too simple for them. Imagine how you would feel sitting for an
hour repeating the names of colors and counting to ten in English! On tests,
they might not do well because they sometimes don't know how to study in
a way that focuses on their deficits in writing. If they are placed in advanced
courses, they are challenged by the oral language but might be far behind
the second language learners when it comes to literacy skills. At that point,
they are likely to drop out and may never return to any kind of formal instruction in their heritage language.

This is the dilemma facing thousands of language teachers in the United
States: how do I teach a class that combines heritage language learners and
second language learners? A veteran high school Spanish teacher honored
regionally for her work confessed to me once, "I still don't have the answer.
I struggle to keep my heritage speakers with our program, and if I can get
them to Spanish 4, everything goes well. But I lose so many before that,"
she said.

The key, I believe, is for us as educators to do all we can to promote the
creation of classes for heritage speakers that use materials designed for
their distinct needs. It is also critical that teachers of heritage learners be
trained in methodology specific to this area. Kim Potowski and Maria Carreira contrast the way we often think of English teacher preparation to that
of teacher preparation in other languages: "It is useful to illustrate this problem through a comparison with the field of English teacher training. Nearly
all English departments maintain a clear curricular distinction between
those preparing to become ESL teachers and those preparing to become
native English language arts teachers. It is not assumed that ESL teachers
will be successful native language arts teachers, nor vice versa. In fact, state
requirements demand separate coursework and award different endorse-
ments and certificates in these two fields" (p. 8).

But no matter how hard we advocate for heritage classes, the reality is
that in districts with limited funding or numbers of heritage learners that
administration does not deem to be sufficient, those classes might not occur (Bateman and Wilkinson 2010). For those situations I believe it is critical to develop a new pedagogy that is grounded in theories and practices
that begin from the presumption that some students will be second language learners and some will be heritage speakers. Carol Ann Tomlinson has

studied the factors that contribute to successfully blending students of different levels and ages in one classroom and has developed numerous strategies that could be applied across curricula and grades. Her research could be extremely valuable in the development of an approach that successfully blends heritage and second language learners. Characteristics of a what she calls a "differentiated classroom" include: flexibility in the curriculum to reflect the differences in the students; the availability of multiple learning materials; variable pacing; student participation in setting goals and standards; a variable grading system; and work assigned to students by virtue of their level of readiness (Tomlinson 1999). Teachers in districts with strict guidelines about assessment and curricula might be challenged in this regard.

Regardless of the particular situation, however, there are some general guidelines that can help you to better teach a class that blends heritage speakers and heritage language learners:

- Assess the needs of the heritage speaker population in your classes.

- Respect their variety of the language.

- Have specific goals for your heritage speakers, such as learning written accent marks in Spanish, academic lexicon in Arabic, the tones in Chinese, and how to write the "unpronounced" letters in French. As time permits, prepare packets of material based on those goals.

- Vary the level of input throughout the class.

- Allow heritage speakers to step into a leadership position in the classroom community.

- Use fun activities.

- Continue to educate yourself in appropriate methodology.

In the remainder of this chapter I will discuss these guidelines and offer examples of how they can be put to use in the classroom.

ASSESS THE NEEDS OF YOUR HERITAGE SPEAKERS

As you go about designing a curriculum that meets the needs of both your second language and heritage learners, it is important to NOT make any assumptions about the latter. Many will have excellent accents and be able to engage in simple conversations that sound fluently native-like. At the same time, reading a simple newspaper article or writing a letter might be real challenges for them. Also, there will be differences in the typical heritage speaker in different regions. For example, some may live in a region where their language is commonly spoken and there is plenty of written material in their world that has helped to develop their literacy skills. Others might come from elementary immersion schools where they have developed a high level of both written and oral proficiency. But some might have little exposure to their heritage language outside their families and close friends.

Coming to an understanding of the academic needs of the heritage students at your school or university might take some time, so give yourself a break if you struggle at first. Their areas of need will emerge in their written work, their exams, and their oral presentations. Keep a notebook where you jot down your observations on a regular basis. But you can start off by getting a feel for their writing during the first week by assigning a brief in-class composition. (Note: If you are working with a population that has little experience with the writing system of their heritage language, you might need to do this initial assessment by putting them in small groups to discuss the questions, then taking notes on the interaction you hear.)

Give them some options for the composition. Don't ask, "What did you do on your summer vacation?" That was probably the first back-to-school assignment every year they were in elementary school, and they might rebel against a topic that sounds so childish. Ask them instead to write about things they care about, such as music, the groups they are involved in at school, their roommates (for college level), or activities they like to do with their best friends. Brainstorm with them about the topics, and write their ideas on the board. Let them know that the essay won't be graded, but that you simply want to get to know them better.

That evening, read over the first few essays to see if some tendencies emerge. For instance, is there a verb conjugation that is problematic? Are there some common spelling errors? Make a list of the top three to five common areas of deficit, and take some specific notes on how those deficits present. Then read all the compositions and keep track of how often those three to five issues come up. Don't make any corrections on their papers, but you can write comments about the content.

When you have read all the essays, return them and tell the students you found the stories very interesting. Spend some time talking about what they have written. Your goal is not to begin correcting and "improving" their language. You want to send them the message that you respect the way they write and talk, and that they have been able to tell you some very interesting things about themselves.

The list you made will be your foundation for beginning to target areas of literacy where your students need the most help. It will probably expand and change over the upcoming years, but this list gives you a basis for searching out extra materials and creating written exercises for your heritage speakers.

RESPECT THEIR LANGUAGE

As you are organizing and preparing materials for your heritage learners, you should continue to strengthen the message you sent when you returned their assessment essays: you respect their language. You can say it straight out, but the best way to make them believe you is by showing it. For instance, if you teach a beginning class, and they are learning greetings, ask the heritage speakers what they say when they see friends. They might say something that is roughly translatable as "What's up?" or "How's it goin'?" or "What's good, bro?" Responses to the greetings might be similar to "Nothin'," or "Just chillin'." Let the entire class hear these possibilities, and write the interactions on the board. Compare them to the formal interactions in the book, and explain that these are two very different ways of interacting that serve the same purpose in two different situations. Have the heritage speakers play the roles of teachers talking to students using the formal interaction and then the roles of students talking to students using the vernacular. These mini-skits will demonstrate that formal language should be used with some people and in some places, and that informal can be used in others. All the students can practice both types of greetings. The non-native speakers will most likely enjoy saying the equivalent of "What's up?"

In this way, you begin to show that there are varieties of a language. Gradually introduce them to the idea that in school everyone has to learn the academic variety and that being able to use that variety in speaking and writing will open many doors to them in the future. Still, throughout the year, allow them to display and be proud of their abilities in the informal variety through some assignments such as skits and poetry.

Permitting and even encouraging "home" language in the classroom is very difficult for some teachers, even those who used to speak that way themselves before they went to college. But it is important to remember that the way we communicate is intimately tied to our identity. If we get the message in a classroom that the way we have spoken since childhood is "bad," the natural impulse is to pull away. If we get the message that we are competent speakers capable of communicating interesting things in our home language, and that in the classroom we are going to learn a new variety that makes us competent in a new way, we are more likely to participate.

If you hear the lexicon and morphology of the heritage variety in your class, never correct it in front of their peers. You can give alternative "feedback" by responding with the academic term embedded in a phrase so that they hear how you would say something and compare it to what they have just said. But don't demean your students by correcting them in front of others.

Our impulses as teachers might be to "fix" what we perceive to be problems—the "wrong" words or conjugations. But the best long-term outcome for your heritage students will occur if they stick with education in the language, and they are more likely to do so if they feel good about their abilities in both varieties. Coming to the point in which they use academic language will be a process, an evolution that will happen with time.

HAVE SPECIFIC GOALS FOR YOUR HERITAGE SPEAKERS

Use the list you developed from the initial writing assessment to come up with the goals you want to target for your heritage speakers. Maybe your first year of teaching you will only focus on one or two general areas and try to push your heritage speakers in those areas during the entire year. I recommend that you target these areas through specific examples of just a few words or utterances in each lesson. The following sections give examples of the types of challenges that heritage speakers face in various languages.

Chinese: The Tones

In Chinese there are four different voice tones as well as a "neutral" tone that can convey meaning. Many heritage speakers have difficulty employing the tones correctly. They understand what their relatives say to them by situational context, but they lose their ability to employ the tones when they speak. In the following examples, using the pinyin system that employs the Roman alphabet and accent marks, you can see what a big difference tones can make:

First tone:	*mā* = mother
Second tone:	*má* = a type of plant
Third tone:	*mǎ* = a horse
Fourth tone:	*mà* = a curse word
Light tone:	*ma* = a question indicator

French: Spelling

One of the most difficult aspects of learning to read and write French for both heritage speakers and second language learners is the fact so many letters, particularly toward the end of a word, are not pronounced. In particular, all consonants except *c, f, l,* and *r* are usually silent at the end of a word, although *r* is silent at the end of the first-conjugation verbs and *aller* (to go). For example, the difference between *trouver* (to find), *trouvé* (the past participle of *trouver*), and *trouvez* (the second-person plural command form) is only distinguishable by context in spoken language.

The imperfect forms in French are particularly problematic, not only for silent word-final consonants but for the fact that the same vowel sound is captured by different letters in different words. For instance, "I made" and "you made" are both spelled *faisais.* But a colleague of mine who has taught heritage speakers has seen them spell the word incorrectly as *fesé, faisez,* or *feisai.*

Spanish: Accent Marks

Correctly employing accent marks in written Spanish is extremely difficult for anyone not educated in a Spanish-speaking country. Accent marks serve different functions, including the indication of question words, the formation of preterit verb conjugations, the difference between two homophones, and as indicators that the spoken emphasis on a syllable in a word varies from the norm.

Examples of differences in meaning that can occur if accent marks or the tilde (the ~ in the letter *ñ*) are used incorrectly include the following:

bailo = I dance	*bailó* = he danced, she danced, or you danced
el = the	*él* = he
tu = your	*tú* = you
que = that	*qué* = what
si = if	*sí* = yes
ano = anus	*año* = year

Arabic: Vernacular Language vs. Academic Language

One of the challenges facing Arabic teachers of heritage speakers is the fact that the variety of Arabic recognized as the standard for education throughout the world is the home language of very few people. Spoken Arabic varies greatly between countries such as Egypt, Syria, Tunisia, Algeria, Saudi Arabia, Qatar, and Lebanon.

Written Arabic is based mainly on that academic dialect. Many heritage speakers learn to read to some degree, particularly for religious texts. But they struggle with producing the standard variety, in both its written and spoken form. One of the main stumbling blocks for them is the fact that there are no written vowels in Arabic, so the same written word could be pronounced numerous different ways depending upon whether the sounds "a," "u," or "i" separate the consonants.

Targeting Your Goals through a Behavioral Approach

One of the biggest problems I see in educational materials is the tendency to present new material in what I call the "laundry list" approach. For instance, a textbook chapter focused on the home and household activities might include a vocabulary list for twenty pieces of furniture. The students would have to memorize that vocabulary list in order to do well on the test. But in what natural world does somebody acquiring a new language learn the names of twenty pieces of furniture at the same time? A child or a language learner would naturally first acquire "chair," "table," and "bed." It would be months before she would learn "nightstand" and the difference between "stove" and "oven."

Likewise, there is a tendency to present the targeted areas for learning to heritage speakers using this laundry-list approach. For instance, all five Chinese tones might be taught at the same time. In Spanish, some heritage textbooks lay out all the rules for written accent marks in the same chapter that includes the rules of syllabic accentuation, homophones, diphthongs, triphthongs, and interrogative words. How in the world could anyone assimilate all that material in one chunk?

Instead, I recommend breaking down your larger goal into much smaller chunks the way a behaviorist targets new skills for acquisition. This can be done with almost any academic goal, whether it is word-final spelling in French, tones in Chinese, accent marks in Spanish, or academic lexicon in Arabic.

For instance, a Chinese teacher could focus on two tones and choose three or four key words for each tone that exemplify the difference. In the example provided above, a teacher could focus on the first and third tones and the difference demonstrated in the words "mother" and "horse." During the input presentations in each class for a month, she could employ stories that contrast the first and third tones with just a few words. During the next month, she might call the students' attention to the difference between the second and fourth tones. In a following month focus could be placed on the contrast between the first and second tones, and the following month the focus could expand to contrasts between three of the tones.

In terms of Spanish accent marks, a teacher might begin by telling students that two words that stand for people (*tú* = you and *él* = he) have accent marks. The other, less "important" words don't have accent marks (*tu* = your and *el* = the). Focus could be placed on these contrasts in every situation in which it could naturally be embedded.

Arabic teachers might use their initial writing assessment to prioritize areas of lexicon and focus on three or four words per week. French teachers might choose a handful of very common verbs in the imperfect and use them often in the input, occasionally stopping to write them on the board. There are numerous ways to employ this behavioral approach, but one underlying rule of thumb is to keep it simple and build slowly.

Using Homework Packets

Preparing separate written materials for heritage speakers might be more than can be expected of a first-year teacher. But if you can find the time, it would be beneficial to your students to have some kind of homework to support the areas you are targeting for them in your classroom. You can turn to textbooks for heritage language learners for ideas and even copy some of their exercises. Be sure to check copyright laws before you do so. (A list of heritage language textbooks in various languages is available on our website.)

Start by giving them some readings that include informal dialogue between characters (Colombi 2009). The best would have dialogue that employs informal vernacular and that is typical of the population living in your region. In that way the readings will be much more accessible to your students, and you can begin to teach them the difference between informal verbal language and academic written language. Little by little the readings could become more formal and more academic. These readings could substitute for or be in addition to the readings that the rest of the class is doing.

Next, develop some written exercises that are tied as directly as possible either to the readings you prepared for them or to the curriculum that the rest of the class is learning. Giving them written work that is disconnected from their readings or their classroom interactions will be frustrating for them and could possibly set them up for failure on the written work.

For instance, if your Spanish class is learning about sports, you could find a short news article about soccer and "white out" some of the accent marks on words that they have studied. Photocopy the article and have the heritage speakers read it at home and write in the accent marks. In class the next day, they could talk in small groups about the gist of the article.

VARY THE LEVEL OF INPUT

As you know, it is extremely important to stay in the target language during class. With practice you will become better each year at shooting for that magical "Input + 1" level where your language is slightly above the level that is easily understood by your students. However, if you have heritage learners in your classroom, they will need more of a challenge, and you can do this throughout the day by bumping up the narrative to a native level.

You will find that they become much more alert, particularly if you employ comprehension checks.

You might ask yourself: But what about my non-native speakers? How will this impact them? You should just as well ask yourself: How does staying at a beginning level of oral language impact my heritage speakers? The answer is that the situation is not perfect for either, but it can work just fine. In fact, it can benefit beginners to occasionally be surrounded by some native-level banter in the language they are learning.

I believe that the best way to provide higher-level input for heritage speakers is by weaving it into stories, conversations, and instructions. At first, you can be satisfied with simply bumping up the level of difficulty in some of your utterances without necessarily targeting specific goals. All the students will come to understand what is going on as they see you make eye contact and engage in comprehension checks with the heritage speakers as you use the higher-level language. But as you become better at flowing back and forth between levels you can start to target the goals you have developed for your heritage speakers. It is important to remember that "bumping up" the level of language for heritage speakers is not the same as bumping up the level for the more advanced second language learners in your class. For instance, if you are working on the simple present conjugation of verbs, turning to the heritage speakers and employing the past tenses is not necessarily a challenge for them. They use the past tenses at home all the time, although they might have trouble with the irregular conjugations. Use your assessments to arrive at your goals.

Below is an example of a typical comprehensible input presentation with the higher-level language marked with "HS" for heritage speakers. In the textbook, the class has begun a chapter about the home and daily activities. This class will focus on household chores using a story about the teacher's three children. The teacher has added on input for heritage speakers that exposes them to the subjunctive mood as it is used in Latin languages. Carmen Silva-Corvalán and other linguists have studied language attrition among Spanish heritage speakers in the United States and found that one of the most striking characteristics of this change is the loss of the ability to employ the subjunctive mood. This form of conjugation is used in subordinate clauses for things such as emotional reactions to an event or the fact that one person tries to influence the behavior of another (Silva-Corvalán 2001). In English, we employ a number of grammatical strategies to capture these concepts. For example, we use an infinitive ("I want you <u>to go</u> to the store"), a participle ("I prevent him from <u>going</u> to the store"), or a simple present-tense conjugation ("I hope that he <u>goes</u> to the store"). In Latin languages, the subjunctive is necessary: <u>Quiero que vaya a la tienda</u>. Many Spanish heritage speakers understand something said to them in the subjunctive, but when they open their mouths to speak, it doesn't come out. For this reason, I believe it is valuable to provide input in the subjunctive whenever possible.

For this presentation, I would use a PowerPoint, photos, or physical movements augmented by props. It tells the story of "my" three children and the chores they must do every Saturday morning.

Saturday Mornings at My House

Every Saturday morning my three children have to clean our house. My husband and I have to work at his business on weekends, so it is up to our kids to get the home in order. Some Saturdays I stay home, so I know what goes on.

First, Natalie vacuums in the living room, the hallway, the dining room, and her bedroom. She does not vacuum in her brothers' bedrooms. That is their job.

<u>HS: Sometimes my son Nathan gets mad that she has woken him with the sound of the vacuum. But she likes to vacuum first, and she figures that he can go back to sleep. Besides, she thinks he should get up earlier.</u>

Next, Natalie dusts the furniture in the living room. She likes to listen to music and dance while she dusts.

<u>HS: This is another thing that bothers Nathan. He just gets back to sleep after Natalie turns off the vacuum, and then she turns on the music. He usually yells, "Turn it off!" But Natalie just turns up the music.</u>

Finally, Natalie takes out the garbage to the bins in the garage. She puts a new plastic bag in the garbage can.

<u>HS: Sometimes the plastic bag is so full of garbage that it breaks, and everything spills onto the kitchen floor. She hates that when it happens and has to use rubber gloves to pick it all up.</u>

COMPREHENSION CHECK:

Who vacuums, Nathan or Natalie? (Natalie.) HS: Is anyone bothered by her vacuuming? (Yes, her brother Nathan.) Etc. etc. Where does Natalie dust? (She dusts in the living room.) What else does she do while she dusts? (She listens to music and dances.) HS: Does Nathan like the music? (No.) Why not? (It wakes him up again.) What does he do? (He asks her to turn it off.) Etc. etc. When Natalie takes out the garbage, where does she take it? (She takes the garbage out to the bin in the garage.) After she takes it out to the garage, what does she do? Etc. etc. HS: What happens on some mornings? (The garbage bag breaks and garbage spills all over the kitchen floor.) How does she react? (It makes her angry when the bag breaks.) What does she do then? (She puts on rubber gloves and picks it all up.) Etc. etc.

Max is the little brother so he has the easiest chores. First he waters the plants on the patio, and then he waters the plants in the garden. Sometimes he puts too much water on the plants, and their leaves turn yellow.

HS: Max says that this is his favorite chore. He likes plants so much that when he grows up he wants to be a gardener.

Next, Max is supposed to wipe the kitchen counter and to wash the dishes. Usually he puts them all in the dishwasher.

HS: I want Max to wash the pots and pans by hand, but he doesn't like to do that, so he puts them in the dishwasher and waits to see if I notice when I get home. It's an ongoing battle.

Finally, Max takes our dog Einstein for a walk. Usually they go around the block and then to a nearby park where Einstein can run.

HS: Einstein always wants Max to take him to the river so he can swim. But I don't like him going so far from home.

COMPREHENSION CHECK:

Does Max water the plants in the house? (No.) Does he water the outdoor plants? (Yes.) HS: Does Max like this chore? (Yes.) What has he told me about plants and his future? (He says that when he grows up he wants to be a gardener.) Etc. etc. After watering the plants, does Max wash dishes or clean the bathroom? (He washes the dishes.) What does he do with the pots and pans? (He puts them in the dishwasher.) HS: Is that what I ask him to do? Do I want him to put the pots and pans in the dishwasher? (No, you want him to wash them by hand.) Etc. etc. What is our dog's name? (Einstein.) Where does Max walk with Einstein? (They walk to the park.) HS: Where does Einstein want Max to take him after going to the park? (He wants Max to take him to the river.) Why does he want to go to the river? (He wants to swim.)

Nathan usually gets up at about noon. After breakfast he starts to do his chores. First, Nathan sweeps the floors in the kitchen and the bathroom. He listens to music on his iPod while he sweeps.

HS: If Natalie has broken the garbage bag in the kitchen, there is usually some garbage on the floor for Nathan to sweep up. He gets angry that she doesn't pick up very well after breaking the bag, and he often complains to their father and me when we get home.

Next, Nathan has to mop the floors. He usually mops the bathroom floor first and then the kitchen floor. He uses really hot water because he can see that it cleans better.

HS: After he mops the floors, Nathan waits on the front porch for them to dry and keeps his eye out for his brother and the dog. He doesn't want Einstein to walk on the wet kitchen floor and get it dirty.

Finally, Nathan has to clean the bathroom. He uses a sponge, hot water, and bleach.

HS: Nathan really hates this job. He has proposed that he and Natalie switch some of their chores and says that he prefers to vacuum. It makes sense, he says, because that way he is the person in charge of all the floors. He is in negotiation about this issue with his father and me.

COMPREHENSION CHECK:

What time does Nathan get up? (He gets up at about noon.) Where does Nathan sweep the floors? (He sweeps in the kitchen and the bathroom.) <u>HS: On some mornings, Nathan gets mad about some-</u><u>thing while he's sweeping. What is it that makes him angry?</u> (He gets mad that there is garbage on the floor from the broken garbage bag.) After he sweeps, does Nathan clean the counters or mop the floors? (He mops the floors.) What does Nathan use to clean the bathroom? (He uses a sponge, hot water, and bleach.) Does Nathan like this job? (No, he hates it.) <u>HS: What has Nathan proposed?</u> (Nathan has pro-posed that he and Natalie switch chores. He wants to be in charge of vacuuming and he wants her to clean the bathroom.)

In the communicative activity that follows this presentation, students will most likely talk about their own lives and the chores that they or their fami-lies do. If heritage speakers are divided equally among the small groups in class, the teacher can encourage them to go into the same level of detail as heard in the presentation.

Constantly keeping in mind the various comprehension levels of your students and providing them with an appropriate level of input can seem daunting in the beginning. But with practice it will become second nature.

ALLOW HERITAGE SPEAKERS TO TAKE A LEADERSHIP POSITION

If the heritage speakers in your class will use the target language, the second language learners are very lucky indeed. They will get more input and have more opportunities for genuine communication. But what do the heritage speakers get from these interactions? They will get some of the same ben-efits that older students in a one-room school house get—the psychological investment that comes from mentoring and the metalinguistic knowledge that comes from teaching something to another person.

We have all heard the adage "You really learn something when you teach it." By working with non-native speakers in pairs and small groups, some of the heritage speakers will strengthen their understanding of whatever they are working on during that class, whether it is a verb conjugation or the for-mation of complex sentences. There can be great benefits from occasionally explaining or teaching a concept to others.

However, you must be careful to NOT use heritage speakers as your class-room aides. It is important to balance occasional activities in which they work with second language learners with activities in which they work with each other on the more challenging packets that you have prepared for them. Watch carefully and ask them their opinions about what kind of role they benefit from most. Even if a student says, "I really like helping the other people in class," that is not a good reason to always use the student as a helper. Keep the academic goals for that heritage speaker in mind.

Another way to encourage heritage speakers to assume a role of leadership in the classroom is simply by treating them as leaders. Ask them about their opinions on language use and about their experiences and knowledge when it is relevant to the chapter (for example, festivals or customs). You can ask them to be leaders of group activities or to help organize something.

Your main goal is to foster pride in what they know already and who they are in your classroom community. If they feel good about who they are in your class, they are more likely to continue studying their home language.

USE FUN ACTIVITIES

One of the primary goals of this book is to help you become a teacher who uses enjoyable communicative activities to promote learning. People almost always learn more quickly and retain that learning better if they are having fun. Your heritage speakers are no exception.

Look at the communicative activity in every lesson plan and ask yourself, "Would this activity in English be engaging to me?" If the activity is to create a list of the different kinds of plural forms that exist in the language, your answer will probably be "no." If the activity is to find out who in the class used to go camping as a child, who played with Barbies, and who stole candy from the store, your answer will probably be "yes." Your native speakers will stay much more engaged if the activity is fun and focused on true communication, not simply on language form.

CONTINUE TO EDUCATE YOURSELF

There is a growing focus on the importance of training language teachers in the methodology of teaching heritage speakers. Few universities offer classes in this approach, but there are workshops, conferences, and numerous publications that teachers can take advantage of on their own. The best clearinghouse I have found is the Heritage Languages in America website of the Center for Applied Linguistics, http://www.cal.org/heritage/. There you will find numerous links to listservers for teachers of various languages, links to upcoming conferences, information about publications, and profiles of heritage programs throughout the country. On their webpage Heritage Voices Collection you can even find descriptions of and syllabi for heritage programs for numerous languages, including German, Chinese, Hindi, and French. The American Council of Teachers of Foreign Languages (ACTFL) also has a Heritage Languages Special Interest Group. You can find the link at their main site, http://www.actfl.org.

◊   ◊   ◊

We strongly advocate the creation of separate language classes for heritage speakers whenever that is possible. Considerable research points to the efficacy of this approach, particularly when taught by educators trained in methodology for teaching heritage speakers and when materials developed explicitly for those students are employed.

However, political and financial constraints often prevent the creation of such classes. In those situations, teachers must strive to develop an approach that teaches to the heritage speakers in a blended class instead of trying to force them to function in a model developed for second language learners. Some of the techniques that will help include: assessing their needs in the beginning of the course, respecting their variety of the language, having specific goals for heritage speakers, varying the level of input throughout the class, allowing heritage speakers to step into a leadership position, using fun activities, and continuing to educate yourself.

Summary Questions

1. What are typically the strengths of heritage speakers of any given language in the United States?

_____

_____

2. What are typically the greatest challenges for heritage speakers in a language classroom?

_____

_____

3. Name the six steps a teacher can take to serve heritage speakers in a beginning language class.

_____

_____

Scenarios

Scenario 1

You were just hired by a high school or community college to teach a beginning-level language course. The administrator told you that typically 25 percent of students in beginning courses at this school are heritage speakers. Develop a general plan for your heritage speakers during the first week of class.

_____

_____

Scenario 2

You teach a beginning-level course for second language learners at a high school or university with a heritage learner program. However, one heritage speaker has signed up for your class and refuses to go to the heritage learners' class that is taught at the exact same time as yours. If you had to venture a guess, you would say that he wants an easy A. There are two problems. First of all, he speaks often and very quickly, and your other students seem to be intimidated. Instead of being drawn to working in groups with him, they pull away. Secondly, he gets defensive when you correct anything he writes. Come up with some strategies to both incorporate him better into your class and to challenge him with reading and writing.

_____

_____

11 • Including Students with Disabilities and Learning Differences in a Language Classroom

DENISE MINOR

For those going into teaching in this millennium, the question is not whether you will have a student with disabilities in your classes. The questions are: How many students with special needs will you have? What kinds of disabilities will they have? How can you best incorporate them into your classroom? How can you best help them reach their learning potential?

According to the U.S. Census Bureau, about 5 percent of children between five and seventeen years of age have significant disabilities, and another 8 percent have learning disabilities (www.census.gov/compendia/statab/2011/tables). Many of these students will go on to college or continue their education through adult programs, so whether you teach at a high school, a university, or an adult school, you must be prepared.

It is best to start with legal basics. In 1990 a sweeping change in policy governing special education was put in place with the passage of the Individuals with Disabilities Education Act (IDEA). This law grew out of previous legislation and was the culmination of decades of work on the part of activists to change the structure of our society to make it more inclusive (http://idea.ed.gov/explore/home). It is hard for us to imagine, but it used to be that some wheelchair users couldn't even go to most schools because they

couldn't go up the front stairs, couldn't get in the front doors, and would not have been able to use the bathroom even if they did get inside. Some teens with dyslexia were matter-of-factly labeled stupid and consigned to manual labor jobs for the rest of their adult lives.

Now people with disabilities have legal rights to accommodations, and teachers of every level should know what those rights entail. For those of you who will teach high school, know this: all children or teens with disabilities are entitled to education that is designed to meet their individual needs in the "least restrictive environment." What does "least restrictive environment" mean? That is very much open to interpretation, but not by you alone. The decision will be made by a team that designs the students' Individual Education Plans (IEPs), and you will most likely be on that team. There are numerous paths the IEP could take in terms of your students, including mandating that all materials be tape-recorded for a blind student or that all exams be given orally to a student with dyslexia.

For those who will teach at the college level, the situation is somewhat different. Not everyone has the "right" to go to college. However, public universities are considered public entities that are governed under Title II of the

Americans with Disabilities Act (ADA), and are more specifically governed by Section 504 of the Rehabilitation Act, which requires institutions of higher education to provide students with disabilities the same opportunity to engage in educational experiences as other students. Students who voluntarily disclose (self-identify) that they have a disability, provide documentation of that disability, and meet eligibility requirements are entitled to receive approved accommodations such as longer time to take tests, modifications to programs, and auxiliary aides.

What does that mean for you? For some students, you will receive word from the school's disability support services (DSS) or a similar office that the student has a disability and is entitled to accommodations. In those cases, use the support of the professionals at your school as much as you can. In other cases, you will have a student who struggles or seems very different to you, but you will not hear anything from the student or administration about a disability. You should handle those situations differently.

From my experience at the university level, there are many students with autism, learning disabilities, and disorders such as obsessive-compulsive disorder (OCD) who either do not have a diagnosis or choose not to disclose it. You cannot say to them, "It seems to me like you have a learning disability" or "Are you autistic? Do you need me to make some accommodations?" But you can take steps to steer them toward the professionals, and you can take SOME steps toward incorporating them better into your class or helping them learn, even without a diagnosis.

At the high school level, if you have a student that you suspect has an undiagnosed disability, you will have a very specific protocol for making a referral that will vary between states and even between school districts. Often you will make a referral to your principal, who will then contact a school counselor and a special education professional. They will most likely look into the student's records and will send someone to do an observation. You simply need to follow the protocol.

At the college level things are a little trickier. In terms of learning disabilities, there is no parent or special education teacher looking out for your students. They have to take matters into their own hands and contact the school's disability support services. I advise beginning a conversation with a student by asking questions such as, "Do you find it difficult to finish the exams on time?" or, "Do you feel like you are really studying hard and still can't seem to learn this material?" If they respond yes, you can say that you have had many students with the same issues, and some of them have gone to DSS and seen their grades go up. I often mention the fact that I have mild dyslexia and have learned strategies to compensate. Their eyes usually light up when I say that because they realize that I am not saying that a learning disability is a bad thing; it is simply something you have to deal with in order to get through college.

Autism is a whole different ball game. My son has autism, and through interacting with many people on the autism spectrum over the last fifteen years, I have been amazed at how varied the characteristics are of people with the same diagnosis. Some people with autism also have significant cognitive disabilities or communication disorders. Support for those issues will be similar to support for students with disabilities or learning disabilities. But with autism there is almost always the additional issue of having difficulty interacting with others. Some people on the spectrum want to intensely interact, and they can't read the social cues telling them to back off. They might stand too close and talk at great length about one particular thing. Others have serious difficulty with any kind of human interaction. They don't want to be touched—even a simple pat on the shoulder—and they can't look people in the eyes. If you are following our instructions in this book and have created a classroom with lots of interaction and communicative activities, your students with autism might struggle. You might not be able to turn to DSS for help, but there are things you can do. Further on in this chapter I will give you some examples.

So, at the bare-bones level, you must comply with the law. But there is another level that I consider just as important, and that is the level at which a teacher goes beyond what is required legally and tries to give a student with a disability the same chance as others at learning the language and at becoming an integral part of the class. It requires not just following the rules but going the extra mile to do what is right. In order to do that, you will have to dedicate some extra time to rethinking the way you teach. In some cases it may be a matter of only a few minutes per week, but in others it might be much more, at least in the beginning.

Now let's move on to some suggestions that might help you do your job. Instead of teaching you generalities, I am going to use the stories of students I have had over the years, as well as a story told to me by my coauthor. (The stories are real, though I've changed the names.) I hope that by studying the specific accommodations that were made for these students, you will gain knowledge of how to think, plan, and create in ways that work for a wide variety of students. The first three stories will focus on students who had received a diagnosis and for whom we received notification. The last two stories focus on students who did not receive any outside support. One did not have a diagnosis, and the other had a diagnosis that was not recognized by her university's disability support services.

Before we move forward, though, I want to pass on one important piece of advice for including someone with a disability into your classroom. The first thing you must ask yourself is what he or she *can* do well, not what he or she cannot do. Everyone has strengths. Is your blind student very good at picking out the words of a song? Maybe you will use music more in class this year. Is your student who uses a wheelchair very social but having difficulty maneuvering in your small classroom to interact in "signature" activities? Then move outside where it is easier to navigate in a wheelchair. Go to an area with benches or take a few chairs outside, and encourage some students to take a seat, and consider doing so yourself. In that way your student won't be looking up at everyone to participate in the interactions. With practice, this way of modifying your class plans will come so naturally that it will require little or no extra work, and the benefits will be tremendous.

MARTIN

Martin was a brilliant young man in my Spanish 2 class at a research university. He used a wheelchair and had very limited control of any of his body, although he could hold a pen or pencil and, with great effort, could write. Resting on top of the arms of his wheelchair was a board with a cell phone attached to it. Because of his physical impairment it was difficult for most people to understand his speech.

Martin was the person who made me realize that the important question to ask myself when thinking about accommodating a person with a disability was, "What can he do?" He wouldn't be able to pantomime Total Physical Response (TPR) activities such as "jump, dance, write your name in the air, and touch your stomach." Therefore, when students were learning the imperative (command) forms of verbs, I replaced commands such as "stand up, sit down, dance" with commands such as "look up, look down, open your mouths, say *ahhhh*." Yes, it is fun for students to stand up and shake around. But they were *fine* with learning commands for people in a seated position, and in this way one of the members of our community was *not* excluded.

I also realized that Martin could use the joystick on the wheelchair to move his chair, so that a good way to practice the imperative would be by creating an activity that moved out of the classroom and traveled into campus. So I developed a treasure hunt in which groups of students practiced the commands on each other. For instance, Student 1 would tell her group members to leave the room, go to the elevator, go up to third floor, go to the Anthropology Department, and say *Hola* to the secretary there. Student 2 would then tell the group to go to the elevator, go down to the first floor, exit the building, go to the statue of the politician in the plaza, and look behind the statue. Waiting there was a bag of chocolates marked *Español 2*. Student 3 and Student 4 would have further commands for the group that eventually brought everyone back to the classroom. Key to the success of this activity was the fact that Martin could participate in everything. Now, ten years later, I continue to use this same activity in my beginning Spanish classes.

I also used skits in my beginning language courses and realized that I could modify all of them to include a person who remained seated. For instance, the skit *Dos Hombres y una Mujer* (Two Men and a Woman) began with two men walking down the street when they see the wife of one of the men walking arm in arm with another man. I changed the skit to begin with two men sitting at a restaurant eating pizza and watching sports on television. In this version of the play, Martin was seated at the table with the husband. At one point a crime occurred and Martin "called" 911 with his cell phone, which was attached to his desk. Martin was not in all of the skits performed in class, but I looked at every one of them to make sure they could be modified to include him if that occurred.

In order to accommodate Martin's difficulties with writing, I made one version of each test in large print and photocopied it on one side only so he didn't have to turn each page over to write on the back. It was in the essay of the first exam that I came to realize that Martin was an excellent writer. He didn't write much, but what he did write was clear, clean, and creative. I read his exam essay aloud to the class, and in that moment I felt a shifting in perceptions. Until then, the other students had seemed to shy away from him a little bit. They had a hard time understanding him and weren't sure how much he understood. When they heard his beautiful essay, many realized how intelligent he was and began to interact with him more.

Martin was a senior that quarter, and at the end of the quarter he received word that he had been accepted into law school. I've since heard that he practices law in a firm that specializes in disability rights.

LAURIE

I didn't realize at first that Laurie, a student in one of my beginning Spanish courses at a university, had a learning disability. From the first day of class she sat in the front row and paid close attention. Her homework was always neatly done and turned in on time. It wasn't until after she failed the first exam that I was notified that she was supported by DSS and had the right to take her exams at the center and receive twice as much time. I'm not certain why she didn't have DSS notify me earlier, but I suspect that she first wanted to see if she could do well without any accommodations.

When we met in my office, Laurie told me that since she was a small child she had a very hard time remembering things, but that once she learned them she never forgot them. This was the most important thing she could have told me. From her failed test, I could see that the hardest thing for her was the verb conjugations. She wasn't acquiring them naturally in our class interactions, and she wasn't able to memorize them by studying.

Together we developed a simple system that you could use in your classroom, or you could teach the system to a tutor who works with your students. I have used it mainly to help students who struggle with remembering verb conjugations or vocabulary. The following system is the one I use for teaching verb conjugations. You will have to modify it with drawings, photos, or translations in order to drill vocabulary words.

1. Make two sets of flash cards, one with the pronouns *I, you, he, she, we, you, they* (in the target language), and the other with verbs on one side and their conjugations on the back. It is easy to buy packs of cards with conjugations, but the act of making them can help a person learn.

2. With the two piles in front of the student, pick one pronoun and one verb and ask her to conjugate them. For instance, in the case

of Spanish, if I picked up *yo* and *ir*, my student would say *Yo fui* (I went).

3. Thus far you might be thinking that this drill is no different from a memorization exercise for all students. But the trick to using this practice effectively to help a person with memory problems is to cycle the cards using a very frequent pattern. Repeat the previously done conjugations over and over. Below is an example using the English irregular present perfect:

I have written.	She has eaten.
She has written.	They have eaten.
I have written.	She has eaten.
She has written.	She has given.
They have written	They have given.
She has written.	She has given.
I have written.	She as eaten.
They have written.	She has written.
She has written.	I have given.
She has eaten.	I have eaten.
I have eaten.	I have written.

If the student makes any mistakes, fold the mistaken cards in to the drill *every other one* until she has it down perfectly.

4. Have the student carry the cards with her to drill for five minutes at a time as she waits for buses, sits on a bench between classes, or is listening quietly to her friend go *on and on* about her ex-boyfriend on the telephone. Impress upon your student that this type of learning must be done in small chunks every day in order to be truly effective.

Laurie and I met once a week to monitor her progress and to make new cards. (As I stated earlier, this is a responsibility that could be taken care of by a tutor, but I prefer to do it myself.) On the next test Laurie got a C, and in our subsequent meeting we decided that she would be able to make her own cards and drill grammar and vocabulary on her own. The week before the final exam I held a study session, and about eight students arrived. I created a conjugation game in which they took turns drawing cards out of a hat and creating sentences according to the verb and required conjugation.

Most of the students caught on quickly, but Laurie was having a difficult time. I was sitting next to her at the table and it was clear that she was struggling when it came her turn. She kept her eyelids down and I could see from the side the tears that were filling her eyes. The group session was another reminder for her that her brain didn't work like everyone else's. I wanted to stop the game, but thought that my reason might be obvious and might embarrass her further.

On the final exam Laurie got a B–, and she came to my office with a thank-you card and a very sweet letter. Her final grade was a C+, a very hard earned C+. As I filled in the grade sheet over semester break, I thought about how much more I admired her than the group of party boys in that same class who barely cracked the book and got the same grade.

Two years later I ran into Laurie on campus. Through our conversation I learned that she had done well in college, in part because she had applied effective learning strategies and in part because she had gotten support from DSS. On that spring day she was very happy to be headed off on a European exchange program that provided both language courses and an internship.

MICHELLE

A few years ago my coauthor, Norma, received word from her university disability support office that she would have a blind student in her upcoming Spanish 1 class. Norma knew that she would have to seriously reevaluate all of her class plans because she relied so much on visual input to provide contextual meaning. Physical movement, facial expressions, gestures, and photos were all intrinsic to communication in her classroom. She wondered if she wouldn't have to break her own NO TRANSLATION rule and translate everything so that this one student could understand.

At the end of class on the first day she asked Michelle for help. "How do you best learn? Do you have any suggestions that can help me to teach you?" she asked. Michelle simply requested that Norma say aloud everything that she wrote on the board or distributed on paper.

Norma got into the habit every day, as she prepared class for the following day, of looking at her plans, then closing her eyes and asking herself, "What will this be like for Michelle?" She found herself explaining things in two or three different ways (always in Spanish) with the hope that Michelle would comprehend at least one of them. As it turned out, she did. Michelle was able to use the extra verbal input to compensate for the lack of visual input.

Norma remembers clearly the day that she had planned for her class to practice vocabulary they had learned in their chapter on sports. She told the class that they would divide into two teams and head outside to the lawn to play a game of soccer. As they played, they would use their vocabulary, such as "Pass it over here!!" Some students did not want to play but instead planned to play the role of fans on the sidelines shouting the Spanish cheers that Norma had taught them. Norma asked Michelle if she wanted to cheer from the sidelines, and she said, "Oh no, I play soccer. I have a ball with bells on it."

The next day Michelle showed up with the ball with bells, and the game began. Both teams seemed to naturally use more language to help Michelle keep aware of where everyone was. The game was a smashing success.

LEE

Lee was a young woman in a beginning Spanish class I taught at a university. Although I received no notification from the disability support office concerning her, and she did not tell me that she had a disability, I noted behaviors that reminded me of autism. I did not need a label for her in order to make accommodations that I believed were appropriate. I have considerable experience doing this, and I know how to make accommodations that do not make one person stand out from the others and are not even noticeable to a class. If you are a beginner teacher, I urge you to get advice from an inclusion professional before making changes or accommodations for a student for whom you have not received official notification or who has not told you herself about her disability.

The first thing I noticed was Lee's reluctance to engage in the interactive activities that required students to move around and talk to different people. That, of course, is not necessarily an indication of autism. But she could not make eye contact with the other students, and her body language made it clear she was very uncomfortable. Some students don't like to engage in these activities for other reasons. For instance, young people who still have a high-school-type rebellious streak will sometimes act like these activities are not cool. They will plop in a chair the first chance they get and check their cell phone. Lee did not send any of those signals. It was clear that she was a dedicated student and was not "too cool" for anything. She simply really struggled with the social interactions.

After another week I announced that some students could stay in a small group for these activities instead of standing up to interact. I chose the left side of the room as the "small group" side, which was, *not* coincidentally, Lee's side of the room. I watched to see if her ease with interactions got better, and there seemed to be a slight improvement. The following week I addressed her after class and said that I noticed that she wrote extremely well (which was true). I told her that I liked to know what went on in the small groups, and that if she would take notes it would help me greatly. For the following interactive activity, she took out her notebook and started writing. I told her group that she was helping me by reporting on their language, and they all looked at each other as if to say, "Uh-oh. We'd better speak well." I was happy to look over her notes at the end of each class and chat about them, even though conversation was somewhat awkward with her in English as well.

I asked Lee to continue to interact with the others even though she was taking notes, and over the coming weeks I noticed that little by little she would look up and speak more and more. I began to think that the pen and paper served as small physical and psychological buffers between her and the other students. Those buffers were not big enough to impede communication, but they were big enough to reduce her anxiety.

I also made sure that students rotated out of the seated groups and that, at most, there were eight sitting at any time. Nobody noticed (I hope) that the only one always seated was Lee. And in fact, I did make everyone stand and move around for some activities during the course of the quarter. I continued to watch to see if these whole-class interactions were getting easier for Lee, but they were not.

It's true that Lee still did not get the level of second language oral production that the others did. But my impression was that in the small groups she got more interaction than she did in the whole-class interactions. Also, in this particular way, her affective filter was low, and therefore more acquisition was taking place than when she was anxious.

As I said earlier, you have to be very careful about making accommodations when you aren't notified through official channels about a student's disability. But having a few students complete an activity by sitting in a small group, as opposed to standing up and moving around, is hardly a radical accommodation, and nobody is harmed by it. This is an example of the kinds of small changes that you can make to accommodate not only disabilities but also different personalities and learning styles.

MARINA

During the first week of Spanish Composition 1, I couldn't help but notice Marina's arms and hands. They were covered with skin that was cracked and flaky. I also noted that during class discussion she would make a point and then have a difficult time moving on. She would raise her hand to make the same point, and wanted to say it again after class to me.

That quarter I decided to add a couple of extra office hours at a coffee shop near my home in order to help those who were struggling. Marina arrived and looked very nervous. She sat down and told me she had to talk about something that was very difficult for her to say. Finally she blurted out that she had obsessive-compulsive disorder. I smiled and said, "Oh, I think my son has that on top of his autism. Tell me more." She said that OCD significantly impacted her life and that, for instance, she had to constantly wash her hands and lower arms. (That explained the cracked skin.) She also said that the rituals she felt compelled to engage in took up a considerable amount of her time, which made it difficult to complete schoolwork. Finally, she said that she could not complete a composition because it was never good enough.

That, of course, was going to be the biggest problem for her in Spanish Composition. Marina said that she had gone to the disability support office but that they didn't recognize OCD as a disability and therefore couldn't provide support. After chatting for some time, we decided that she would come to my office at scheduled times to work on her compositions. When the time was up, she had to stop, and I would print the composition. What was there on the page would be graded. As it turned out, her compositions were quite good except for the fact that they always lacked a conclusion. She received a B in the class.

Three years later I was walking down a street when a woman with long dark hair ran out of a shop and yelled my name. It took a few moments to recognize Marina because she had changed so much. She said that she simply wanted to tell me how much I had helped her at an important juncture in her life. For one thing, with our system for helping her turn in compositions, she learned to let go a little bit of that particular obsession. In addition, she was able to convince other teachers to make accommodations because one teacher already had done so.

Are these accommodations extra work? Of course they are, particularly before you get good at it. Is it worth it? In my opinion, they are more than worth it. We go into teaching because we want to make a difference in people's lives, and there are few places where we can make as big an impact as in the lives of people with learning or physical differences. On top of that, learning to be a good teacher for students with disabilities will make you a better teacher for all of your students.

Summary Questions

1. What percentage of students in the United States has significant disabilities? What percentage has learning disabilities?

_____

_____

2. What does the law mandate for accommodating and including students with disabilities in K–12th grade? What does the law mandate for accommodating and including students with disabilities at the university level? What is the difference?

_____

_____

3. What are some common accommodations made for students with learning disabilities? What are some ways to make your class activities more inclusive for a student with physical limitations?

_____

_____

4. What is the most important question to ask yourself as you evaluate your lessons plans with the goal of including a student with disabilities as much as possible?

_____

_____

Scenarios

Scenario 1

You receive word from the special education teacher at your school or the disability support services office at your university that you will have a deaf student in your next beginning language class. She has cochlear implants and has very limited hearing, but she is able to speak, although sometimes her speech is difficult to understand. Your new student is fluent in American Sign Language and will have an aide with her in half of the classes who signs ASL.

What are some ideas you have for including her as much as possible in your class, particularly on the days when her aide is not present?

_____

_____

Scenario 2

On the first day of class one of your students hugs you tight and then backs up very slightly and begins to talk quickly while staring you in the eye. He talks for a long time in great detail about his class schedule and does not pause for you to respond in any way. During class you can't help but notice that he is very different from any student you've ever had, both in his body language and in the things he says. It is clear that he is making some people uncomfortable, particularly the young women when he stands very close to them during the interview activity. It occurs to you that your student might have autism, but you have not received notification about it.

What will you do? Will you rethink your class plans and activities?

_____

_____

12 · The Use of Technology

NORMA LÓPEZ-BURTON

THE PLACE OF TECHNOLOGY IN THE CLASSROOM

Technology does not make a great teacher. From the lowly piece of chalk and the venerable printed word, all the way through to the most spectacular, digitally enhanced, online collaborative learning space you can imagine, technology is simply a tool. It can make you look cool; it can make you look the fool. Ultimately, what you do with it is what makes all the difference.

Used properly, technology can be a wonderful tool for language teaching. We've got PowerPoint, document cameras, music CDs, DVDs—digital media of all kinds. And now, of course, we have the Internet—we can find almost anything instantly! The Internet also allows for the use of Skype, e-mail, chat rooms, Twitter, discussion boards, YouTube, blogs . . . What will be next?!

In this chapter I will explore some of the current technologies and the advantages and pitfalls of using technology in the classroom. I will also include practical communicative activities for the language lab. But first . . .

A Word to the Technophile . . .

I know your pupils dilated when you read the first part of this chapter. You probably did a little fist pump of excitement: "Yeesss!" Well, before you blast up too high into cyberspace, come back to earth for a second and ask yourself two important questions: Have I first mastered the art of teaching? And,

Do I want to use technology to truly enhance my delivery, or just to look flashy?

New technological advances are exciting, but the gadgets themselves are not the answer to better teaching. Technologies are only *tools*. You first have to have a strong sense of what teaching is all about. If you aren't already a good teacher, all the technology that black-T-shirted Silicon Valley technocrats can cart into your classroom will only be a waste of computer chips and hard drives.

In the 1950s the tape recorder was the new technology that promised to revolutionize language instruction, and in some ways it did. Many a lab was filled with this exciting apparatus. Not long after the tape recorder came television and videos, and they were great. But unless a teacher knew of the importance of a pre-viewing, a while-viewing, and a post-viewing activity, he or she would not be truly using technology to enhance the acquisition process. Entertainment would certainly be taking place, but not necessarily learning.

Learn well the mechanics of teaching, teaching strategies, and class management, and understand how a student learns a language, before you use new technology! First learn and practice how to do things no-tech—just you and the chalkboard—before going digital, because technology is guaranteed to fail some time, and you will have to carry on without it. What are you going to do when it fails? Cancel class? Start crying?

And then there's the second question: Will technology make you look cool? If it works, of course it will! And when technology fails and you carry on with grace, you are still cool. Now, will it help your delivery? Ask yourself this question, because sometimes no-tech is better. Story-telling (comprehensible input), for example, is more meaningful from the teacher than from an audio file. The student gets the facial expressions, gestures, and interaction that an audio file or video cannot provide. A good general rule is: if it makes no difference, go no-tech; if it enhances your teaching, then by all means, go low- or high-tech.

. . . And a Word to the Technophobe

When you read the title to this chapter, I bet you sighed loudly, maybe went into heart palpitations, or even broke into a cold sweat and thought, "I am SO not doing this. I'm not any good at this computer stuff, plus, I don't have the time to learn how to use all that software. I am a good teacher who employs a variety of instructional strategies without digital help. I can still have strong lessons and achieve my learning objectives without all these bells and whistles. I don't have to learn this . . ."

Yes you do, and for several reasons:

- Using new technology will help you connect with your students. Their lives have been completely submerged in technology, just like fish in the water—they don't even know it's really there. It is an undeniable daily aspect of their lives, and most respond naturally to all things digital.

- New technologies give us the opportunities to present concepts in new, effective, and efficient ways. We are not just teaching our old material in new ways.

- These new technologies are here to stay; you can't ignore them. Can you imagine a teacher back in the 1980s and '90s, ignoring the fact that CDs and DVDs came out? If that teacher stubbornly stuck to cassette tapes and VHS videos, where could she or he play them now?

- You can't be left behind in the advances of your profession, and should keep up and stay informed. It is part of good professional development.

- Your school administration, in the name of efficiency, economics, or even public image, may go all digital.

- You have to be knowledgeable and be able to relate your experience using these tools in a job interview.

- You will be so cool!

But, who will teach you? If your school has a lab, start with the language lab director. If there is no lab, talk to colleagues who use technology and pick their brains; they may be willing to share materials and ideas. Attend language conferences and listen to talks on a particular tool you are interested in trying out. Learn one tool at a time—search the Internet and see how others use it. And remember, when you learn how to deal with a new piece of hardware or language learning program, because of what you just learned, the next technology will be easier to master.

And if all fails, remember too that everything is on the Net!

Now, let's go to the classroom and see what technology can be useful to enhance your teaching. I personally view technology tools as having three levels: no-tech, meaning just you and your gestures or you and your chalkboard; low-tech, meaning anything that needs electricity but does not require an Internet connection; and high-tech, which is anything that requires a laptop or opening an account to access it. Since no-tech is not an issue in this chapter, we'll just jump directly into low-tech.

LOW-TECH

By low-tech I mean CDs, iPods, DVDs, and document cameras hooked up to digital projectors. These used to be considered high-tech but now are just so last millennium. And before CDs we had cassette tapes. Cassettes were nice because they were more portable than film, they would not scratch as would vinyl records, and the rewind feature was a godsend. But now CDs have replaced the cassette tape, and the iPod is slowly replacing the CD. One big reason is cost for the latter: if you want to use just one song from a CD, you have to buy the whole thing ($$), while with an iPod you buy just the one song you need, download it at home, and later connect it to the classroom media panel in the classroom—voilà.

There is no doubt both CDs and iPods can lend a lot of flexibility to the classroom. For example, with both you can introduce songs from your target language and can build whole exercises around the songs. For a complete communicative exercise, provide pre-listening and while-listening exercises as well as a post-listening task, such as a fill-in-the-blank exercise that emphasizes questions on content and culture. And if you like to watch your students squirm, make them do a sing-along. (They'll complain and roll their eyes, but when they see you make everybody sing, they get into it. Try it!)

As audio evolves, so too does video. VHS was the new technology of the 1980s. It replaced film. You remember film—a projector with two large reels, with the teacher having to thread the film through two sprockets, maybe even needing a student (usually the teacher's pet) to help run it. (If all this is before your time, watch some late-night reruns of the TV program *M*A*S*H*. It's funny—on movie nights on the army base, Radar, the hapless orderly, could only get the movie projector to work half the time.) Back to real life: VHS replaced film projectors because encased tapes were easier to use, the machines had a rewind feature, and the only thing needed was a TV and a videocassette player. And now DVDs have replaced VHS tapes. DVDs let you quickly jump to a relevant scene without having to wait to rewind. But most importantly, you can choose the spoken language and the language of the subtitles. This flexibility makes it a great language tool.

CDs, iPods, and DVDs are all great, but a document camera connected to a digital projector is my favorite! It is convenient, it saves paper, and it's a great teaching tool. It's convenient because, instead of parading back and forth with the open book in front of me like I had to do decades ago, I just put the book on the document camera bed and with a pencil point out what I want. The projector makes the image bigger than life and easy to see, and some have a freeze-image feature that will digitize an image of what I am projecting and freeze it. This allows me to walk away from the document camera and roam around the classroom as I speak, which is more my style. So remember, you don't have to be chained to the document camera.

If your school does not have document cameras and projectors because they think they can't afford them, point out that this device saves a surprising amount of money in paper costs. Instructors project images or activities for all to see but don't have to cut down a forest to make everyone a copy. Just think what a hero you'd become if your school adopted document cameras and projectors!

THE USE OF TECHNOLOGY

Document cameras are also great tools for in-class editing. For example, during a group writing exercise, project what students have written, comment on the writing, and improve it right then and there with everybody's involvement. For variety, I sometimes ask one student to come up and display his or her paragraph on the document camera bed, read the story, and have the whole class comment. The student erases and modifies the writing on the spot. The other day I asked my students to interview one of their classmates and draw their family tree. Years ago a follow-up without a document camera would have required the student to go to the chalkboard, draw the family tree with all the names, and burn up a lot of class time. Now I just have the student use the document camera to explain to everyone the family tree that he just created. They are also great for showing small cultural objects that a student or I have brought to class. The object does not need to be passed around, minimizing handling and the possibility of damaging it. Document cameras are my low-tech favorite tool that I use every day.

HIGH-TECH

When I use the term high-tech, I am referring to software applications like PowerPoint and to the Internet, which gives access to YouTube, Skype, chat rooms, discussion boards, e-mail, social networking, Twitter, blogs, and more.

PowerPoint

I use PowerPoint quite a bit—in fact, almost every day. PowerPoint replaced what we used to call "picture files." Ahh . . . the good old days; for years I collected images from magazines and used them to help introduce vocabulary or simply invent a story. Images had to be clear and big enough for all to see at once, and these were not easy to find. It took me years to create a decent stock of images. For a good while I was looking at magazines not for the articles but for the pictures! Once I found an image, I taped it to a piece of cardboard to make it easier to handle in class. To display the image I had to walk around holding it up in front of me, like the women who announce the next round in boxing matches. Students stretched their necks trying to see what I was holding. Then PowerPoint arrived . . . ahhhh . . . heaven. PowerPoint is stable, it is on almost every computer, it's not too hard to learn, and everybody can easily see the image. Once you learn to use PowerPoint, picking up images is easy: just type anything into Google, select "images," and wow yourself. You have a nice string of images for your story. And once you compose a file, you can use it over and over again; it is a good investment of time.

Some advice about PowerPoint:

- Don't put too much text on each slide. An image and a caption is all you need—you say or narrate the rest. If you put in a lot of text, the students get confused between listening to you and reading what is being projected, so they don't do either well.

Too much text.   Image and caption is all you need.

- Use fonts larger than 28 point.

- Don't use busy backgrounds. If the background has too much going on, it competes with the information.

The background here is distracting.   Simple background and large font.

- PowerPoint can be set up to have cute transitions from one slide to the next. Limit the transitions, as they can be very distracting and make it difficult for the students to remain focused on what you are saying.

- Don't insert big memory images into your slide show. The larger the file, the more difficult it is to e-mail it, and the greater the chance of the whole thing crashing. I like to stay around 500 $\times$ 500 pixels. If you have to have a really big image, modify the size before inserting it into PowerPoint. Almost any image manipulation program (Photo-Shop is the biggie) will allow you to manipulate file sizes.

- And most importantly: even though it is pretty reliable, PowerPoint can fail. If not the program, your laptop will poop out. If not the laptop, the projector will act up. There is always something! And because there is always the possibility of something not working, always print all your images as a backup, and when the inevitable happens carry on without much fuss because you know how to do things no-tech too. Your students, being technologically savvy, will understand and accept any equipment malfunction.

YouTube

I have found that you can find just about anything on YouTube. Try it! There is a video for everything: how to make someone fall asleep instantly, how to build a homemade flamethrower, how to make a person stop talking to you . . . You can find a lot of silly things on YouTube, but you can also find very helpful teaching tools. For example, to brainstorm for an activity on a particular tense or vocabulary, just as you would do in Google, type in "songs," "preterit," and "France" into YouTube and see what treasures pop up. Remember, even if you can't find what you are looking for, the Internet machine is great for coming up with new ideas.

What else is on YouTube? Watch short films, music videos, commercials, TV episodes from all over the world, individual scenes from movies, and clips from TV events, like music or film awards. Many YouTube clips are posted by regular folk, and you can do that too. The next time you go on vacation to a country where they speak the language you teach (it seems like teachers are never truly off duty!), consider filming yourself with a digital camera doing anything: cooking and explaining a recipe, ordering at a restaurant, buying something at a store, checking into a hotel, filming your friends and relatives during a meal. Post your videos on YouTube, and with Internet access, they will be there for you to use anytime you want in class.

Or ask your students to film themselves in small groups doing a skit and then post their work on YouTube. Be sure to screen their work first to make sure it is appropriate—you don't want to show raunchy content or something so linguistically poor that it is not comprehensible. Show the best one, or the best three; ask students comprehension questions, and have them vote which is the best.

Music videos are a little tricky to use in class: they include both audio and visual inputs that students have to process. Maybe they can process two inputs, but you can't ask students to process a third by including writing too, like a fill-in-the-blank exercise. There's just too much going on, too many stimuli. The students will overload and stop the writing task because the visuals and audio are too alluring.

The right way to employ music videos (or any video, for that matter) requires you to have a pre-viewing activity that could include new vocabulary or information about the type of music to be seen and heard, the artist, the cultural background, and the content of the lyrics. Show the video a first time, so they enjoy it and get a general understanding of what is going on. Then show it again, but this time minimize the window on your laptop so the video disappears and only the audio remains. Now you can carry out an activity where your students search for specific words or verb tenses while they listen. Students will concentrate on what they are hearing and will not be distracted by the visual component. End the activity with a post-viewing or follow-up exercise.

A few dos and don'ts:

- Don't show any clip you yourself have not first seen, just because a colleague recommended it.

- Don't show an entire movie. Instead choose a scene or part of a scene that is one to five minutes long and is culturally or linguistically relevant to your secret agenda. If the clip is short, it can be repeated to assure comprehension without wasting too much class time.

- Do have a pre-viewing, a while-viewing, and a post-viewing activity.

- Don't show scenes with nudity even at the college level. (I am sure your students have seen countless R-rated movies by the time they get to college, just not with you. It is like uncomfortably watching a sex scene with your parents, and in this case, you are the parent.)

- Do have a pedagogical purpose every time you show a video.

- Don't show something just for entertainment; your students can do that at home.

- Do show something new, engaging, and interesting; you don't want the students to catch up with sleep by napping during the clip.

Communication Tools

And then there is e-mail, Skype, chat, blogs, Twitter, discussion boards, and more. With these tools we foster communication and collaboration. Often, to manage them better, they are integrated into a single system called a Learning Management System (LMS), such as Moodle (open source, i.e., no cost), Blackboard ($$), and others. These systems allow the teacher to consolidate assignments, monitor student interactions in discussion forums, make announcements, and download files. LMSs have calendars, rosters, student e-mail lists, and capabilities for online quizzes and exams. LMSs are especially useful if your school does not already have a course management system in place, or if you have a job in more than one school, because it allows you to access all your teaching materials wherever there is Internet access.

Let's look at each of these communication and collaboration tools individually.

E-mail

E-mail is ubiquitous—it seems everybody and their cat have e-mail accounts. Why not take advantage of e-mail's reach to connect with a professor in France, Spain, or Japan, and have your students dive into an authentic cultural exchange? It is best not to leave the assignment as an open conversation; rather, you should have guided questions adjusted to the linguistic level and vocabulary limitations of the students. Decide on the number of exchanges, provide deadlines, and have the students turn their work in. This is culturally enriching and fun for the students.

Skype

Skype lets you use the Internet to talk to others while you see them on your computer screen in real time, just like in the 1960s cartoon *The Jetsons*. To use Skype, first open an account, download and install its software, and make sure there are webcams installed on the computers that will connect to each other. Then you can Skype one of your friends in the target country and have the class come prepared to interview him or her. I have connected with friends in Spain through Skype (a little difficult with the time difference, but possible), and had the class ask questions about their house, since that was the vocabulary we were studying. My Spanish friends actually took the camera around (it was embedded in their laptop) and gave us a tour of their house. My students were jazzed. Here we were in our windowless classroom, talking to live people 6,000 miles away, and they were speaking in Spanish, showing us their house, their bathroom, their bedroom . . . It was the real thing, not a grainy picture in some stale textbook. Wow! How great is that?! I've done the same thing for vocabulary about food and clothing—the possibilities are endless.

If difficult time differences don't allow for easy connections, you can set up a call with a native speaker of your language who lives in the United States. That person can show your students their pantry and what foods from the old country they still like to eat. They may have pictures of their families hanging on the walls or might want to describe favorite places they liked back home. Make sure to guide the questions so your contact uses the vocabulary you want the students to hear and use.

Twitter

Get your students involved by having them follow a famous native speaker of your target language. I once had a lethargic athlete who was taking my class as a requirement, and nothing I did in class could reach him. He was a college baseball player destined for the majors, and so for my Twitter assignment, he followed a baseball player named Albert Pujols. I don't know much about baseball, and I certainly didn't know who Pujols was, but the important thing is that this guy tweeted in Spanish, and by following him, my student's interest in Spanish shot way up. He told me excitedly, "I wonder what he is saying?" He started looking up words in the dictionary to find out. I assure you he would not have done that to find out about Salvador Dalí!

For the above assignment it is important to provide a list of celebrities that tweet in your target language, so do your homework first. Also provide students with a worksheet that they will have to turn in, and set a deadline.

Chat rooms

Chat rooms are real-time media. Once a time to meet online is set up, everybody links up and starts typing away. I don't use this tool in my regular classes, but I do use it a lot when I take students to the language lab. (See the lab activities below.) Outside class, I have used this tool to hold extra office hours (yes, more work for us!), or to provide an extra review session before an exam or a final exam. I tell them I will be in the chat room at a specific day and time for anyone who has a question about the exam.

Discussion boards

Discussion boards—also called forums (or for you Latin snobs, *fora*)—are asynchronous, that is, one student posts a comment and the other students chime in at a later time. Students aren't allowed to simply post opinions willy-nilly; they usually have to first respond to a question you post and then write something in response to other students' postings, creating a new way of discussing a topic. Discussion boards are especially useful for shy or weak students who feel intimidated about speaking up in class. Because they now have the time to think, and then write, they can engage with a classmate at their own pace from the comfort of home.

Remember, technology is adaptable to any linguistic level—just insert easier or more difficult requirements as needed. In an advanced class the teacher could post a question for discussion based on a reading, a film, or a cultural point presented in class. The teacher can monitor their involvement without necessarily grading everything. The important thing is to get the students to communicate in the target language using a different medium. It adds variety and brings home the message that this new language is not just for use during classroom hours.

A QUICK REVIEW: ADVANTAGES AND
DISADVANTAGES OF USING TECHNOLOGY

The Good: We connect with our young students' digital world; we add variety; we can connect with live culture better than any textbook can; it is current; it adds authenticity; language is for communication, and these tools emphasize the skills of communication; it is engaging; it motivates, it is fun, and it is cool.

The Bad: There is a learning curve with all these technologies, and we teachers have to invest time to learn. This can be intimidating for the technophobe; technology creates a little more work for the teacher in the beginning because we have to brainstorm for ideas to better take advantage of technology's benefits; we also have to do something with the work generated by the students using these media; however, once an activity is fully developed, it can be used over and over again without ever wearing out.

The Potentially Ugly: Technology will fail, and we will be left high and dry with an awkward smile in front of twenty-five students, waiting in anticipation: "Is something supposed to happen?" But, no worries—you will have Plan B ready. Make this a habit. If the virtual world does not want to cooperate that day, it's no problem. Just like the quarterback who stands up after a thunderous tackle and thumps his chest, bellowing "I'm good," you and your chalk must carry on with grace: "I am good!"

So, other than language labs, which I talk about next, this concludes my (very personal and opinionated, but obviously correct) review of the use of technology to teach language.

LANGUAGE LAB ACTIVITIES

Here are some general guidelines for lab activities:

- Give students worksheets to fill out. This will keep the student focused on the task rather than just surfing the Net.

- Limit the time. Especially with the Internet, students face a lot of temptation to click away to powerful distractions. Give your students a challenging time limit so they get busy and don't go off course.

- Collect work. To make sure they put in some effort, tell your students from the beginning that they will have to turn in their work. Collecting their work may mean a little more work for you, but you don't have to spend a lot of time grading it. If the work does not have any weight in the grade, then create the illusion that you have looked at it; just circle, check, and underline a few interesting things here and there.

- Where possible, adapt lab activities to different linguistic levels. For example, to challenge advanced students, a simple activity could be spiced up to require more detailed and specific work.

- Make sure all Internet sites you are counting on to use are up and working.

- In lab work, be sure to have a pre-lab activity so students are busy while you set up the main computer and take care of the pairing or grouping.

- Have a Plan B ready. Technology is wonderful, but when it fails, it can hang you out to dry. You must have a no-tech alternative for every activity.

Sample Lab Exercise 1

Famous Person

Secret agenda: To practice physical descriptions and formulate questions.

Materials:
1. Twenty-five printed cards you give your students, each with a name of a historical or important character culturally relevant for the language you teach. (The cards do not have to all be different: think of just seven or eight names and repeat them to fit the class enrollment.)

2. Images of the characters for projection in the lab.
3. A worksheet with directions for the student. *[See Appendix B, Worksheet 12.1.]*

Procedure:

1. While students surf for images and write descriptions of their celebrity, you set up the pairs or groups.
2. Once the students are done writing their descriptions, instruct them to share them using their headphones. Students try to guess who each other's character is.

Follow-up: Ask a student to read his or her description out loud and project any image. Ask the students if the description matches the image. Why does it or doesn't it?

No-tech alternative: If the Internet is down, be ready with printed copies of the characters to give to the students. They still can write their descriptions and then share the information. If the headphones don't work either, have students sit back-to-back and read their descriptions to each other.

Sample Lab Exercise 2

More Information on the Famous

Secret agenda: To practice physical descriptions, preferences, and question words.

Materials: A worksheet to fill in information and instructions for the search. *[See Appendix B, Worksheet 12.2.]*

Procedure:

1. While you arrange lab computer groupings or pairings, ask the students to think of their favorite artist, politician, or

celebrity, and to write down three important characteristics of that person on the worksheet.

2. Model the activity: "Where is s(he) from? Where was s(he) born?" Then ask them to chat with their partner or group to guess who the character is.

3. Once they have guessed each other's characters, students must pick one and search the Internet (in the target language) for more information. Still connected by headphones, they can transmit their findings to each other and fill in more information on the worksheet.

4. Using the chat room, both students cooperate to create a paragraph with their findings.

Follow-up: Have two or three pairs of students read their descriptions out loud for the class to guess.

No-tech alternative: If the lab hardware isn't working, place students sitting back-to-back and have them share their information. For step three, if the Internet is down, ask the class how many of them have smartphones. If only half the class does, then pair the ones who don't have phones with those who do. If there are not enough smartphones, ask the students to pair up and use paper and pencil to compose a description just using the information they have.

Sample Lab Exercise 3

What Is the Weather Like?

Secret agenda: To practice weather expressions and expressions in the future.

Materials: A worksheet for Student A and Student B. *[See Appendix B, Worksheet 12.3.]*

Procedure:
1. As a pre-activity, ask students to individually write down what they will be doing the next weekend. This helps students review the future construction and allows time for you to arrange student lab pairings.
2. For the first activity, direct students to use their headphones to ask each other the information they each need to complete their worksheets.
3. The next activity requires that each student search for weather information of a specific country. This will be shared via headphones so that they can answer their worksheet questions.
4. As a writing activity, ask the students to use the chat room to compose a paragraph detailing their plans for a visit to one of their target countries, the activities they are planning, and how the weather could impact their trip.

Follow-up: Ask a pair of students to read their paragraph out loud without mentioning the country, and have students guess which country the pair is describing.

No-tech alternative: If the network is down, you must come to class with already-printed weather reports from several countries and distribute them. If headphones don't work, pair the students with their backs to each other as they share information and complete their worksheets. If you can't use the chat room, pencil and paper will have to do. Remember, no-tech is your savior.

Sample Lab Exercise 4

World of Foods

Secret agenda: To practice food vocabulary.

Materials: Worksheet with instructions. *[See Appendix B, Worksheet 12.4.]*

Procedure:
1. While you arrange the lab pairings, have students carry out an Internet search with the links you provide and complete the missing information on the worksheet.
2. Students communicate with headphones and tell each other about their recipes. Each student must take his/her own notes to complete the worksheet.

Follow-up: Ask the class about what was found: "Which was an interesting recipe? A healthy one? Which had an obscure ingredient?"

No-tech alternative: Come to class with many recipes already printed and distribute them.

Sample Lab Exercise 5

Let's Go Shopping

Secret agenda: To practice indirect object pronouns.

Materials: Worksheet with instructions. *[See Appendix B, Worksheet 12.5.]* You will also need some extra information. Find out before class whose birthday is coming up soon, or who was absent because of illness, and provide an e-mail about that, also before class.

Procedure:
1. While you arrange the lab pairings, students search the Internet for three things they would like to buy if they had the money.
2. With a partner, each student is to say what he/she is going to buy and why. Each takes notes.
3. Students negotiate what they will give the people listed in the worksheet.
4. Think of a gift for the student whose birthday is coming up soon or the student who was recently absent.
5. Following the example in the worksheet, students are to send an e-mail through an electronic card company (link given) to the birthday or sick student, copying you on their message.

Follow-up: Ask what the students are giving you, and why. Be amazed, be horrified, or be grateful.

No-tech alternative: Bring printed copies of several pages from the website of the store you would have sent your students to. Because you don't want to waste paper, instead of pairs, put them in groups of four or five. That way you have to print only four or five "catalogues" of store items.

Trust me on this one. The bottom line is, learn good teaching skills first because all the best equipment in the world will not make a difference if you are not a good teacher. Don't use technology for technology's sake, but only if it will enhance your lesson and your delivery.

As with anything new, there is a learning curve that could prove to be a little frustrating at the beginning, but plow through and persevere because once that is surpassed, the results and the improvement in your classes will make you a hero.

Summary Questions

1. Are you a technophile or a technophobe? Which of the technologies mentioned in this chapter do you think you might use in the classroom?

_____

_____

2. What should we make sure is in place before we decide to use technology?

_____

_____

3. List three problems and three benefits of using technology.

_____

_____

Scenarios

Scenario 1

A teacher finds a great music video on YouTube. She is dealing with the past tense, and this video is loaded with it. Not only that, the song is a current pop hit, the artists are very popular, and the video itself is pretty cool, with a lot of special effects and animation. Nice! She has a pre-viewing quiz to review some troublesome verbs, and also includes some questions to prepare them for understanding certain expressions in the video. Next she hands out a sheet with the lyrics and thirty blanks for the students to fill out the verbs in the past tense while watching. She dims the lights and they all watch. During the follow-up she notices that very few students have filled in the blanks. Thinking that the song was too fast or that they needed more light, she plays it again, but the same thing happens. She decides to tell the students the missing verbs herself. She shows the video yet one more time and asks them to sing along. Very few do. What is going on? Don't they like the activity?

1. Why aren't the students writing?

_____

_____

2. What would you have done differently?

_____

_____

Scenario 2

A teacher is introducing weather and activities vocabulary. He finds great images on the Internet depicting different weather patterns and people doing different activities, like barbecuing, walking, jogging, sunning themselves, children jumping rope, etc. He is all set to go, but because his laptop has been acting up lately, he implements Plan B by putting the presentation on a memory stick. So if his laptop acts up, he will ask one of the students to lend him theirs, use the memory stick, and that's it.

As he had feared, his laptop misbehaves, so he goes to Plan B. A student lends him a computer. The laptop works fine, but the PowerPoint doesn't come up on the screen. The computer isn't the problem, it's the projector! With no Plan C, he is most embarrassed, and desperately starts drawing on the chalkboard some of the things he had in the PowerPoint presentation. He draws as fast as he can, apologizing every thirty seconds, but the whole Picasso-thing takes some time. When he is done drawing, he proceeds with his story, pointing at the drawings. Because he was drawing in haste, the drawings are not very good, and the students are frowning and squinting, trying to guess what each scribble is. Since the drawings don't work, he carries out the whole input with gestures. That actually makes it funny and, at the end, he is able to engage the students.

1. What contingency plans does he have in case PowerPoint doesn't work?

_____

_____

2. Why do his backups fail, and what backups would the reader suggest?

_____

_____

13 · Assessment

NORMA LÓPEZ-BURTON

I can't say I ever liked taking tests in school. Not because I didn't know the material—I was a bookworm after all—but because I was afraid the test would not adequately measure what I studied. Sometimes the test would be too long, and in a hurry to finish, I'd make silly and costly mistakes, fall for the unfair trick question, or be surprised by some question I didn't know was going to be included. Argh! If any of those things happened, I knew I would be unfairly classified as a B, C, or D student, which brought unpleasant consequences from all sides.

Because I remember those days, and because I am a proponent of the golden rule, I hate inflicting pain on my students when I give them exams. The problem is that I am required to do it. Assessment is part of our educational system, and there is no way around it. Through the years I have learned how to minimize students' stress of taking tests by following some principles that I pass on to you now. In this chapter we will explore the types of tests that assess the four skills: listening, speaking, reading, and writing. I will also show you how to assess students' progress in class, how to craft a valid exam, and how to score it as fairly as possible.

FORMATIVE ASSESSMENT

There are two kinds of assessments that are commonly used in language classrooms: summative and formative. Summative assessment comes in the

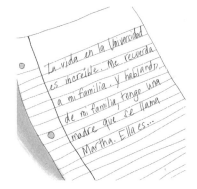

form of midterms and final exams. It measures what the student has learned after a certain section, chapter, or level. Formative assessment is daily and ongoing. With formative assessment, the teacher constantly checks students' comprehension so the instructor can repeat, clarify, paraphrase, or improve an explanation or input. Great teachers are very aware of their audience and constantly check to see if their students are getting the message or developing misconceptions.

How do we go about assessing every day? Most of us do it without even realizing it. We assess when the students answer our questions; we assess during the warm-up if it includes a mini-review; we assess during the input phase with comprehension checks (see Chapter 2); we assess during guided practice and follow-up as we roam around in the classroom; and we assess during communicative activities when we monitor students' performance. The follow-up to communicative activities also tells us volumes: whether a well-planned activity is not working, or students simply are not getting it, or they are not yet ready to deal with difficult material.

At the end of each class, most of us usually ask, "Any questions?" Most students don't want to open a new can of worms when everybody is packing their books to leave, so they don't answer, which mistakenly confirms our impression that our students have understood everything. A better alternative is to first summarize what they have learned so far, and then ask a specific question, such as, "How do we express the future?" or, "Tell me two ways to form a question." With a specific question and its revealing answer, we see if our students got the lesson for that day.

Here is a twist to the end-of-class question: A few years ago a teacher friend of mine introduced me to "exit quizzes." Before her students leave the classroom, each one has to respond, translate, or produce a sentence based on the day's lesson. Her students had come to expect this and because of it, their attention spiked. They no longer just cruised along, spaced out, or planned to cram before the test. They had to pay attention because they knew they had to take the exit quiz. If they answered incorrectly, the teacher was going to get on their case the following day, and the students knew they were going be called on more. For us teachers, yes, it is more work, but not that much. You only have to read twenty-five sentences which, once you get the hang of it, can be done very quickly. Just stand in front of the recycling bin, read the strips of paper, and discard the ones with correctly written sentences. Keep the ones that contain errors. Now you know who is not understanding what you are teaching and can make adjustments accordingly, such as calling on the person more and watching his or her reaction more closely when you speak.

I have recently modified this "exit quiz" device for a freshman seminar on cultural differences. This is not a language class, but I have since applied the same idea for my language classes. One of my goals in the seminar, besides achieving the general objective of having students reflect on cultural differences, was to have the students learn the locations of many world countries, their capitals, and the names of their national leaders. I noticed that if I gave the students all this information and tested their retention with a traditional paper quiz, they would sigh, groan, and sometimes be upset if they didn't do well; the happiness meter showed no movement. So I decided to go against the grain and see how my students performed if the quizzes did not count for their grade, but just for their own edification (what a revolutionary concept!). I started every class with an "entrance quiz." For example, I would give them a schematic map of Europe, and in groups of three, my students had to name and locate as many countries as possible. Out of over twenty countries, they would invariably only get three or four correct (sad, but true!). After giving them the answers, I would give them a minute or two to memorize everything (between twenty and twenty-five countries), and then continue on with my regular class.

At the end of class would come the exit quiz. Since there is no grade incentive, I've had to replace it with another incentive or consequence. A positive consequence: The group with the highest score gets a standing ovation, and/or wins a mystery prize (I give them some chocolates or cute pencils). A somewhat negative consequence: The group with the lowest score has to erase the board, straighten out all the chairs, or my favorite, go outside (with the class watching) and in a crowd of students shout in unison "I LOVE THIS CLASS!!" and quickly run inside. I have used both, but I prefer the negative because all but three students win and there is a more general sense of accomplishment, which generates a lot of smiles and high fives. They also have the pleasure of seeing three of their classmates do something silly. Even shy students will be good sports and do the penalty if all three have to do it together. Very important: always vary the groups to avoid the same three students winning or losing! The penalty I choose is innocuous, really, but you would think it was "Off with their heads!" because they really work hard to avoid being last. Exit quizzes work so well that during class I sometimes see students glancing every once in a while at their notes, memorizing the map. In what grade-incentive-driven class could you see that eagerness to memorize anything?! The distaste of a test has been replaced by the possibility of winning!

The first time I did this, I feared the students were storing this information in their short-term memory and that they were going to forget it, just as they do with regular tests. Therefore I reminded them every once in a while that we were going to have "the mother of all exit quizzes" the last day of class. So, the last day of class we had a potluck and a Jeopardy game with all the categories covered during the term. I divided the class in groups of three, and the penalty for the losing group was to clean the potluck table. I was so pleasantly surprised that they had not forgotten the information and that they were excitedly and fervently competing as if $50,000 were at stake! I did this as an experiment and have kept doing it because it has always worked, as confirmed by positive student evaluations, the obvious positive results of the exit quizzes, and all the smiles and fun I see around me.

For my language classes I have found that it works well to do exit quizzes occasionally—particularly on Fridays, because it gives students that "end of the week" feeling of accomplishment. It works really well for vocabulary (foods, parts of the body, professions, parts of the house, etc.). Your students will find the quizzes fun, will learn the vocabulary, and will remain engaged. But, most importantly, it is a great formative assessment tool.

SUMMATIVE ASSESSMENT

This formal type of assessment summarizes what the students have learned, using exams, midterms, and final exams. We cannot tell you what your exams should include or what format they should have, since it all depends on the particulars of your language and your approach to teaching. Your test should reflect *what* and *how* you teach. If you favor emphasizing grammar over a more communicative approach in the classroom, your test should reflect that by having mostly closed exercises such as fill in the blank, true or false, multiple choice, or matching columns. If your teaching approach is more communicative, your tests should reflect that by providing opportunities for the students to create with the language by answering more open-ended questions such as "describe this drawing," "write a letter to . . . ," or "answer these interview questions." If your course is more of a hybrid in which you make room for grammar but also have plenty of communicative activities, your exam should also be a hybrid and test grammar as well as communicative skills. If your daily classes place importance on culture, that should also be included on the test. Remember, according to students' logic, "If it's not on the test, it's not important, so I can tune out during cultural instruction."

Exam grading also needs to reflect the importance you place on each skill in the classroom. If your emphasis is on oral or written communication, don't count every single grammar mistake on an exam; the grading should be more holistic, focusing more on what the students are trying to communicate. If you spend a lot of time in class making sure the students are spelling correctly and are learning where all the accents go, then that is where your exams' emphasis should be. Whatever your approach or type of exam you give, don't forget to inform students of the class objectives, the type of assessment they will encounter, and what will be emphasized in class.

For language exams, teachers usually test reading ability, oral comprehension, writing skills, grammar, and cultural knowledge. Each section has its own special considerations and pitfalls that we will cover in the remainder of this chapter.

TESTING READING

You will have to find a short but interesting text to test reading. The first time around, finding the right text can be time-consuming. But don't worry, after a few years you will develop a collection of appropriate and interesting texts you can choose from to use. With any text you choose, make sure it is not too complicated, that it relates to the topic you have been teaching, and that it is interesting. One of the secondary effects of really being into teaching language is that you are constantly on the lookout for good articles, stories, and essays that might be used either in class or on an exam. If that is the way you are, you will already have a pile of possIbIlItIes waItIng for you when it is time to create an exam.

Real Over Fake

When choosing a text for an exam, it is best to try to find something that mimics real life, as opposed to teacher-invented stories. Try to find texts that your students would normally read in real life, such as restaurant menus, want ads, advice columns, recipes from a book, blogs, tweets, e-mails, personal profiles in magazines, horoscopes, obituaries, or weather reports. All those items have a more real feel than reading about a fictional Alice Smith and her summer trip with her parents. Seriously, who is Alice Smith and why should I care?

Consider the text in Sample Test 1:

Sample Test 1

Reading comprehension: Josephine is in Colombia! Read the following paragraph and answer the questions in complete sentences.

My name is Josephine Ramírez. I am 22 years old and I am from Cali, Colombia. I live in Cali, but I was born in Chicago. My father is from Chicago, and my mother is from Cali. I was born in February, and that is why I like winter so much.

On weekends I go out with my friends and ride bikes, play tennis, or swim. At night I like to dance salsa in some discos in Cali. I don't have a boyfriend right now, but I like a guy named Mike in my math class. He has brown eyes and curly hair. He is very handsome!

1. How old is Josephine?
2. Where was she born?
3. Is she single or married?
4. Describe Mike.

This is obviously busywork, and since it doesn't inform us of anything out of the ordinary, it is meaningless and boring. There is no context either, except for "Josephine is in Colombia." (Who is this Josephine, anyway?)

The questions that follow the text are very explicit. There is no need to think! Question #1: <u>How old is Josephine?</u> Text: <u>I am 22 years old</u>. No other mention of any other number anywhere, so that has to be the answer by default. Question #2 is also explicit: <u>Where was she born?</u> Text: <u>I was born in Chicago</u>. Question #3 is a little better; the student has to understand the word "boyfriend" and consider the words "right now" in order to answer correctly. Question #4 can be answered by a five-year-old.

A better text would contain information about the life of a real person from the target culture, like a politician, an artist, a TV personality, an athlete, an actor, a singer, or an inspiring true story of an ordinary person. Contrast the text of Sample Test 2 with the text in Sample Test 1. Consider the content and the questions. Is the content edifying? Is it something a native speaker of the target language would look up? Are the questions implicit or explicit?

Sample Test 2

Reading comprehension: Who was José Martí? Read this article, adapted from Wikipedia, about this famous person and answer the questions below in your own words.

> José Martí (1853–1895): Martí is considered one of the great turn-of-the-century Latin American intellectuals. In his short life he was a poet, an essayist, a journalist, a revolutionary philosopher, a translator, a professor, a publisher, and a politician. Through his writings and political activity, he became a symbol for Cuba's bid for independence against Spain in the 19th century. From adolescence, he dedicated his life to the promotion of liberty, political independence for Cuba, and intellectual independence for all Spanish Americans.
>
> Born in Havana, he would travel extensively in Spain, Latin America, and the United States, raising awareness and support for the cause of Cuban independence. His unification of the Cuban émigré community, particularly in Florida, was crucial to the success

of the Cuban War of Independence against Spain. He was a key figure in the planning and execution of this war, as well as the designer of the Cuban Revolutionary Party and its ideology. He died in military action on May 19, 1895.

1. What types of writing did José Martí do?
2. What did he want Spain to do for Cuba?
3. Where was he trying to gather support for the cause?
4. Who did he seek in the United States to support his cause?
5. How did he die?

The text in Sample Test 2 is about a real person who can be searched on the Web. The information has some significance. The questions are not explicit. To answer question #1, the students have to state their response in their own words, because it is not explicitly stated (it only says that he was a poet, journalist, translator, professor, etc.) The student then has to write: Martí wrote poems, wrote articles for the newspaper, etc. The rest of the questions are also implicit.

Authentic Over Teacher-Generated

We must avoid texts that are generated by teachers or that include information that is common knowledge. If you are the one who writes the text, the student will only be capable of functioning or surviving in a classroom environment, not the real world.

Authentic texts are so much better. By "authentic text" I mean one that was originally published for a native speaker audience. They are more relevant for your students and make for a better test of real-life understanding. Some educators believe authentic texts are too complex, but students don't have to understand every single word of the reading; the important detail is being precise in *what* you ask. Your students must be able to understand the questions and be able to find answers embedded in all other information they might not understand. If the text includes sentences A, B, C, and D, and sentences C and D have structures or vocabulary beyond the students' level, then only ask questions based on sentences A and B. Either do that, or gloss some words in sentences C and D. Contrast the exams in Sample Tests 3 and 4.

Sample Test 3

Reading comprehension: Read the following paragraph and decide if the sentences are true or false.

The Life of a Plant

A plant has several stages of life: it sprouts, it grows, it reproduces, and it dies. Many plants produce flowers and fruits such as cherries, lemons, and tomatoes. Plants require water and food in order to grow. Sometimes plants need extra nutrients to grow, so a person has to prepare the land with the appropriate fertilizer. From some plants we eat the seed, plants like corn and peanuts; from others we eat the fruit, think of apples and oranges. From lettuce we eat the leaves, and from celery we eat the stem. In some cases we eat the root, as in the case of potatoes and carrots.

True or False

1. A person could help a plant grow by adding fertilizer.
2. We eat the seeds in apples and oranges.
3. Plants only need water to grow.
4. When we eat lettuce, we are eating the root.
5. When we eat celery, we are eating its seed.

The text is overly simplistic, and the questions are testing our knowledge of elementary biology, perhaps not the most interesting of topics. If these exam questions were in any Romance language (remember, I speak Spanish), their inability to challenge me means I probably could figure out the answers having only a rudimentary knowledge of the language. Also, because the true/false format limits my choices, it probably would increase the chances that I would score well without really knowing the answers.

The following are examples of authentic texts (they were originally in Spanish and have been translated for the purpose of this book):

Sample Test 4

Reading comprehension: Read the following want ads and match the person to the best job.

LOOKING FOR MONEY? Bilingual salesmen. Growing company in the beauty industry. Must own car. May work in your own area. Call 1-862-555-2558.

CHAUFFEUR needed to drive truck with "A" license. Must be very familiar with Los Angeles. Good salary, great benefits. Apply in person. 1318 First Street, San Fernando, CA 91340.

COOK needed to work in Hawaii. For more information call (862) 555-0006.

WAITER/WAITRESS Up to $600 a week. No experience or English necessary. Call after 8 a,m. Club Galaxie. 902 Olive and 9th. (555) 489-2944 or 489-2945.

Help the following people look for jobs:

1. Nina needs money. She does not have a driver's license, does not speak English, and would rather work in her area. What job would be best for her?
2. Kim is bilingual and has a car. She wants to work near her house. What job would be best for her?
3. Ben needs money. He lives in California, but wants to try his luck in another state. He likes to cook and is pretty good at it. What job would be best for him?

The above text was taken directly from newspaper want ads. It is something a native speaker of the language would read. It is a text that our students would encounter if living in the target culture. The questions are implicit, and in order to match job seeker to job, they require the test taker to evaluate each job seeker's abilities and desires.

TESTING ORAL COMPREHENSION

One of the four skills to be tested is oral comprehension. To test this, think of something that you would normally hear in real life: a weather report on TV, or an advertisement on the radio, a message on an answering machine, boarding calls, flight or train announcements, a funny story, a phone conversation, a phone survey, a waiter describing the special of the day, phone-tree recordings, etc. Look at the examples in Sample Tests 5 and 6, and for each determine whether: (1) the example is something you would normally hear in real life, (2) the content makes sense, even though created by the teacher, and (3) the questions are too explicit.

Sample Test 5

Oral comprehension: Listen to a waiter in a fine restaurant and decide whether the sentences below are true or false. If they are false, provide the true answer.

> Hi, my name is Ryan, and I will be your server tonight. Could I start you with something to drink? Just to let you know, we have three specials tonight: The first is grilled salmon with a wonderful apple chutney sauce, resting on a bed of rice pilaf. We also have a filet mignon cooked over an open fire with peppercorn sauce, and it comes with a choice of creamy garlic potatoes or wild mushrooms. For our third special, we are pleased to introduce a new creation by our chef: an Italian-inspired lasagna featuring spinach, morel mushrooms, and a blend of three cheeses. I will give you a few minutes and return with your drinks.

True or False

1. The waiter brought drinks to the table.
2. The first special includes dessert.
3. The second special has a choice of side dishes.
4. None of the specials are for vegetarians.
5. If you are lactose-intolerant, you can only eat the third special.

Sample Test 6

Oral comprehension: Listen to the letter that Elvira's grandfather has written to his granddaughter with advice to have good health and live many years, then answer the questions.

> Dear Elvira,
>
> Yesterday I turned 90 years old, and your grandmother invited all of my friends over. I thought about you and I am writing this letter to tell you my secrets to stay healthy.

First: I get up at six o'clock every morning. I usually drink a cup of coffee with milk (with a little bit of sugar) and two pieces of toast.

Second: I eat fruit every day because your grandmother goes to the market every day and buys pineapple, strawberries, and apples. But I like oranges better.

Third: I drink a glass of wine with my dinner because it is good for the heart.

Fourth: I have not smoked for many years, and I exercise every Monday, Wednesday, and Friday.

And lastly: I drink eight glasses of water every day.

Hugs and kisses,

Your grandfather, Fernando

1. At what time does the grandfather get up?
2. What does he eat every morning?
3. Does he drink alcohol? Why?
4. What does he think about smoking?
5. Does he drink a lot of water? Explain.

Let's examine Sample Test 5. A waiter telling the specials of the day is something you would normally hear in the real world. The content makes sense; we all have heard waiters say things like that. The questions are implicit. Question #1 is about the drinks. The text never mentions that the waiter brought the drinks to the table, but it does mention the word "drink" twice. That is a fair distracter, and it is not too confusing. Question #2 is about recognizing dessert vocabulary. The text mentions apple chutney, but only as part of the main dish. The word dessert is not in the text, and there is no separate description of a dessert. "Apple chutney" is a fair distracter. Question #3 is the only easy question, and it is straight from the text. I believe in having at least one very easy question per section. In questions #4 and #5, the student has to recognize food vocabulary in order to determine what has no meat or recognize what is not a dairy product. They are not explicit questions because they require some critical thinking.

In Sample Test 6, the text is something we would normally write, not hear; remember, this is an oral exam, not written. The content is forced. It looks like the teacher who prepared this part wanted to test daily routine and just listed a few activities. It does not have a feeling of reality to it, and I don't think a grandfather would write something like that. All the questions are explicit, as all the answers are clearly spelled out in the text. The student does not have to deduce anything.

GRADING ORAL AND READING COMPREHENSION

When questions are explicit, students tend to write answers verbatim. They write down exactly what they hear or lift it directly from the written text. But when questions are implicit, the students have to think a little more, and there is more room for error because the students have to write the answers in their own words. Therefore, when grading reading and oral comprehension, we have to keep in mind *what* we are testing: we are testing the students' ability to understand what is being said or what is written and . . . *nothing else*. To also test grammar or linguistic accuracy would be too demanding. Because the students have to prove they understood what they read or heard in writing, marking corrections becomes tempting for us teachers. Our hands automatically grab that red pen and mark away, pointing out every imperfection with teacherly duty. Remember that in a communicative environment, as long as the sentence communicates, and as long as the learner proves she or he has understood the oral or written text, we have to let it go and not mark down for anything else. So, when you see that misspelled word, just repeat, "I am one with the universe, I am one with the universe, I am one . . ."

TESTING AND GRADING WRITING

If you follow a communicative approach, your exams will most likely include an open-ended question for students to develop into a short essay. Here are some practical dos and don'ts for creating short essay questions.

Don't provide just one question and hope that the student will write enough for you to evaluate. With the time pressure of finishing a test, one question without any guiding subquestions will produce mixed results, and the exam will be difficult to grade fairly. For example, "Where did you go last summer?" is such a broad question that it is hard to tackle within just a few minutes, and results will be hard to evaluate. It is best to include some subtopic questions. See Sample Test 7.

Sample Test 7

Composition: You just came back from a summer trip and want to e-mail a good friend about it. Write an e-mail addressing each topic fully:

- Greeting
- Say where you went
- Tell your friend who was with you
- Tell him or her how long you were there
- List a few activities you enjoyed
- List a few things you did not like
- Tell your friend whether or not you recommend the place for him or her
- Closing

Don't specify a number of words or paragraphs to answer the question— students will waste exam time counting. It will also make for an awkward piece, because if the student is short in the count, he or she will have to add more text (usually uninteresting and written only to meet the limit). As the example above illustrates, just direct the students to answer the topic fully. When grading, you can mark down if the student did not address the subsection or did so very weakly. The direction "address each topic fully" is relative, but it clearly suggests more than one sentence. This somewhat normalizes the information required of students and helps them write something coherent in a short amount of time.

Do make sure the students have the linguistic tools to answer each subquestion. If the exam is for a beginner level, make sure your questions don't require the use of complex structures.

Do make sure students have the vocabulary necessary to develop the essay. If you think they may need a few words they may not know, provide them at the beginning. Consider the following example:

Sample Test 8

Composición: *Mira los dibujos y describe qué pasa. Asegúrate de desarrollar cada punto completamente.* (Look at the drawings and describe what is going on. Address each subtopic fully.) *Vocabulario útil* (Useful vocabulary):

una cita (a date)
un malentendido (a misunderstanding)
Él la quiere. (He loves her.) *Ella lo quiere.* (She loves him.)

- *Describe al hombre. ¿Cómo es físicamente? ¿Qué lleva?* (Describe the man physically. What is he wearing?)
- *¿Qué piensa?* (What is he thinking?)
- *Describe a la mujer. ¿Cómo es físicamente? ¿Qué lleva?* (Describe the woman physically. What is she wearing?)
- *¿Qué piensa?* (What is she thinking?)
- *¿Qué va a pasar después?* (What is going to happen next?)
- *¿Qué va a pasar con su relación en el futuro?* (What will their relationship be like in the future?)

If your approach is communicative, don't count every single grammar error when grading this part of the test. If you do, it shows the student that grammar—and not communication—is important to you. In this section of the test, we want the student to use the language creatively to describe a drawing, to write a letter, or to write a dialogue. The method that works best for me is holistic, where I circle all mistakes (feedback for the students), and put brackets around what does not truly communicate. What is enclosed in brackets is more important than what I circle. Depending on the length of the composition, I may count five or six circles (grammar mistakes) as minus one point. Each bracket, depending on the length of the sentence, would be a range of minus two to minus four points.

There is no one correct way of grading. It depends on the language you teach, because you'll have different details to test. In French the students have to prove they know how to spell each word since many sound the same. For example, the word *parler* sounds the same as *parlais, parlait, parlient, parlai,* and *parlé,* but all are different subjects or tenses. And to think this used to be the language of diplomacy! Orally, the student can get away with murder, while in written form the sentence would not communicate because of the misspellings. Obviously, you must adjust your grading to your language needs.

TESTING GRAMMAR

If your focus in the classroom is on grammar, or if you have a hybrid approach, then one way or another grammar will have to be featured in your exam. One way to test grammar is with closed exercises, such as fill in the blank, matching columns, multiple choice, true or false, short-answer questions, or dehydrated sentences. But it doesn't all have to be so one-dimensional; as we shall see, grammar can also be tested with more open-ended, and more challenging, contextualized exercises.

Closed exercises are easier to grade because they are very straightforward: either right or wrong. More open ended exercises such as complete the sentence, describe this comic strip, write a letter, etc., are more subjective and harder to grade, but they are a better measure of students' ability to create with the language. I'm still a language learner, so I know that with closed exercises you are able to hide. Been there, done that. If I don't know the answer, I can guess with True or False; I write down letters in matching columns; I can choose something that is already written with multiple-choice exercises. I don't have to provide sentences or even put two words together. With more open ended exercises, everything has to come from me; I have to reveal what I know . . . there's no place to hide! Exams with closed exercises test what the students *know*, but the open ones test what the students can *do*. I argue that the latter is the true test of language proficiency.

Let's examine some closed exercises. Note that some are better than others.

Sample Test 9 (fill in the blanks)

Le subjonctif

1. *Mes parents ne voulent pas que je (faire) _____ des folies pendant le week-end.*
2. *La prof désire que j' (avoir) _____ une bonne connaissance culturelle des pays du Maghreb.*
3. *J'ai peur que tu ne (prendre) _____ le problème de l'immigration au sérieux.*
4. *Les étrangers sont tristes que certain français (être) _____ racistes.*

The subjunctive

1. My parents do not want me (to do) _____ crazy things on the weekend.
2. The professor wants me (to have) _____ good cultural knowledge about the countries of the Maghreb.
3. I am afraid that you do not (to take) _____ the problem of immigration seriously.
4. The foreigners are sad that some French (to be) _____ racists.

Sample Test 10 (fill in the blanks)

Blog del viaje: *En el avión Natalia empezó a escribir un blog sobre su viaje a Guatemala. Para saber qué escribe en el blog, llena los verbos en la forma correcta del **pretérito**. (7 × 2 = 14 puntos; –2 verbo equivocado; –1 verbo correcto pero forma incorrecta; –1/2 por punto error ortográfico)*

comprar   **llamar**   **tener**   **estar**   **decir**   **poder**   **pedir**

Querido Blog,

*¡Qué ilusión! Por fin estoy en camino a Guatemala, pero ayer
1)_____ un día muy estresante (stressful). El
mes pasado, yo 2)_____ un billete de avión
(airline ticket) por $700. Qué buen precio, ¿no? Pero ayer por la mañana,
la agencia de viajes me 3) _____ por teléfono.
¡Ellos me 4)_____ que hubo unos problemas
con el billete! ¡Qué horrible! Entonces les 5)_____
ayuda a mis amigas Rocío y Cristina. En la oficina del agente de viajes, por
fin 6)_____ resolver los problemas al pagar
$300 más. Yo no 7)_____ muy feliz, pero ahora
quiero olvidar los problemas, y pensar en Guatemala.*

Travel blog. While on the plane Natalie started writing a travel blog of
her trip to Guatemala. In order to know what she is writing on the blog,
fill in the blanks with the correct form of the verbs given in the **preterit**.
(7 × 2 = 14 points; –2 wrong verbs; –1 wrong subjects; –1/2 mechanics)

to buy   **to call**   **to have**   **to be**   **to say**   **to be able**   **to ask**

Dear Blog,

Finally, I am starting my trip to Guatemala, but yesterday
1)_____ a very stressful day. Last
month, I 2)_____ an airline ticket for
$700. Good deal, wasn't it? But yesterday morning the travel
agency 3) _____ me on the phone. They
4)_____ that there were some problems
with the ticket. How horrible! Then, I 5)_____
my friends Rocío y Cristina for help. In the end the travel agency was
6)_____ to solve the problems, but I had to
pay $300 more. I 7)_____ not very happy, but
now I want to forget my problems and think about Guatemala.

The exam part in Sample Test 9 seems to be a mechanical exercise without context. The exercise calls for the conjugation of the verb provided.

Think about this: If the verb is provided, the students don't have to understand the sentence or verb meaning at all. The only thing they have to do is to see what the subject of the verb is and . . . apply the rule! That's it! This is exactly how a student can do well on exams and not be able to speak the language at the end of the semester. The sample provides no indication how the work will be graded, an important factor for uniformity in large language programs (more about exam scoring later in this chapter). And finally, each sentence has nothing to do with the other—there is not even the illusion of sentient communication.

The exam section in Sample Test 10 is also a fill in the blank, but the premise gives us something that could happen in real life: writing a blog. The verbs are given at the top, so the students not only have to know what the verbs mean, they also have to know what the sentences mean so they can conjugate the verb in order to complete the sentences correctly. Fill-in-the-blank exercises are not creative and remain mechanical, but at least in this second example the student has to understand several concepts in order to do well.

True/false exercises are heaven for the lucky students who did not study. One way of thinking about it is that chances are 50–50 they will get it right, which is a nice boost to start out with. A better alternative is to ask the student to provide the right answer if they think the sentence is false.

With matching columns there is less guessing, and having an unequal number of entries in each column further reduces successful guessing.

Multiple-choice exercises are closed and will not test what the student can do, but rather how well they retain information. The usual fair format is to have four choices: one is the answer, one is clearly the wrong answer, and the other two choices should have some factor that could allow them to be a partially right answer.

Dehydrated sentences are "sentences" without pronouns, conjunctions, or articles. The verbs are in the infinitive, and there is usually no subject-verb agreement. It is the job of the student to provide all that. Dehydrated sentences are very similar to fill in the blanks because students do not have to know what the sentence means. They just have to check agreement, add an article before a noun (whatever the noun may mean), and conjugate away according to the rules. See the following example:

Sample Test 11 (dehydrated sentences)

¡Fernando el materialista! Describe los objetos que poseen Fernando y sus amigos. (5 × 3 = 15 puntos; –1 cada error de concordancia)

1. *Javier / yo/ tener/ cuatro / casa / bonito*
2. *Mi amigo/ María / comprar/ maleta / nuevo*
3. *Yo / vender / mi / mochilas / viejo*

¡Fernando the materialist! Describe the objects owned by Fernando and his friends. (5 × 3 = 15 points; –1 agreement errors)

1. Javier / I / to have / four / house/ pretty
2. My friend / María / to buy / suitcase / new
3. I / to sell / my / backpacks / old

The point being tested doesn't really translate well into English. In Spanish, the student has to solve the agreement issue with number and gender; in English it would be more of a syntax problem, but you get the idea. These types of sentences do not require too much creativity but a lot of grammar knowledge. So if you are testing for grammar, they might be acceptable, but you wouldn't use them in a communicative setting.

Open Formats

Open formats measure how well a student can deal with a situation based on what she or he has learned. Open formats are a little harder to grade because the student has to write more, and that tempts teachers to count everything that is wrong. The key here is to concentrate on the ability to communicate, along with the grammar point we are testing, and forget about the rest. Here are some examples:

Sample Test 12 (open format 1 – giving a few words as guide)

*La preparación del guacamole. Por fin (finally) llegas a la casa de los padres. Tú les dices que aprendiste a hacer guacamole y como les gusta mucho el guacamole, te piden que les enseñes (teach) cómo hacerlo. Usa el **se impersonal** para describir los pasos. Usa los siguientes verbos en el orden apropiado:* ***aplastar, poner, comprar, agregar, picar.*** *(5 × 2 = 10 puntos; –1/2 errores de ortografía; –1/2 concordancia verbal incorrecta; –2 verbo incorrecto)*

How to cook guacamole. Finally you arrive at your parents' house. You tell them you learned how to make guacamole and, because they like guacamole a lot, they ask you to teach them how to make it. Use the **impersonal "se"** to describe the steps. Use the following verbs in the appropriate order: **mash, put, buy, add**, **dice**. (5 × 2 = 10 points; −1/2 spelling errors; −1/2 agreement; −2 wrong use of the verb)

1. _____

2. _____

3. _____

4. _____

5. _____

Sample Test 13 (open format 2 – answering questions)

Casi listos. *Asegúrate* (make sure) *que tienen todo listo para el viaje. Usa los **pronombres de objeto directo**. (4 × 2 = 8 puntos; −1 pronombre incorrecto)*

¿Llevaste nuestras plantas a la casa de la vecina? _____

¿Pusiste el flan en el congelador? _____

¿Pusiste mis zapatos negros en la maleta? _____

¿Sacaste tu chaqueta de mi maleta? _____

Almost ready. Make sure you have everything ready for the trip. Use **direct object pronouns**. (4 × 2 = 8 points; −1 incorrect object pronouns)

Did you take our plants to the neighbor's? _____

Did you put the flan in the freezer? _____

Did you put my black shoes in the suitcase? _____

Did you take your jacket out of my suitcase? _____

Sample Test 14 (open format 3 – given some information, the student has to compare items)

El vecindario Villaverde. *Llegan al vecindario Villaverde unos nuevos vecinos: Don Lorenzo López Lugo y el Sr. Mario Mares Moreno. Llamas a tu hermana y le platicas* (chat) *de los nuevos vecinos. (6 × 2 = 12 puntos; −2 error de comparación; −1 palabra que falta; −1/2 ortografía)*

The Villaverde Neighborhood. Some new neighbors move to your neighborhood: Don Lorenzo López Lugo and Sr. Mario Mares Moreno. You call your sister and chat about the new neighbors. (6 × 2 = 12 points; −2 wrong comparisons; −1 missing words; −1/2 spelling)

Escribe comparaciones entre los vecinos. (Write comparisons about the neighbors.)

Don Lorenzo López Lugo

Tiene $100 (He has $100)

70 años (70 years old)

1. _____

2. _____

Mario Mares Moreno

Tiene $100 (He has $100)

30 años (30 years old)

Escribe comparaciones entre las casas de los vecinos. (Write comparisons about their houses.)

Casa de Don Lorenzo (Don Lorenzo's house)

3 baños (3 bathrooms)

5 habitaciones (5 rooms)

1 piscina (1 pool)

Casa de Mario (Mario's house)

1 baño (1 bathroom)

3 habitaciones (3 rooms)

1 jardín (1 garden)

3. _____

4. _____

5. _____

6. _____

Sample Test 15 (open format 4 – given a drawing, students describe it)

¡La fiesta de la clase de Español 2! Identifica quiénes están en la fiesta y qué están haciendo. Usa la forma del **presente progresivo**. *(6 × 2 = 12 puntos; −1 falta de verbo; −1 concordancia; −2 no comunica)*

1. Yo _____

2. Mi profesor/a _____

3. _____ y _____

   (compañero/a de clase)   (compañero/a de clase)

4. _____

   (compañero/a de clase)

5. Todos nosotros _____

A party in the Spanish 2 class! Identify who is at the party and what they are doing. Use the **present progressive**. (6 × 2 = 12 points; –1 verb missing; –1 agreement errors; –2 does not communicate)

1. I _____

2. My professor _____

3. _____ and _____
   (classmate)   (classmate)

4. _____
   (classmate)

5. We all _____

Open-ended exams force your students to communicate with the vocabulary and grammar you have taught them. If we imagine that grammar and vocabulary are construction tools, we are asking the students to build a fence with the tools, not to tell us what the tools are for.

TESTING CULTURE

Culture is not normally counted as one of the four skills, but if culture is important to you and you have endeavored to present cultural information and perspectives throughout the term, it must be included on the test. It is your way of saying to the students that this is important enough for them to memorize and understand. If it is not included on the test, your cultural points will just become background noise.

In Chapter 4 we talked about cultural knowledge and cultural proficiency. Cultural knowledge includes facts such as dates, location of countries, names of cities, and so forth. Cultural proficiency reflects what we can understand or interpret in a culture, given those facts. Since we should test what we teach, think of the ways you teach culture and test accordingly. Compare Sample Tests 16 and 17.

Sample Test 16 (testing for cultural knowledge)

1. **Multiple choice**
The Spanish tortilla is made of:
   a. Corn
   b. Eggs
   c. Flour
   d. Tomato

2. **True or false**
   a. Baseball is popular in the Spanish Caribbean.
   b. Soccer is the number one sport in Argentina.
   c. All Spanish speakers eat picante sauce.

3. **Specific factual questions**
   a. What is the capital of Honduras?
   b. What is the name of the prominent mountains in South America?
   c. Which countries fought in the Cinco de Mayo battle?

Sample Test 17 (testing for cultural proficiency)

1. Given the situation below, explain what is happening.

One night three children in Spain are terribly excited about something. Before going to bed, they each leave a shoe near a window. The next day two of the kids are very happy, but one of them pouts, touches his elbow with his hand, and walks away.
   a. What is this day called?
   b. Why are the children putting shoes near a window?

    c. Why are the two children happy?

    d. What is the third child thinking?

2. Given what each of the following characters says, determine the information asked.

José: *En casa, la especialidad de mi madre es la paella.* (At home, my mother's specialty is paella.)

Julián: *Mi padre, Juan, come mucho conejo.* (My father, Juan, eats a lot of rabbit.)

Jaime: *¿Quieres más mate?* (Do you want more mate [a tea from Argentina]?)

Pepe: *Mi tío cocina un postre riquísimo que se llama tembleque.* (My uncle cooks a delicious dessert called *tembleque*.)

Carlos: *Pues, en mi país es difícil ser vegetariano.* (Well, in my country it is hard to be vegetarian.)

1. *José y Julián son hermanos. ¿De dónde crees que son?* (José and Julián are brothers. Where do you think they are from?)

2. *¿Cuál es el nombre y apellido del padre?* (What is their father's first and last name?)

3. *Carlos y Jaime son primos. ¿De dónde crees que son?* (Carlos and Jaime are cousins. Where do you think they are from?)

4. *¿De qué país es Pepe?* (What country is Pepe from?)

Testing culture knowledge or proficiency depends on what you have covered in class as well as on the importance you have given it and the amount of time you have dedicated to it.

IN-CLASS COMPOSITIONS

Some language programs set aside a few days for two or three in-class compositions per term. This is a creative process that requires special procedures. First, we cannot spring this task on our students on some random day and then ask them to write a masterpiece by simply giving them a topic. Writing is a really challenging task (even in our native language!) that must first be practiced with daily communicative activities and homework assignments that require writing. (For sample writing tasks, see Chapter 3.)

This is what has worked for me. First I prepare my students so that they have a good idea of what I expect. On the day of the in-class composition I write the topic on the board and carry out a brainstorm of ideas. Let's say the topic is "A day with . . .". I tell the students, "We are going to write about

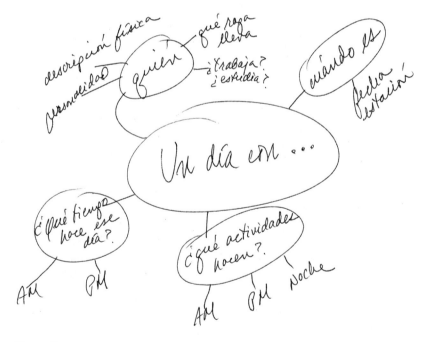

Figure 3

spending a day with someone. It could be a real person, like your mother, a cousin, a friend, a boyfriend, or a classmate. It could be a famous person we really don't know personally, but we can imagine spending a day with, like Angela Merkel, Antonio Banderas, or Carla Bruni. Or it could be a fictitious character such as Mickey Mouse, Cinderella, or Darth Vader. What can we write about?" The students then suggest subtopics, as they have done for other in-class practice essays. See the sample brainstorming web generated by my students in Figure 3.

Generating this web gives the students a lot of material to write. Writing is no longer the lonely and daunting task in which the learner has to race against the clock and come up with ideas all alone. Brainstorming also reminds your students what they are already able to do with the language. They can describe a person, describe what they wear, describe the weather, mention activities, talk about the future, and so forth.

As with regular exams, students should be well informed of what is expected of them, including the composition's length and format. This reduces stress and brings out their best performance.

Grading In-Class Compositions

If your approach to teaching language is communicative, then communication should have the greatest weight when determining a student's grade. *What* they are writing should be more important than minor details such as accents, commas, capitalization, spelling, etc. (This will vary depending on the language you teach.) My program at the University of California, Davis, is more of a hybrid, where we place the greatest importance on communication, but we also pay attention to grammar, and because of that, just like with exams, we have a combination of holistic grading and grammar awareness in grading.

First, when we grade, we read the in-class essay for content and write comments in the margins. Because we want to validate and give importance to what the student is trying to say, our comments are not about grammar, but about content. Just imagine reading a letter from your nephew, an eight-year-old who is writing about his first trip to Disneyland, and the letter he sends you is full of grammar mistakes. Yes, we will see all the errors (we're language teachers, after all!), but are we going to point out spelling or grammar mistakes right off the bat, or are we going to respond about what a great experience it must have been to go on a Jungle Cruise at Disneyland?! The kid is trying to tell us something! Our students are not little kids, but linguistically, they are, and just like children they are putting a lot of effort into telling you something. Let's acknowledge that. I write comments like: "That is so funny, Mark!" "Wait, you chose Jason Bateman, but he is spending the day with me!" or "Wow, what an interesting idea, Kim, I may do that too one day!"

Second, we grade for grammar. Just as we all did in writing assignments in our first language, it is best that your student figures out the error with your help, instead of simply providing the corrected sentence. You can discreetly mark (by the way, I don't use red pens) with a code what the error is that the student needs to correct and provide in their second draft. Following is a sample grading key for Spanish essays that you may adapt for your language.

Grading key

∧	missing word
ac	accent missing or misplaced
conn	connector word missing or wrong
op	wrong or missing object pronoun
G	gender error
N	number error
pp	wrong or missing preposition
sp	spelling
sva	subject/verb agreement
T	tense
wo	word order
ww	wrong word
P/I	preterit or imperfect choice
S/E	*ser* or *estar* choice
M	indicative or subjunctive mood
Ang	Anglicism
[¿?]	does not communicate

Un <u>día</u> con Cindy Crawford
<u>ac</u>

Hoy es un <u>día</u> excelente porque Cindy
      <u>ac</u>
Crawford y yo vamos al zoo en la <u>mañana</u>,
                                  <u>SP</u>
<u>Bogóta</u> a las once de la mañana, <u>París</u>
<u>ac</u>   <u>ac</u>
a las dos de la Tarde, y ∧bailar en New
york a las <u>neuve</u> de la noche. Todo en
           <u>SP</u>
<u>la</u> mismo <u>día</u>.   Es ∧<u>julio</u> 04, mi cumpleaños. Es un
<u>G</u>   <u>WO</u>
día en el verano y <u>es</u> calor. Cindy
                    <u>WW</u>
no necisiba <u>mucho</u> ropa porque <u>es</u> calor.
            <u>G</u>   <u>WW</u>
Cindy es muy bonita y simpática. Ella
<u>esta</u> <u>enmorada</u> conmigo. ←¡ <u>No me digas</u>! ⌣
<u>ac</u>   <u>SP</u>   <u>WW</u>

   En la mañana yo voy a <u>Cindy's casa</u>.
                                <u>ANG</u>
Vamos al zoo muy rápido y Cindy mira∧
los animales y yo miro ∧Cindy. Entonces,
vamos a <u>Bogota</u> para almuerzar en un
         <u>ac</u>
restaurante <u>fantastico</u>. Cindy dice, "Ryan,
             <u>ac</u>   <u>SP</u>
tu eres <u>muy</u> <u>guapísimo</u> y inteligente,
<u>ac</u>   <u>ac</u>   <u>WW</u>
¡yo quiero tu [body]." yo digo, "¡Cindy,
<u>parate</u>, vamos a París ahora!" Vamos
<u>ac</u>
a París y Cindy quiere <u>mucho</u> besos
                        <u>∧</u>
de mí. Hablamos mucho y yo <u>dice</u>,
                             <u>SVA</u>
"no quiero <u>casarse</u> contigo." Cindy
           <u>PP</u>
llora y llora y llora, y Cindy dice
Ⓜ¡ por favor, por favor!" <u>Finalamente</u>,
                            <u>SP</u>
vamos a New york. Bailamos y
hablamos mucho y regresamos a
California. "<u>Adiós</u> Cindy!" "¿Hasta
mañana Ryan?" Ⓜ ¡Yo Cindy!"
<u>ac</u>

   ¡ Eres un rompe-corazones
        Ryan! ⌣

¡Wow, Ryan, qué día!

Figure 4 shows what a student essay looks like when marked with the symbols in the grading key.

For the actual grading, we have a hybrid way to mark, with the greatest importance given to communication. Following are the teacher and student versions of a grading rubric I use for scoring in-class essays in my undergraduate classes.

In-Class Essay – First year: Instructor's Copy

CONTENT (10)   _____   _____

       length (too short) (from –3 to –5)

       off assigned topic (from –3 to –5)

       expand on some ideas (–2 per idea not developed)

ORGANIZATION (10)   _____   _____

       missing title (–1)

       missing introduction   (–2)

       no logical order (–2 if paragraphs do not follow logical order)

       paragraphs not coherent (–2 if it is choppy)

       missing closing sentence (–2 if there is no conclusion)

GRAMMAR (14)   _____   _____

       spelling

       verb forms   (–1 for 4 to 6 spelling, verb form, and/ or

                           punctuation errors)

       punctuation

COMMUNICATION (16)   _____   _____

       sentences don't communicate (–2 to –4)

       some phrases don't communicate (–2 each non-communicative phrase)

       some words don't communicate (–1 each non-communicative word)

       usage of English (–1 each non-Spanish word)

                     _____ + _____

1st version (60)   2nd version (40)

TOTAL _____

Grading results are recorded on the student version of the rubric and given to the student with the first and second drafts.

In-Class Essay – First year: Student's Copy

CONTENT (10)   _____ _____ _____

      length (too short)

      off assigned topic

      expand on some ideas

ORGANIZATION (10)   _____ _____

      missing title

      missing introduction

      no logical order

      paragraphs not coherent

      missing closing sentence

GRAMMAR (14)   _____ _____

      spelling

      verb forms

      punctuation

COMMUNICATION (16)   _____ _____

      sentences don't communicate

      some phrases don't communicate

      some words don't communicate

      usage of English

              _____ + _____

1st version (60)   2nd version (40)

TOTAL _____

GENERAL CONSIDERATIONS ABOUT GRADING

I remember a friendly discussion I had with a graduate student about a particular point on an exam. This teacher was unusually generous in his grading. Looking at some of his students' exams, I remember pointing out some errors he didn't catch, and I remember him saying, "Yes, I know it is wrong, but he just probably forgot. Why should I punish him for forgetting something?" Punish?! Is that the attitude he held about grading?

I see grading not as punishing anybody, but rather classifying students by "excellent," "good," "fair," and "language is not really your thing." If your exams are valid, have meaning, you test what you teach, you prepare the students well, you have ample practice beforehand, the test is a fair length, etc., then there are no surprises come exam day. It is up to the students to prove what they are capable of doing. They will perform according to their God-given ability and how much they crammed the night before. That ability and/or diligence may be excellent, good, fair, or poor, and your job, after making sure you have given a valid exam, is to add up the numbers and classify the student with a grade. You are not punishing anybody or being mean. We wish all our students could get As (or maybe our deepest wish is that we didn't have to give a grade at all), but that is unrealistic.

As a young teacher I remember feeling bad about returning exams with low scores. I had one particular student who I thought was pretty smart get a C on an exam. I feared seeing the disappointment in his face, but when he saw the grade he said, "YES!" He had expected a lower grade! Immediately I had a flashback to one of my calculus classes back in college. I was never good at math. (And why in the world do they call a subject that has more letters than numbers "math" anyway?) In that class I remember being ecstatic about getting a C. I was so bad at it that I was happy I did not fail! From then on I realized that most students expect and accept their grade because they know they didn't have the time to study for a particular exam or they just don't have talent for the subject. On the other hand, you will encounter students who, in spite of their performance, unrealistically think very highly of themselves. Or you may encounter students who will ask you why you are "giving" them a B and not an A. If you construct valid exams, remind them that you are not "giving" them a grade, but rather "reporting" what they earned. That is why it is so important that you hold the moral high ground on this one. You must have valid exams and a fair assessment procedure because if you don't, your complaining student will have a point, and rightly so.

CHEATING

This is very distasteful and painful for me, but we teachers have to deal with cheating, and as educators, fight it for the sake of all the honest students and in the name of fairness. Some students will use the old favorite "cheat sheet" with all the verb conjugations listed, but the latest trick I have seen is students using their smartphones to take pictures of the test and e-mail it to their buddy who will be taking the exam in the next class period. I have also seen students texting answers across the room to others. Even if their phone is silenced, you sometimes see one student "checking to see how much time they have left" (but they are really texting). A few seconds later another student "checks the time" and flashes a smile because they now know the answers. As a result, I prohibit smartphones during exams.

Another form of cheating is having some excuse for not taking a test on the prescribed day and asking to take it later. That way a student can get the inside scoop from somebody who has already taken it. Excuses vary greatly, but the most common is the death of a grandmother. I have noted that exams are particularly fatal for grandmothers, and it is at this time that this unfortunate population's death rate peaks, especially during final exams. If a student has four grandparents, it is easy to say one of them has died once a term.

I usually tell my graduate TAs to be sympathetic and give the student the benefit of the doubt the first time. If another death or illness happens again the day of an exam, it becomes a pattern, so their excuse is probably not true.

EXAM CHECKLIST

- Are you assessing the students' understanding daily? Exit quizzes tell you which students do not understand what you are teaching.

- Have you informed the students about the exam's format, its content, and the skills to be tested? There should be no surprises on the test.

A True Story from the Front Lines: Excuses, Excuses

A few years ago, a student told me he could not take the first midterm because his mother was very sick and he had to go visit her. Because this was his first excuse, I was sympathetic and gave him a make-up exam. For the second exam, he said he had a very important job interview he had to attend. That to me established a pattern, and I told him I was not giving him a make-up exam. Amazingly, he was able to reschedule his interview! For the third exam, he said his grandmother was dying and he had to run to her bedside before she passed away. Being an expert on grandmother excuses, I did not believe him and refused to give him a make-up. So, he took the exam. And finally, a week before the end of class, he e-mailed me saying he had been in a truck accident and attached a note from the hospital giving a list of his injuries. They included a broken leg, a broken jaw, a broken spine, and various other horrible conditions. I thought nobody

- Are the direction lines clear and simple? The student can't spend precious time reading a long paragraph of instructions.

- Have you provided a context for every exam part so it somewhat reflects real life?

- Is the oral comprehension test based on something you would normally hear in real life?

- Is the reading comprehension part something you would normally read?

- Is the essay something you would normally write?

- Are the questions implicit or explicit?

- Is the exam too long? If it takes the teacher more than ten minutes to do it, it is too long.

could possibly make this up. It had to be true, so I e-mailed back offering my heartfelt sympathy for his accident and offered him an Incomplete, which he could complete next quarter. To this he said he just wanted to take the final a week later, not next term. What?! He wants to take the final a week later? If all these injuries are true, he would have to be in bed for three months, not just one week. I felt so foolish falling for this lie! I e-mailed back and told him that he either had to take the Incomplete or take the final on the scheduled day, and that I was getting tired of his lies.

Anyway, the day of the final he showed up wearing a back brace, with his face all black-and-blue with bruises, in a wheelchair pushed by his mother, handed me his grandmother's death announcement, and through clenched teeth said, "I want to take the final!!"

Yes, I was wrong!!

- Are all blank spaces the same length? Sometimes we inadvertently provide a small space if we know the answer is a short word and a long space for a longer word. We are giving a big hint if we do this.

- Have you included grading instructions so the students know how much something is worth?

- Are some answers embedded in other parts of the test?

- Does it test the four skills and culture?

- Are you testing what you taught?

Exams can be stressful for students, but we hope to minimize stress by making sure we design a valid test that will fairly measure students' language ability.

Summary Questions

1. What is formative assessment? Give examples.

_____

_____

2. What is summative assessment?

_____

_____

3. What are some examples of closed exercises and open exercises?

_____

_____

4. How can we make essay writing easier for the student?

_____

_____

Scenarios

Scenario 1

A teacher gives the following two-part exam. After grading the exams he sees the students did pretty well. In Part A some students missed question #5, and in Part B #4 was a problem too. Overall the teacher considers this a fair test, since the first part is a little more grammar oriented and the second one more open, which reflects his hybrid approach to teaching.

Examine and evaluate these exam parts below. What type of exercises are these—open or closed? What do you think about the direction lines, the context, the level of difficulty for the students, and the grading instructions? What do you think of the fact that the students did well overall? Was it a valid test?

Parte A. *Escriba el pretérito de los verbos en paréntesis recordando cambiar el pronombre reflexivo a la forma correcta.*

1. *Fernando y Lucía* _____ *(instalarse) en su apartamento.*

2. *Mi mujer y yo* _____ *(verse) obligados a trabajar.*

3. *Yo* _____ *(preguntarse) si había hecho bien en decírselo.*

4. *El joven* _____ *(enamorarse) de Lucía.*

5. *La turbulencia política* _____ *(producir) cambio.*

Part A. Write the preterit of the verbs in parentheses, remembering to change the reflexive pronoun to the correct form.

1. Fernando and Lucía _____ (to install themselves) in their apartment.

2. My wife and I _____ (to see ourselves) obligated to work.

3. I _____ (to ask myself) if I had done well in telling it to her.

4. The young man _____ (to fall in love) with Lucía.

5. The political turbulence _____ (to produce) change.

Parte B. *Conteste en frases completas.*

1. *¿Estudió usted la lección de español?*

2. *¿Tomó usted café esta mañana?*

3. *¿Cantó la clase una canción española?*

4. *¿Hacen ustedes siempre la tarea?*

5. *¿Bebiste leche hoy?*

Part B. Answer in complete sentences.

1. Did you (polite form) study the Spanish lesson?

2. Did you (polite form) drink coffee this morning?

3. Did the class sing a Spanish song?

4. Do you (plural) always do the homework?

5. Did you (informal form) drink milk today?

Scenario 2

A teacher gives an exam she thinks is valid, but many students do poorly. She goes through the exams again and sees that most of the errors occur in the essay at the end of the exam. Many students lost up to 18 points out of 20 because of so many grammatical errors. She thought she had prepared the students well, and she was pretty sure the structures she taught were answered correctly in the grammar part of the test. However, since the essay had an open format, some students were very ambitious and creative, making many spelling errors that were not necessarily covered in class.

How do you think she graded this exam? What do you recommend she do differently?

_____

_____

Part IV • The Future

14 • Hitting the Job Market
Getting a Job at a University

NORMA LÓPEZ-BURTON

The last job interview I had was over twenty years ago. Much has changed since then, so my advice in this chapter comes from graduate students who have been successful at getting the jobs they wanted. I especially want to thank Kelly Bilinski and the other graduate students who have candidly told their experiences to their fellow students in panels and talks. I thank all these students for graciously submitting to my interrogations so I can better prepare each new crop of job seekers.

I also speak from the point of view of someone who has had numerous interactions with young scholars who interview with our department. I have to be truthful with you: in an ideal world we should only judge people by the content of their character and the level of their qualifications. But we don't live in an ideal world, and the fact is that we also judge based on other less lofty characteristics, such as the way others dress, their manners, their physical appearance, and the way they comport themselves. What can I say? We are faulty human beings—"Forgive me, Father, for I have sinned!" All too often we interviewers see young men and women with dirty fingernails, wearing ill-fitting clothing, or with new shirts still sporting the packaging creases, and we can't help but roll our eyes after the interview is over. I have asked myself why we care about appearances. Are we that shallow? Maybe, but in our defense, if an interviewee does not take the time to polish his or her manners or to look his or her best for the interview, it feels as if we are

not that important. Do we really want an unsophisticated person working with us or representing our university? I think that we all try to look beyond appearances, but we subconsciously are searching for a person who is not only intelligent and qualified for the position, but who also took the time to look good for us. If there are two equally excellent candidates to choose from, the one who looks the part will get the job. So, accepting the fact that the world is not going to change soon, I would like to tell you what you can do to maximize your chances of getting the job you want.

There are many things you have to do before applying for a job. The steps listed below should be completed months before stepping foot on campuses for interviews. Many of these points are discussed in greater detail in other parts of this chapter, but here's the abbreviated version:

- Check and update your curriculum vitae. There is plenty of help online for this. Just search for "curriculum vitae academic."

- Write and perfect your teaching philosophy statement.

- Write and finish your research statement. Seek the advice of your dissertation director.

- Scan and organize your teaching evaluations.

- Set up an online account with a digital dossier, a credentials and a letter of recommendation service, such as Interfolio. This may be a little pricey for some graduate students, but many swear by its convenience. Your university may also have a similar free service; check into that.

- Ask at least four professors for confidential letters of recommendation, and give them the information to upload to your chosen agency.

- Set up a personal website. Upload all your documents and show any favorable personal information you would like the committee to see.

- Draft and perfect two syllabi for courses you would like to teach. Make one of them a senior seminar.

- Shop for nice business attire ahead of time.

- Make sure your dissertation is at least halfway finished by the time you go to the MLA. Be prepared to talk about your goals and self-imposed deadlines to finish.

- Arrange for one or two mock interviews with your professors; it is important to practice.

- Adjust the content of your answers to the type of institution with which you are interviewing. Different research institutions will not only ask different questions and expect different answers, they will also focus on different aspects of your teaching or research.

- Rehearse for interviews on Skype. Make sure one of your mock interviews is online so you can work on your posture and background. Practice looking at the webcam instead of at the computer video image.

TEACHING PHILOSOPHY STATEMENT

What is the ideal teaching philosophy statement? The teaching philosophy statement is all about you as well as your teaching style, teaching goals, and

this is the core of who you are, the overall content

to each institution doesn't change much. But that

ybody gets the exact same application package from

to tweak the statement a little to fit the institution. Look

ctive employers' websites to find their areas of interest. See

oks they are using.

a couple of examples of how to customize your teaching state-

tenure-track research university will have top students who can be

"p   ed" a little more. So in your teaching philosophy, mention that you expect a lot from your students, you believe in maintaining high expectations, and your research will ensure that your students get exposed to the latest developments in their field. You might also mention all the technological tools you use in your teaching. Finally, convey that your love for research equals that of teaching, thus implying "don't worry, I also plan to publish."

In contrast, students in community colleges may be somewhat older, have families, or may not be as academically oriented as those at research institutions. Remember, in this environment research is secondary to excellence in teaching, and so that is what you should emphasize.

Note that in the two above examples, the core of the teaching philosophy is the same, and it reflects you and your style, but adding or deleting key sentences that reflect the institution to which you are applying really could make the difference in whether you get the fat acceptance package in the mail, or the thin, polite rejection letter.

The basic elements that I recommend you **do include** in your teaching philosophy are: the most important skills you want students to learn in class and why this is important to you; what you have taught and how many years of experience you have; your passion, happiness, and enthusiasm for the profession of teaching; the fact that teaching matches your personality and that it is personally rewarding to teach; how you are able to relate to your students; your teaching approach or rationale of why you do what you do at each of the levels (elementary, intermediate, advanced, and lower division), including specific examples; your feelings about the importance of culture (how you make it come alive); and the use of technology to enhance your teaching and professional development.

You could also include: the name of a very effective professor who influenced your teaching, and the qualities you have adopted from him or her; and a specific interesting, humorous, or sublime event in the classroom that makes your teaching philosophy statement stand out and compels the reader to remember you.

Do not include: any type of excuse for evaluations or shortcomings of any kind; any boring generic terms to describe your teaching; a long laundry list of what you do in the classroom; or any efficiencies you may have developed in order to cut corners in teaching and meet the demands of your publishing schedule.

YOUR PERSONAL WEBSITE

Set up a personal website. This shows you are technologically literate, which is important in this profession. Be careful only to include personal information you want the search committee to see. **Include** in your website links to your CV, your philosophy of teaching statement, syllabi for future classes, your research abstract, and a few personal "safe-to-hire" items such as your sports activities (shows you are active and in good health), travels (shows you are curious and adventuresome), and hobbies like cooking, quilting, and drawing, along with any photos or videos of your creations (shows you have a balanced life). **Do not include**: links to political organizations or charities that might disclose your political inclinations; images in which you are smoking or drinking; unflattering photos; links to your Facebook page. **You could include**—but not front and center—a picture of you and your spouse if you want committee members to know you are married; a picture of you and your partner if you want them to know up front about your sexual orientation; a picture of you and your children if you want them to know that fact. If you would rather let prospective employers know about your personal life later in the interview process, or if you know it could affect your prospects (legally and ethically it shouldn't, but remember how this chapter started out—we are all just human), leave the personal data out.

THE INTERVIEW

There are many things to keep in mind and to practice before you take on your first interview. First, shop for adequate clothing and work on your appearance. Then do dress-up mock interviews with several people in which you rehearse your job talk and practice explaining your dissertation in both languages. To help you prepare for specific interview questions, I have collected a long list of questions I have heard (or asked) over the years, which I provide below. Some may apply to you; others might not. Practice answering them in a confident, firm, and strong voice; don't meekly raise your eyebrows, expecting the interviewers' approval, hoping that you have answered their question correctly. You are not a graduate student anymore, so don't act like one.

- Tell us about your dissertation.

- Tell us about your research. How did you come to this project?

- Where do you see your project going?

- How would you teach your research?

- What is your teaching philosophy?

- Tell us about yourself.

- We're looking to establish a minor in sub-discipline X. If you were to help us structure this minor, what three or four courses would you see as essential to a program of study in that minor and why?

- We have quite a few first-generation students at our school. How has your previous teaching experience prepared you to serve the needs of such students?

- Your article on X seems quite far from your current research. Is there any connection between the two, or do they simply reflect two very divergent research interests that you'd like to continue exploring?

- What experience do you have teaching literature?

- How do you teach writing?

- What would you say if a student came to you and said that she wanted to work on an independent study on Sartre?

- What is the most influential book you have read in the field of X lately?

- What subjects can you teach that might normally be outside your field?

- What do you have to offer graduate students?

- Our department has high expectations for publication for tenure. How do you see yourself handling the expectations?

- What is the difference between teaching graduate students and undergrads?

- We have a faculty reading group that picks two or three books a year that cross disciplines. What book from your field might you suggest that would spur discussion among people in other disciplines?

- How do you see yourself in five years?

- What is your favorite book? Why?

- What animal would you like to be?

- Do you think your private life/sexual orientation might be a problem in this job?

- Why do you like to teach?

- How would you teach our methods course?

- What is your favorite level (elementary, intermediate, or advanced) to teach?

- How do you facilitate the learning process? How do you grab students' interest?

- What do you still struggle with?

- Why is it important to read literature and how do you plan to teach students how to interpret it?

- Are you familiar with the ACTFL guidelines? How would you implement them in a language program?

- How would you teach X class?

- What would be your favorite class to teach?

- We don't have a lot of funding for the kind of travel you require for your research. How would you work around this?

- How would you deal with language instructors that are full professors and do not want to follow your guidelines or change the way they have been teaching for the last twenty years?

- How would you contribute to our community? What kind of service do you see yourself providing? (Usually asked at smaller universities . . .)

- What methodology do you prefer/use in language classes?

- What are the implications of your research in the profession?

- Why would you like to work with us?

- Which textbook would you use in X class?

- Have you ever had a problematic student in your class? How did you deal with him or her?

- Are you familiar with the European framework? (vs. ACTFL guidelines . . .)

- How would you teach a methods class attended by graduate students from different language programs? Which text would you use?

- Tell us about your experiences as a senior TA.

- What first-year language textbooks have you worked with?

- What student behaviors do you expect in your class? What are things you do not want to see in your class?

- What are your best/worst attributes?

- Would you be OK with having to teach elementary language every now and then? (This was asked for a combined assistant professor + language coordinator position.)

- What would you teach in a freshman seminar?

Lastly, they will ask:

- Do you have any questions for us?

You must come prepared to answer that last question. Do not say, "Not really." Have two or three questions in mind. Do not ask about salary or about their spousal hiring program. Do not ask about compensation packages or benefits at this point. You could ask, "What funds are available for research or for conference travel?" or, "I saw on your website that you have an active Spanish Club (or any undergraduate or graduate organization). What kinds of activities do they do? " or, "I understand that the responsibilities for your French program rotate among professors each semester. Could you tell me more about that?"

What to Wear

Someone will probably pick you up from the train station or airport, so you have to be well dressed from the start—not super dressed-up, but wearing something appropriately nice. Prior to landing, check your appearance: check your hair, your makeup, and your teeth. Pop in a breath mint, too. Your materials should be stored in a briefcase, not a backpack. Remember, you don't want to look like a student.

Men: Not too many things can go wrong with men's attire. Just pack one or two good ($300–$500) suits. The fact that you buy an expensive suit does not guarantee that it will look good on you; it must be tailored to your body. Don't wear a suit for the first time at an interview. "Break in" your new suit by wearing it to a restaurant or around the house for a while until you feel comfortable. Pack three shirts. You will probably only need two . . . the third is an extra, just in case you get the first two dirty. Iron out any creases caused by packaging. Pack two ties, nice dress shoes (people notice), and a belt in good condition (not cracked and old). Don't wear cologne.

Women: Pack one or two tailored suits. Just as the men, you should invest in good suits that are tailored to your body. Do your shopping early but make sure you maintain the same weight so your suit still fits when interviewing time comes! Take three blouses. You will probably need just two, but pack an extra for any contingencies. See that the blouses don't gap, especially around the bust area. Tight clothing looks tacky and you don't want any member of the committee distracted because of your wardrobe. Also, buy blouses that are long enough to minimize the chance that they may come out from your skirt or pants. That looks very sloppy. When you try them on, do a "reaching high test" before you buy them. See if the blouse stays in or not. If the gaps are persistent, try fashion tape, available on the Internet. This takes care of clothing gaps, but prepare for hem or popped-button emergencies too.

Buy nice closed-toed shoes, one- to three-inch heels. If you are tall and wear three-inch heels, making you even taller, that can come across as intimidating. General rule of thumb: no stilettos, no flats, and no pointy-toed shoes. Make sure your shoes are comfortable. If they are new, break them in first.

Are pants or skirts better? Wear whatever you think you look best in and what is more comfortable for you. This could be a matter of body type. If you decide to wear a skirt, make sure it doesn't rotate. That has happened to me. Very annoying! Wear neutral-shade stockings. Jewelry should not be big or loud. Bra straps should be completely hidden, and make sure your slip doesn't show. If you wear makeup, apply it as you always do; now is not the time to experiment. If you wear lipstick, don't go too bright, but with more of a natural color. And when you apply lipstick, remember to wipe it from the inside of your mouth so it doesn't get into your teeth. I had a teacher whose lipstick always smeared. She looked like a vampire (and acted like one too).

Both men and women: If your briefcase has a strap, use it just on one shoulder, not across the chest. The strap wrinkles your shirt or blouse and can mess up your hair when you take it off—overall, an awkward movement. If you are the sweating kind of person when you get nervous, buy underarm shields. Carry a handkerchief to wipe the sweat off your hands and brow. Check your fly, please! Consider a manicure: clear nail polish for men, neutral tones that don't stand out for women. And again, invest in good suits. Looking good will boost your confidence!

A few final words: The above are guidelines that have worked very well for my graduate students. When it comes to appearances, the overall goal is to act as if you were a fully functioning, well-rested, comfortably affluent seasoned professional, i.e. the complete opposite of what a grad student normally is! Look and act the part of a professor, not a student.

The MLA

"The MLA" sounds like a terrorist group, but it stands for Modern Languages Association. Some feel the MLA is the ultimate meat market for higher education jobs. I would say it's more like speed dating. Graduate students who have finished or are close to finishing their dissertations anxiously await the

MLA listings that come out each September. These soon-to-be PhDs apply to several universities and wait nervously to see if they are judged worthy of being interviewed. The lucky applicants will attend the conference, offered once a year during the first week of January, and will be interviewed by several universities. Many schools send their committees to interview all the candidates and then offer campus interviews to a short list. So, to make sure you are among those who get that all-important second date, follow the checklist below:

- Find out if your institution is able to help cover expenses to travel to the MLA. Many do.

- Find a hotel near the MLA convention center so you don't have to worry about walking anywhere in cold weather and ruining your hairdo.

- Consider arriving a day early to avoid feeling rushed and tired.

- Print out and bring a crisp copy of your dissertation, as well as enough copies of sample syllabi and CVs for each interview.

- Become an expert about each department and institution that you are interviewing with. Before the interview, e-mail the department secretary and ask who will be interviewing you at the MLA—then look them up online. See if they have written important articles or books that you should be familiar with. Find out about their areas of research.

- You will be interviewed both in English and in the language you will be teaching. Be ready to talk about your dissertation and philosophy of teaching in both languages without too much code-switching.

- MLA speed dating means you may have back-to-back interviews, so take protein bars to hold you over between interviews.

- Do not over-caffeinate. The caffeine combined with your nerves will turn you into a jabbering automaton.

- Take a laptop computer bag instead of a backpack. Remember, you don't want to look like a student.

- Send a thank-you letter to the committee within two days of the interview, expressing your enthusiasm for the position.

- The interviewers will always ask if you have any questions about them. It is not good to say, "No, I don't." Prepare at least three specific questions. It shows your interest in their institution.

Phone or Skype Interviews

Some universities may opt for a phone or Skype interview instead of sending a whole committee to the MLA, which can be a pricey proposition when you consider the costs of airfare, lodging, and meals.

Phone interview: Even though you might not see your interlocutors face-to-face, phone interviews can lead to that coveted campus interview, so they are very important. The good thing about a phone interview is that you can have your cheat sheets in front of you in case you forget something. The bad thing is that the interviewers don't get to see the enthusiasm in your eyes or the gestures you are making as you emphasize something. Your voice alone might not adequately reflect the way you are, a problem I used to have. I consider myself an upbeat and outgoing person, but more than once during a phone call, people would ask me, "Are you OK? You sound sad," when I was in a perfectly good mood. The way I solved that problem was by purposefully smiling when talking on the phone. Somehow that changes the tone of my voice, and I never got asked if I was OK again (unless I was truly having a bad day). So, if you have a "downer" voice, smile!

I also highly recommend you take the call on a landline phone instead of a cell phone. If this is not possible, search for the best area of reception ahead of time. If you don't have good cell phone reception, you run the risk of misunderstanding a question and answering it incorrectly. And be sure to choose a spot that doesn't have any background noise.

Skype interview: You'll have to dress up for this one. And don't be tempted to wear your pajama bottoms because you think the other person will only see you from the waist up. What happens if you have to stand up to get something? That could be kind of embarrassing, right? Pick a good background with shelves filled with books, not clutter. Watch your posture, and don't slouch! Practice looking at the webcam instead of the computer screen. That's harder to do than you think! Practice doing this because it looks best to make "eye contact" when answering questions. So, remember, chin up (or down, depending on where the camera is).

Have a tablet and a pen or pencil available to jot down any important information the interviewers might give you, or to remember the second part of a compound question. It is also OK to take notes using a second laptop computer to the side. It looks professional.

Campus Interviews

Congrats are in order: you landed some campus interviews! You, and perhaps three others, will be competing for the position that should belong to you! Consider the advice below, and go get 'em, tiger!

- A campus interview usually means you'll actually have many interviews, and before the dust settles, you could have been introduced to twenty or thirty people. Typically an office assistant will e-mail you the schedule of your visit ahead of time so you can prepare yourself for the marathon.

- Ask for a contact number before you leave home to make sure you have someone to inform of any changes in your flight schedule or lodging.

- During the flight, quiz yourself with flash cards with names of the faculty you will be meeting and their areas of interest.

- For peace of mind, carry on your luggage and don't give the bag handlers a chance to lose your wardrobe. Remember that if anything gets wrinkled, hotels have irons.

Big Sibling Is Watching . . . At All Times!

From the moment someone picks you up from the airport to the moment you get dropped off, you are "on stage." You are being looked at and scrutinized, whether it is in a formal setting (at the job talk or one of the many meetings), or during the informal chitchat that occurs while walking from building to building and during meals. Consider this your Miranda warning: "Anything you say or do can and will be held against you." With the seemingly innocent small talk you have to demonstrate that besides working nonstop on your studies, you also have kept up with regular life.

When meeting the search committee members for the first time, start with a firm but not bone-crushing handshake; don't pump-shake as if you were meeting your long-lost cousin Eddie for the first time. Smile and make eye contact. Don't forget, your handshake is the first impression. Too soft a handshake or failure to make eye contact shows lack of confidence. The same is true for women: make it a firm handshake. And if the recipient pats the back of your hand (a sign of condescension), you go ahead and pat his back. All in good fun!

Small Talk

Let the games begin! My strong advice is to keep politics, religion, and sex off the list of topics—one misstep and it can land you in someone's bad graces. Safe topics are headline news, recent films, national sports (Go Giants!), the university's (hopefully winning) sports teams, pets, or a well-reviewed best-selling book. A good source of safe topics is what you hear on NPR (National Public Radio). If you don't yet have the habit of listening to NPR, listen to it a few days before so you at least can say, "Yes, I heard about that. What do you think?" Also, small talk requires full conversations, not monologues, so don't go on and on about your favorite TV show. Listening is also a skill that needs to be developed; after all, we have two ears and just one mouth. Everybody likes to be listened to, so ask what others think about the subject of conversation. That way you flatter them and you get to eat your meal. But remember to look interested in what the other person is saying; listen carefully and ask follow-up questions. Make eye contact occasionally when they talk, and pause to ponder every once in a while.

Table Manners

Ah . . . the obligatory faculty dinner. Don't worry, you don't have to be an expert in dining etiquette (although, it wouldn't hurt); you just need to know the basics, which I outline below.

Depending on how long your interview stay is, you might have one or two informal lunches with one or two professors, and two dinners with various faculty members. Even here, you are under the microscope, so make sure to not order sloppy foods like ribs, spaghetti, lasagna, or soup that drip and may stain your clothes. Scan the menu for the neatest, easiest-to-handle foods.

Guys, watch your ties when leaning over to eat; it's the most likely piece of clothing to get dirty. I recommend a tie clip and eating slowly and deliberately. No need to rush. Beware of flaky breads. Breadcrumbs will get all over you. So when biting into that crunchy ciabatta loaf, lean forward a bit so crumbs stay on the bread plate.

Learn how to cut meat. Don't hold the fork like a cello. Use your index fingers to hold the fork and the knife. Also, cut your food while hiding any effort; you don't want to look like you are a Neanderthal stabbing his next meal. Elegantly hide the toil.

Don't use your thumb to push food forward against the fork. Use your table knife as a backstop.

Don't stuff big chunks of food in your mouth. You have to be able to offer a response to a question within three bites, more or less, so put small morsels in your mouth. Some waiters (and professors) have such bad timing: you just stuffed that big piece of lettuce into your mouth, and the waiter (or professor) invariably asks if everything is OK. With a waiter it's perfectly fine to nod, but with a potential colleague, the uncomfortable silence as you chew your cud is embarrassing.

Every once in a while, check your teeth with your tongue. You will not be able to detect small particles between your teeth, but you'll be able to tell if you have a spinach leaf completely covering a front tooth. We've all been in that uncomfortable position of trying to focus on the conversation, only to be distracted by the remnants of our companion's meal front-and-center. When you get done eating, go to the bathroom and make sure your teeth are clear for the rest of the afternoon or night. Also, pop in that breath mint!

As the guest of honor, you will be asked to order first. That's OK, but don't be the first to order wine. If you like wine with your meal, check to see if others will be drinking too, then partake, but limit yourself to just one glass. If you don't drink, decline. No need to explain why. Same with dessert; don't order unless they do.

And finally, the obvious: 1) Don't talk with your mouth full. This is common knowledge, but I am amazed some people still do it. It is so unsightly for the person sitting in front of you. 2) No loud burps, but if one slips out, say "excuse me" and move on. 3) Don't lick your fingers. Use your napkin that, by the way, belongs in your lap the moment you sit down.

Interviews

Usually you have the teaching demo the first day, and then individual or small group interviews interrupted by meals, followed by the job talk. Sometimes the job talk is the following day. A few things to consider:

- By law, no interviewer should ask you about your marital status, children, or religious affiliation, but it happens. Someone will "mistakenly" let slip this question. Other interviewers might ask you about those topics bluntly and straight out. The questions are both illegal and unfair. For example, let's say you are female and you say you have children or plan to have them soon. That may put you at a disadvantage, but not answering this question could antagonize the interviewer. What to do? A professor friend of mine suggested smiling and jokingly "scolding" the interviewer by saying "Naughty, naughty, you are not supposed to ask that." Or you might say something like "and for whatever reason would you ask that?"—again followed by a big smile. Unfortunately, discrimination continues to this very day. Recently, one of my grad students was asked this type of question, answered truthfully (that she was married and pregnant at the moment), and was not offered a job. But that could have been a blessing in disguise. Ask yourself if you want to work in a place with such discriminatory policies.

- Remember to pack small breath mints and pop one in especially after a meal and before you have to talk to anyone up close.

- Smile. Be on your best behavior with everyone you meet whether they have a say in your hire or not. You never know who could influence the outcome of your visit (and besides, it's just good karma to be nice to everybody).

- Campus interviews can be exhausting. If you have more than one campus interview, if you can help it, don't schedule them back-to-back.

Talking to the Dean

During your visit, you will be talking individually to professors and graduate students, giving a teaching demo, visiting the town or city with a real estate agent, meeting with the chair of the department, and most likely also meeting with the school's academic dean. What do you say to the dean? Be careful: this is not the meeting to negotiate salary—you only do that when you have an offer in writing.

I have heard good things and bad things about talking to the dean.

The good: After so many meetings, some candidates may be relieved to see that the dean is the one doing most of the talking. She or he will talk about the compensation package of the job—things like benefits, retirement plans, general policies about reviews for tenure, raises associated with promotions, and campus life.

The bad: The dean will talk about budgetary issues, the sources of grant money you will be expected to seek, funds available (or not) for your research, money available (or not) to travel to conferences, the effects of teaching large classes—that kind of thing.

The not too ugly (because you will be prepared): Some deans will test you about your expertise in your field. So you must be prepared to speak in general terms about current issues and challenges in your field or where you think the profession might be headed in the next five to ten years, and why. Other questions might be thrown at you, for example, your take on a text that has been published lately, and why it is important.

After the Ordeal

Send a thank-you letter within two days of the campus interview. It is also appropriate in this letter to ask for the time frame of the decision-making process.

Once you get a written offer, it is appropriate to contact the other universities you have interviewed with, informing them that you are giving yourself ten working days to make a decision, and that you still would like to be considered for a position in their institution. This will allow you to make a better decision as it may get the second school to commit earlier, and might even give you leverage as you negotiate salary, research and travel funds, and workloads.

Summary Questions

1. What paperwork must be completed before applying to a job?

_____

_____

2. What three major activities do you have to prepare for before you get on campus?

_____

_____

3. What three things do you think you personally need to attend to in order to give a polished appearance?

_____

_____

Scenarios

Scenario 1

You were advised to take a "carry-on" several times, but you decide to check your luggage because you are also visiting relatives who live near the school, and some of their gifts can't get through security. As luck would have it, your luggage did not arrive with you. You are wearing decent clothing at your arrival: a nice sweater, a tie, nice slacks, and shoes. The faculty member who picked you up at the airport understands your predicament and is sympathetic. You are told your luggage will arrive the next day, but you know you can't pick it up since you don't have a car and your day has a full agenda at the university. Other than carry on your luggage, what could you have done to have prevented this inconvenience? What would you do the day of the interview to pick up your luggage? What could you do about being underdressed?

_____

_____

Scenario 2

You have several interviews at the MLA. You are confident and well prepared for most of the most common questions. Everything is going well until one of the interviewers asks you an illegal personal question that throws you off: "If you have children, won't your family life get in the way of your professional life?" You don't want to antagonize the interviewer, but you don't want to answer either. What do you do?

_____

_____

15 • Hitting the Job Market
Getting a Job at a High School

DENISE MINOR

The moment has arrived for you to marshal your efforts and begin the very important step of launching your job search. Allow me to begin by offering three pieces of advice: start working on your curriculum vitae (CV) *tonight*, begin breaking in a new pair of leather shoes for your interviews, and start thinking about the possibility of taking a job farther away from home than you previously considered viable. These three recommendations are simply the tip of the iceberg when it comes to stepping into the secondary education market, but they are also symbolic of three processes that you must begin as you transition into becoming a professional.

First of all, you are most likely to make a good impression if you are good at boiling down your experience, education, and opinions to their essence both in succinct writing, as you will do with your CV, and in speaking, as you will do during your interview. Second, you must turn your attention to your appearance and begin dressing like a professional when the need arises. The beat-up athletic shoes, tousled hair, and shirts that show off your tattoos might look very hip on campus, but they could make a bad impression on a high school principal. And third, for your own long-term financial and professional well-being, you must consider applying for and accepting jobs far from the place you now call home.

I will discuss many other essential steps and recommendations in this chapter as well, but they all follow naturally from those three points. The

316

Last day of college

Morning of the job interview

advice listed here has come from numerous sources, including counselors, a former principal and superintendent, and new teachers who have recently gotten jobs. Principal among these sources is career advisor Kate Buckley of California State University, Chico, whose sound advice permeates almost every section of this chapter.

PLACEMENT FILE

All states have websites that list teaching positions. For each state in which you wish to apply for jobs, you must establish an electronic placement file that will contain information about you such as a profile, a list of references, and your teaching license or credential. Within that file you will create what is often known as your "electronic library," which will include, in order of importance, your curriculum vitae, a cover letter, and letters of recommendation. In order to get your foot in the door for an interview, it is essential that you make this "library" as professional as possible. Most importantly: it must be free of grammatical and spelling errors. Do not rely on a spell-checker. Do have a counselor or English teacher edit it. One career counselor told me that a student had mistakenly written in his CV that he was a "stalker," when in fact he had been a stocker for shelves at a large department store. The spell-checker did not catch that problem. Some principals believe that having errors in such important documents is a sign of sloppiness and will toss your application into the circular file on that basis alone. They will not expect perfection once you are on the job, because they know we all make mistakes. They simply expect solid candidates to do what it takes to make these three documents clean and professional.

Curriculum Vitae

Of the three documents, almost all school principals agree that the CV is the most important. It shows them not only your experience but also your ability to condense that experience into a one-page document that is easy to absorb. "Principals know that you did more than three bullet points of work in your life. They want to see how you choose which of your work experiences to put on the CV and how you frame those experiences," said Buckley. "It's an example for them of your writing abilities."

Nobody expects you to have much teaching experience because you are just now finishing your credential or licensing process. But they do expect to see other work experience and a synopsis of how that experience will contribute to your ability to be both a teacher and a stable employee. Were you a cocktail waitress for three years? Highlight the fact that you were able to remain cool and professional in handling numerous clients during six-hour shifts. Were you a lifeguard every summer at a community pool for six years? Highlight your safety training and your ability to interact well with children at the pool.

Because many future teachers know that the CV is extremely important, they have a tendency to think about it for months but do nothing about it until the last minute. That is a big mistake, because a good CV usually takes months to polish. If sitting down to try to boil your entire life down to one page is too daunting, start tonight with simply the outline. You can find an example at the end of this chapter plus other examples on the Internet. Put your name and address at the top and then create sections such as

1. Education
2. Goals
3. Work Experience
4. Awards
5. Community Service and Volunteer Experience
6. Interests

These sections can vary, depending on what you want to highlight. For now, simply concentrate on the sections, the fonts, and the design. Move forward a little at a time, each day sitting down to add a few things. Don't worry if the document runs over one page for now. After you have put everything on the CV that might be important, you will begin the process of choosing which points stay and which points get deleted or combined.

When you have a working draft, make an appointment with a career counselor or professional educator to look over your CV, correct your spelling, and make suggestions. Once you have taken that advice into account, show it to colleagues in your program and ask to have a look at their CVs. You will get great ideas from one another.

Letters of Recommendation

As you are in the process of polishing your CV, you must begin making contacts with the cooperating teachers and supervising faculty that will write your letters of recommendation. Even though these letters are third in importance on the "library" list, you have to start asking for them as soon as possible because some professors and teachers might take months to get around to them. Unlike letters for graduate school or jobs in higher education, letters of recommendation for secondary teaching positions are not confidential, and you will get to read them, which is probably one of the reasons that they are not considered as important by principals as the other documents. You will only need two, but you should ask as many people as you can for letters because it will give you some breathing room. For one thing, some well-intentioned, hard-working people are terrible at getting around to writing letters of recommendation. They either don't do it or they get them to you late. Then, too, some people are not good letter writers or will not write the kind of recommendation that you had hoped for. It will be best if you have options in choosing which letters to place in your file.

You might consider asking professionals such as your former professors to observe you teach (if your mentor teacher and school permit this), letting them know in advance that you both want their input and would like a letter of recommendation. Ask all of your references to print two original, dated and signed recommendations on letterhead stationery, and tell them that you will pick them up.

Cover Letter

As you are applying the last bit of polish and shine to your CV and waiting for your letters of recommendation, it is time to turn your attention to your cover letter. "Let this letter be your voice," advised Buckley. "You should convey your passion for teaching and your excitement, as you would in a conversation."

Remember, this letter that you write yourself is more important than the letters of recommendation. Use it to show a principal or a hiring panel that you love the subject you will be teaching, that teaching is your "calling," and that you care very much about young people. Also, just as you did with your CV, you must think about being concise. Don't repeat the same idea over again using different language, but rather push further into specifics and details that *show* rather than just tell your main points. For instance, you might describe the moment when, as a student teacher, you stood back and listened to the excellent interaction among pairs in the classroom as students designed their dream houses, and you felt more certain than ever that this was your chosen profession.

After you have finished all three of these documents, save them or scan them as PDF files and download them into your placement file in each of the states where you will consider taking employment. (More on looking for work in other states later in the chapter.)

MOCK INTERVIEWS

After you have created a "perfect" CV and written an engaging, well-crafted cover letter, it is time to further hone those skills of synthesizing your knowledge and experience in the verbal area. You must practice engaging in job interviews. I recommend that you first do mock interviews with classmates from your program. In this way you will begin in a less stressful environment and will get ideas from one another. Then you should contact a job counselor or attend an education job fair where you will practice interviewing with professionals. The more practice the better, because different principals have different interview styles.

Below is a list of typical interview questions, divided into four different topics. Most of them are the type of general questions that principals or interview panels will ask all candidates for job openings in a variety of subject matters, but I have included a few that are specific to languages. The interview will be in English, so you must practice first in English. But sometimes the principal will speak the language you teach, a teacher from your language area will come to the interview, or there will be another person on the interview panel to ask you questions in the language you teach to test your oral proficiency. Those questions will almost certainly come from the Curriculum / Subject Knowledge section below, so it is a safe bet to prepare those in your target language.

Curriculum / Subject Knowledge

- If you were hired to teach starting this September, what are the first materials you would begin to prepare for teaching the beginning level?

- What textbooks do you have experience with? What do you like or dislike about them?

- What does individualized teaching mean to you?

- How can you tell students are learning to understand German (French, Chinese, Spanish, etc.)? How can you tell that they are learning to communicate? Describe some evaluation techniques.

- What are some of the language teaching methodologies that you use?

- Name some ways that a student working in a group can show you he or she can communicate in German (French, Chinese, Spanish, etc.) or has understood a concept.

- In which curriculum area do you feel particularly strong?

- What goals do you hope to achieve in your subject for this school?

- How would you incorporate students of different levels or heritage speakers into the same class?

- If you were asked to get in-service experience in one area of the curriculum, which area would you choose?

- What are the various ways you would present new material to a class?

- Describe what diagnostic and proscriptive learning means.

Classroom Management

- How would you go about setting standards at the beginning of the year?

- How do you get students to do what you want them to do? Describe your system of classroom management.

- How do you get students to develop self-discipline? Can this ability be taught?

- Who should be responsible for the discipline in the school?

- If you have a student disrupting your classroom, what steps would you take to solve this problem?

- What is your attitude toward individual vs. total class punishment?

- Compare negative and positive reinforcement and describe some effects of each.

- Describe a high school student at a grade level of your choosing—his or her personality, study habits, or attitude toward learning and behavior characteristics.

- What steps would you take to get a student who has been tardy to be more punctual?

- What would I expect to see in your classroom's physical environment? Describe the way you would set up your classroom.

Parent Relations / Communications

- Describe some ways you can inform parents of what is going on in your classroom.

- Tell me some ways you would involve parents in your classroom.

- How do you let parents know the progress of their child?

- In your opinion, how effective are parent conferences in solving student problems?

- Imagine that you replace a teacher during the middle of the year. Describe how you would become acquainted with parents and students.

- What would you tell a parent who complained about his or her child not having enough homework or having too much homework?

Personality / Personal Attitudes / Professionalism

- Describe an "ideal" teacher.

- Why do you want to teach in our school district?

- What is wrong with education today? What is right?

- What do you expect from the school principal, psychologist, and superintendent?

- Describe what your closest teaching associate would say about your getting along with adults? With teenagers?

- What are the greatest teaching strengths you would bring to a teaching position?

- Why should you be selected for this position rather than someone else?

- What were you hoping we would ask you but didn't?

- What talents do you bring to this position?

- If your friend was describing you, what three adjectives / descriptive phrases would he or she use to describe you both personally and professionally?

- What do you believe is the major purpose of teacher evaluation?

- What are some personality characteristics you find unbearable in people?

- You have heard students complaining constantly about another teacher. What would you do?

JOB SEARCH AND NETWORKING

Education Job Fairs

The best way to find out about teaching jobs in your region is to attend an educational job fair. Most of these job fairs are sponsored in the spring by universities with large teaching credential or license programs. If the university where you are receiving training does not have a fair, ask a counselor for recommendations or visit the websites for other universities in your state. A typical fair will involve a CV/résumé workshop, mock job interviews, panel presentations by superintendents and principals, and a luncheon with the same panel presenters.

Arrive for the job fair well-prepared, well-dressed, and with copies of your CV. You can be assured that the principals in attendance are on the lookout for teachers to fill open positions at their schools, and those "mock" interviews are in truth preliminary interviews. In fact, some principals choose all the candidates to be considered from the teachers-in-training that they meet at the job fairs.

Employment Websites

Even before your placement files are ready, you should be keeping your eye on the state websites that list job openings. Most of them list jobs not only by specialty but also by region. If you learn of a position that interests you in a school not far from where you live, make an appointment and go visit. "Eighty percent of principals we surveyed said they are very open to visits from interested teachers," noted Buckley. "It's a great way to get to know more about the school and to make a first impression on a principal. The pressure is off, because you're just going in for a discussion."

Another advantage to visiting a school that interests you is that, even if you don't get a job there, it could lead to a connection at a school where you could get a job. Every principal that you talk to might not have a job available, but they probably know somebody that does.

Regular Contact with Other Teachers

Keep in contact with friends you have made who have gone into teaching. One of my former students here in California got word from an old buddy who taught at a middle school in Colorado that there was a Spanish teaching position opening up at his school. My student contacted the principal, sent her his file, and had a telephone interview. He was eventually offered the job. That student's story reinforced for me an awareness that had been growing over the past few years: beginning teachers must consider leaving their region in order to maximize both their prospects of getting a job and also their earning potential. There is a trend I have seen over and over of students graduating with good credentials but being unwilling to move. Some would prefer becoming long-term substitute teachers to leaving their hometowns. On the one hand, it seems logical that a person interested in becoming a teacher would be of the personality type that would be closely tied to his or her community. But if you don't open yourself up to the possibility of leaving, you will be competing with all the other teachers coming out of the credential or license program at your university. You also might be starting at a salary much lower than you would receive elsewhere. In California, for instance, the difference between the highest beginning teacher salary (Mountain View—Los Altos Union School District) and the lowest (various districts) in 2010 was about $32,000. That difference is not typical, but a $10,000 annual difference between neighboring school districts is very common. You can check out these figures at the California Department of Education website (http://www.cde.ca.gov/index.asp); most states similarly publish the beginning, average, and highest salaries of their teachers and administrators on their respective department of education webpages. Do your homework on this issue. Knowing who pays what is an extremely important factor to consider as you make choices in your job search.

Finally, you are closing yourself off to new experiences if you are unwilling to move. If you have been educated in Michigan, why not try living in Florida and learning about a place where many of the residents are of Caribbean origin and people spend New Year's Day on the beach? If you have been educated in a Northern California town, why not try living in an East Coast city with a vibrant theater district and thousands of excellent ethnic restaurants? Remember—you can always go back and your life will be richer for having had the experience of teaching young people in a different part of the country.

Other States

The training and certification process of secondary teachers varies greatly, so if you are willing to move you will have to find out if there is a "reciprocity" agreement between the state where you have been educated and the state where you want to work. Even if there is an agreement, you will still need to go through the steps of applying for a license or credential from that state. Often there is at least one additional step, such as passing an exam that demonstrates knowledge about your new state's history and constitution.

There are two basic systems of training teachers in the United States: either you receive your teacher training as part of your bachelor's degree, or you receive it in a program that typically lasts one year beyond an undergraduate education. Different states have different names for the qualification authorization, but most are called teaching credentials, teaching licenses, or teaching certificates. In the first system, students decide as undergraduates that they want to become teachers, so they enter a program that requires both education classes and upper division courses in their specialty. Often the requirement is about eight upper division courses in the target language. Student teaching is completed during the senior year. As students near the completion of their BS or BA, they must pass a battery of standardized tests to demonstrate writing proficiency in their subject matter, knowledge in the field of education, basic math abilities, and English writing proficiency. Upon receiving their degree and passing the tests, they apply for a teaching license/credential/certificate from the state.

In the second type of system, a student completes a bachelor's degree in the language he or she plans to teach. As is the case with the first system, people who plan to be teachers must pass a series of tests to prove proficiency in their subject matter, math abilities, and English abilities. Often there is also a series of extra prerequisite classes in education that students must then take before continuing. With their degree in hand, and with the extra prerequisite classes and the results of their standardized tests, future teachers then apply to a credential/certificate/license program. If they are accepted, they receive one year of instruction in education classes and work during that year as a student teacher under a credentialed mentor. Upon finishing their program, they apply for a teaching credential/license/certificate from their state.

Some of the states whose credentials/licenses/certificates are recognized by most other states are California, Texas, Florida, and North Carolina. If you complete your education in a state whose programs are not recognized by the state where you hope to live, you might need to move there and get at least one extra year of training.

THE INTERVIEW

Unlike jobs in higher education, you will most likely have to finance your own travel expenses for interviews. If you plan to cast your net far and wide in this process, you should begin now to budget for this expense. The time you spend at the school site will probably be just a morning or an afternoon, long enough for an interview, a tour of the school, and (possibly) a teaching demonstration. There are three areas in which you must prepare yourself for the interview: your appearance, the interview itself, and the teaching demonstration.

Exactly who will conduct the interview can vary greatly. Some districts are assured of the funding for a position in the spring, and in that case it is more likely there will be an interview panel. I have heard of interview panels made up of teachers, a parent, and the principal. Other times, districts must wait until just days before classes start in the fall to make sure they have funding to hire someone new, and in those cases the interview is usually conducted only by the principal. Find out before you go what the situation will be for you and whether you will be interviewed in both languages. You will perform better if you know what to expect.

Appearance

I will state the obvious: you want to look your best for an interview. I will also state the difficult: you might increase your chances of being the winning candidate if you make some changes to your hair, your makeup, and the type of clothes you wear on that very important day. I am not advocating that you fake anything, but I want to remind you that we all change over time (check out your photos from high school!), and this might be the right time to start evolving your own professional style. Most young people on university college campuses look exactly like what they are—college students—and you might be no exception. That is a good thing. We all display our identity through choices we make about our appearance. But if we want to be successful in a new environment, we often have to make changes, at least for that eight-to-three shift Mondays through Fridays.

If you are a man who sports long, unruly hair and a constant five-day growth on your face, consider cutting your hair and shaving. If you are a woman with long, straightened locks, consider cutting your hair, at least a little. Shorter hair will make you look older and more professional. If you have more piercings than just one in each earlobe, consider removing the extra jewelry. If you have tattoos, cover them. If you are a woman and usually wear thick eyeliner and dark eyebrow pencil, use a much lighter touch when you pull out your makeup kit the morning of the interview.

Remember that if a principal has narrowed a job search down to two highly qualified applicants including you, her final choice might come down to which person presents a more professional appearance. Her decision will probably not be based just on what she herself thinks of piercings and a youthful hairstyle, but also on the first impression she believes you will make on parents and students. She wants a person who looks like a teacher standing in front of those classes, not a person who might be confused for one of the twelfth graders.

As for clothing specifics, the typical "dress code" for a junior high or high school interview is business casual. For women, dress pants, a skirt, or a dress is appropriate. For men, dress slacks or khakis, a button-down shirt, and a tie are good basics. Everything that could display a wrinkle must be ironed. For both genders, comfortable leather shoes are a must, but do not choose athletic shoes or high heels.

The Interview Itself

You have prepared for this interview and you have all the necessary qualifications to do this job. Even if you are nervous or you make a mistake in a response, the interview will almost certainly go well if you follow the guidelines below.

1. Before the interview begins, do a reflective inventory of your unique abilities and your core values. When opportunities arise you

will emphasize these points, although once they have been said they don't need to be repeated. For instance, if one of your dreams is to create classrooms where the needs of both heritage speakers and second language learners are addressed equally, say it. If you feel very passionate about the reduction of bullying in schools and have had training in recognizing the subtle signs of bullying and intervention techniques, say it. These things might be in your cover letter or your CV, but a verbal reminder is helpful.

2. If you have the tendency to fidget, put away all fidget material such as pens and notebooks. You can simply clasp your hands together in your lap.

3. Take a deep breath and smile when you enter the room. If you entered the room separately from the principal or the panel, shake their hands. If you are good at small talk, you might make a pleasant comment about the school or town. If you are very nervous, it will be fine if you sit quietly until the questions begin.

4. When you begin to answer a question, reflect for just a moment on the skills you have practiced in condensing your ideas and experience. Decide where you are going with your answer as if you were spotting a point on the horizon, then head for that point in as linear a fashion as possible. Don't repeat yourself and don't meander. If the question provides an opportunity to segue into your core values and skills, do so briefly.

5. If you are asked a question and your mind goes blank, simply ask, "Would you mind repeating that question? I'm a little nervous and am not thinking as clearly as usual." In this way you are showing the principal or the panel a few things. First of all, they can see that you are willing to get clarification about something before responding rather than guessing and rambling on with a decontextualized answer. Secondly, you show them how you gather yourself in moments of stress. Thirdly, you are showing them that you are honestly nervous, which is something they expect. One principal said that if a candidate was not nervous, it was a red flag to him that the person was overconfident.

6. At the end of the interview, if you have not been asked a question that you had hoped would be asked, use the moment to offer the information you had planned to tell them. The best way to do this is by first asking the principal or committee a question and then,

if appropriate, giving them that information. For instance, if you saw no evidence of a French club on the school website or in your tour of the school, you could ask if a French club exists and what its activities entail. If it doesn't exist, you could express your interest in starting a club. If it does exist, you could offer to add to the parameters of club activities. For example, if you also have journalism experience, you could offer to help students create a French newsletter.

7. If you are asked whether or not you have any questions, you must ask something. Have at least three ready based on the investigation you have done of the school. Choose the one that seems most appropriate given the direction that the interview has taken. Examples might include questions about the ethnic backgrounds of the student population or the areas of greatest need for faculty involvement.

8. When you get home, send a thank-you card.

Teaching Demonstration

From the counselors that I have spoken with, teaching demonstrations for secondary positions are becoming less common, particularly in large districts. However, some districts rely heavily on the demonstration in making their decision. "I would never, ever hire a language teacher without seeing them teach," said Holly Johnson, the former foreign language coordinator for the Clark County School District of Nevada, the district that contains Las Vegas. "It's not just an issue of oral proficiency. Some candidates can talk a really good game, but it's not the same as teaching. You need to see them operate."

Whatever the case, it is still a good idea to have a general demonstration for a beginning level class ready to go in case you are called for an impromptu interview. You probably have plenty in your files from your student teaching. However, I recommend that, if you are given sufficient notice, you tailor your demonstration specifically to the school where you are applying, the textbook that they use, and the audience that you will be teaching to.

If you are told that your teaching demonstration will be for the hiring panel, they will most likely expect the presentation to be beginning level because there will probably be at least one person on the panel who does not speak the language. In that case, a safe bet would be to use the First Day of Class plan described in Chapter 1. If you are told that your teaching demonstration will be in front of a class of students, send an e-mail to the teacher whose class you will teach. Ask which textbook he uses and where they are in the book. Also, ask some general questions about his teaching style and about some of the noticeable characteristics of the class. Your main goal with these questions is to find out if the teacher employs the methodology you have been schooled in (i.e., input in the target language, the communicative approach) or if he teaches in English and uses the grammar-translation method. Your audience might be students accustomed to hearing and engaging in the target language, or it might be a group that stares at you blankly as you talk. You should be prepared for both situations, but it is good to have an idea of what to expect.

Try to find a copy of the textbook, but if you can't find one, e-mail the teacher and ask for some general parameters of what the students are studying at that moment, such as food, clothing, or talking about the past. Your demonstration will go much better if it is based on something familiar to the class. Study the material that they are being currently taught and what they just learned over the past two weeks. You will take that material and create an engaging activity. The key to a winning teaching demonstration is NOT teaching the students something new but rather showing how well you can interact with young people in the language they are learning. You will show that best if they are somewhat familiar with the material.

When you step into the classroom, introduce yourself and then immediately start asking students their names. Go down the aisles and shake hands with a few of them. This is your chance to probe their level. For instance, if you ask a young woman her name and she responds, you might ask her a few simple questions, such as what other classes she takes. If she doesn't understand, you could repeat her name and say something like, "That is such a beautiful name. I like it." Move on. Continue to probe their comprehension level with three or four more students. If this type of seat-of-the pants interaction with a group of students makes you too nervous, stick with simply asking their names and shaking hands.

Next, step back to the front of the class to begin your story. KEEP IT SIMPLE. The fewer number of variables there are, the less likelihood that something will go wrong. You will use visuals (whether from a PowerPoint, photos, or objects that you take), and you will use plenty of cognates which will facilitate understanding for those who either aren't used to hearing the language or those who have a hard time understanding your accent. But if you found in your introductions that the average level of comprehension was quite good, push beyond the cognates to give additional information, and watch for their reactions. Do some occasional comprehension checks to help guide you as your presentation unfolds. For instance, if the class recently learned about clothing, you could tell a story about the recent reunion of your eccentric family and the things that each of your relatives wore. If students haven't yet learned to communicate about the past, describe a typical family reunion. It is easy to find photos of outlandishly dressed people on the Internet.

Afterwards, have the students play a guessing game in which they describe the way a person in the class is dressed, and their partner has to guess who the person is. If your reading of the class is that they are not used to standing up and moving around, you could keep them in pairs to do this activity. But if the "energy" is high, have them stand up and circulate to take turns engaging in the activity with different people. Play the game with them and do things like describing yourself and/or their teacher. Watch closely to spot a couple of extroverts. When the activity is finished, ask two or three of the extroverts to stand up and describe a person's clothing, and have the entire class guess who they are talking about. For other ideas consult the first section of this book. One final note: if some of the students speak only English you can encourage them to use the target language, but don't push too hard. Just keep speaking the target language. This isn't the place for you to display your behavior modification techniques. The key point you want to communicate is that you interact well in this target language with these young people.

BEFORE CHOOSING A JOB

The guidelines provided in this chapter should help you get that coveted job offer, and if you have played your cards right, you will get more than one. If that is the case, you will undoubtedly have to weigh numerous factors in making your decision, such as salary, region, your family, and the type of job. But there is one factor that new teachers often don't give enough credence, and I want to encourage you to move this consideration to the top of your list. Place your estimation of the school principal near the top of factors to consider.

There are few things that will impact the quality of your work (let alone your life!) as much as the abilities and fairness of the principal. The school where you are applying to work might have ocean views, salaries at the top of the scale, or be in a town with great schools for your children. But if your principal is ill-tempered, capricious, or unsupportive, you will suffer. My entire working life I have had really good supervisors or chairs, so I was oblivious to how important this was. However, the stories I have heard while conducting interviews for this chapter have made my jaw drop. From these I have come up with what I consider to be the two most important qualities that you should look for in a principal or department chair.

First, the person should be someone who fosters a feeling of community at the school or in the department. Earlier in this book we have written about the importance of fostering a positive feeling of community in your classroom, a place where students are allowed to shine for their strengths and where each one feels that he or she is valued. You want to work for someone who can do that same thing for a department or a school. One teacher told me about the amazing way her boss was able to make all the temperamental egos in her school feel "special." On the other end of the spectrum, I heard from a school counselor about a principal who regularly gossiped about both his teachers and students and even pitted them against each other. These were two very different work environments.

How will you know about this issue with the limited amount of time you spend on campus for an interview? At the risk of sounding very Californian, I will say, "Pay attention to the vibe." There are numerous tiny messages that our subconscious can pick up on from the facial expressions, body language, and voice tone of people when they interact. Do the relationships seem friendly and positive? Do some of the students light up, wave, and yell, "Hi, Mr. Patel!" when they walk down the hall? Good sign. Do the other teachers look directly into the eyes of the principal and smile when they cross paths? Another good sign. It might be hard to concentrate on this issue when you are very nervous about the impression you are making, but try to do so because it is important.

And second, the person should be someone with a logical and fair leadership style. The impact of having a principal with a balanced leadership approach will affect you in a number of ways. To begin with, a fair supervisor is cognizant of the difficulties you face as a new person in the profession and will not burden you with an unreasonable share of service responsibilities or extra work. I have heard a number of stories from teachers and professors who thought they were given an inordinate amount of service work to do and felt they couldn't complain because they wanted tenure.

In addition, it is very important that your principal be an advocate for all of his or her faculty, both with the administration and with the students and parents. If a parent comes to the principal's office in a rage because her son maintains that you "wrote him up" unfairly, you do not want a boss who calls you to the office to defend yourself in front of the angry mother. If it is necessary, a meeting can be set up after she cools down. If a student goes to the principal to complain about the fairness of your exams, you do not want a supervisor who sits you down with that student to have the three of you go over an exam. That puts the student in a very powerful position that will undermine your authority with him and, most likely, with the class. You DO want a supervisor who steps up to your defense in meetings if your name is brought up in a critical manner and you are not in attendance. You DO want a principal who listens to a complaint about you, takes notes, and says, "I'll get back to you." If he or she speaks in your favor before saying "I'll get back to you," all the better. In addition, the quality of your work life will be greatly improved if your principal is the kind of leader who, when he or she does bring up a complaint with you *in person*, does so in a very respectful manner.

Again, how will you know this from such a short visit? For one thing, you can judge by what the other teachers and staff say. There is a palpable loyalty that I have observed at schools where those working there have been treated fairly and supported by their principal. They say things out loud such as, "I always feel like she's got my back."

You can also ask questions to learn more. Don't ask, "Is Ms. Ramirez the kind of principal that criticizes some teachers to other teachers?" But you can ask, "What are some of the challenges that teachers face in this school?" Maybe you will hear only stories about budget cuts, but you also might hear about conflicts and how the principal has handled them. Another possibility would be to investigate if the principal has received some kind of recognition for leadership. Did the PTA come together with teachers to thank the principal for all of her hard work and create a plaque for her? That is a good sign. This is the kind of thing that is easy to find out because people like talking about it. You might say to a teacher or staff person, "It sounds like this is a good place to work. Has there been any kind of official recognition of this?"

Important reminder: Principals don't keep their jobs forever. Before placing importance on this issue, find out if he or she is PROBABLY going to return next year.

As you finish up the program that is preparing you to become a teacher, start thinking of yourself as a professional—it will impact the way you behave and present yourself. Begin work as soon as possible on your curriculum vitae, and get feedback from professionals. Ask for double the necessary number of letters of recommendation from your mentor teachers and professors, and begin to craft a cover letter that captures your voice and personality. In the meantime, begin looking for appropriate clothing and shoes for the interviews.

The best place to both find out about open teaching jobs and to network with principals and superintendents is at an education jobs fair at a university that offers teaching credentials, licenses, or certificates. You should also regularly check the education department website of all the states where you are willing to apply for work. Keep in contact with friends from your department who have graduated and are now teachers, because they will have their ears to the ground about new jobs.

Lastly, prepare well for the job interview and teaching demonstration. Do as many mock interviews as you have time for in both English and the target language. If you have time, prepare a teaching demonstration that is grounded in the material that the class you will teach is studying at the moment. However, if you will give your demonstration to a panel, stick with a beginning level plan such as the one presented in this book.

Good luck!

Summary Questions

1. In order of importance, what are the three documents that make up your placement file? Name one important factor to remember about each of these documents.

_____

_____

_____

2. What are the four areas that usually make up the sections of a job interview? Name at least one important factor to remember as you frame your answers.

_____

_____

3. How will you find out about open teaching jobs in your region? How will you find out about open teaching jobs in other states?

_____

_____

4. Name the two basic kinds of secondary teacher training available in the United States.

_____

_____

Scenarios

Scenario 1

You have arrived for an interview as a language teacher at a high school with a hiring panel of two teachers, two parents, and the principal. You were told ahead of time that the interview would be in both English and the language you teach. The interview goes well until the principal switches to the target language. She seems proud of her ability to speak but has a heavy English accent. It sounds to you like she has asked, "What is your hope for the horses when you learn to speak?" How will you handle the situation?

_____

_____

Scenario 2

In two weeks you have a job interview followed by a teaching demonstration. The classroom where you will give your demonstration is a second-year language class, and they have been learning to communicate about future plans. You have not been able to find the textbook but the teacher told you that vocabulary for the current chapter includes vacations and travel. Prepare a fifteen- to twenty-minute demonstration.

_____

_____

Elias Maestro

elmaestro@hotmail.com

210 C Street, Chico, CA 95973 Phone: 530–824-####

EDUCATION

California State University, Chico	Chico, CA
Single Subject Credential: BCLAD	May, 2012
GPA: 4.0	

California State University, Chico	Chico, CA
BA in Spanish and BA in Latin American Studies	May, 2011
GPA: 3.4	

Cosumnes Community College	Sacramento, CA
AA in Social and Behavioral Sciences	May, 2009

CERTIFICATIONS: CBEST (2011), CSET (2011), CPR (2010)

TEACHING EXPERIENCE

Directed Teaching—Spanish 1	3/2012–5/2012
Cesar Chavez High School	Chico, CA

- Planned and taught units focused upon weather, vacations, and past tense conjugations. Assessed students with two chapter tests that included grammar, vocabulary, reading comprehension, and listening comprehension.

Spanish Tutor—Level 3	8/2009–5/2011
California State University, Chico	Chico, CA
Student Learning Center	

- Tutored Spanish students in grammar, spelling, essay writing, listening comprehension, and reading comprehension. Worked with small groups to prepare for exams.

OTHER WORK EXPERIENCE

Merchandiser / Team Lead Merchandiser	2007–2009
Clancy's Department Store	Sacramento, CA

- Began as part-time merchandiser replenishing stock in all departments. After six months became full-time team leader overseeing five part-time associates in replenishing stock.

SPECIAL SKILLS: Bilingual Spanish/English; Microsoft Word; Excel; Power-Point

INTERESTS: Soccer, foreign films, and travel

REFERENCES: Available upon request

16 • Surviving the Political Jungle

DENISE MINOR

Congratulations! You landed the position! You are ready to take on this exciting job and show the world what you are made of. But beyond the responsibilities of planning classes, studying the textbook, developing syllabi, starting committee work, and getting to know your students, there is one essential element you should keep in mind as you move into your professional future: politics.

High schools and junior highs do not have the reputation of being difficult places politically (at least not for the adults!), as long as the principal is supportive. Universities, on the other hand, have very bad reputations. The stories I used to hear about department warfare and sexual liaisons before I went into academia made me imagine pulp movies from the 1960s. The movie posters would be large and in dark tones, with characters such as an evil-looking, gray-haired man sneering down on a campus from high in a bell tower. They would have names like "Revenge of the Jilted Adjunct" or "Professors Gone Wild."

But after having been around the block—after teaching at a community college, a research institution, an adult school, and two state universities—I have one thing to say: I'm not buying it. I don't think professors behave any worse (or better) than anybody else. It doesn't matter if they have a PhD or a GED, people behave badly and also behave well, depending on their temperaments and the circumstances. Some work environments are terrible and some are wonderful. It is simply a function of what human beings do in

338

groups, no matter the education or the age. We all have to learn to negotiate the complex social terrain of a workplace, with the exception being that of the lone wolf that owns her own business and has no employees.

In this chapter I am going to give you some advice to help you negotiate the first two years of teaching at the secondary level or at a college or university. My recommendations are informed by my own experience (although those particulars will not be included here), but they come mostly from interviews I have done with teachers, lecturers, and professors over the course of a year. I have met with my participants over cups of coffee, in their classrooms during lunch break, and in hotel lobbies during conferences. I have had very long weekend conversations with professors I went to graduate school with who now live in other parts of the country. From their stories have emerged a few common themes.

GENERAL RECOMMENDATIONS

As I said above, politics can be very different at a high school or junior high school from politics at a college or university. One of the principal differences is the fact that at the secondary level you are teaching juveniles, and their parents are a big part of the picture. If you teach in higher education, you will probably only interact with parents at graduation or other formal occasions. Another difference is the fact that at the college/university level you might be competing with your colleagues for things such as teaching assistants, grants, and administrative responsibilities that provide release time. This can add some extra friction to the mix.

But there are other issues that are very similar at both of these levels, and I will begin with recommendations that are common to everyone. Following that there will be separate sections aimed at high school or junior high school teachers and at college or university professors.

Find a Mentor

Over and over I have heard this recommendation from teachers and professors: find someone a bit further on the professional path than you, someone who can encourage you and give you good advice. You might be assigned a mentor (some institutions have a system for doing this), and if so, you must graciously accept that relationship. Your assigned mentor might be a perfect match, but could just as easily be someone who has a very different teaching philosophy than you do. Or maybe the two of you won't get along that well. Continue to try to foster this relationship, but you might need to develop another as well. I believe that mentoring usually works best when people come together of their own volition. Have you studied Lev Vygotsky's theory of zones of proximal development? Although originally developed to understand the way children learn, I believe that it is an excellent model of how humans of any age become better at what they do because of their interaction with those slightly more advanced. It is true for your students in the classroom and it will be true for you as a teacher.

There are SO many things you can learn from your mentor:

- Teaching techniques

- Classroom management strategies

- How to deal with administration

- Good ways to handle difficult parents, students, or colleagues

- The history behind what appears to be psychological warfare between two co-workers

- How to stay out of the aforementioned war

- Tips for focusing your research and getting published

- A plan for getting tenure and doing well in the evaluation process

Invite your mentor out for coffee on a regular basis, and always pick up the tab.

Watch and Listen

For the first year or two it is advisable to maintain a low profile and simply watch and listen to learn more about the hierarchy, the priorities, and the modes of interaction among your colleagues. You will want to know the ropes before you jump in with opinions or proposals. For instance, a high school teacher with three decades of experience told me that she learned very early that a new person is not supposed to propose new ways of doing things. She clearly recalls her first teaching job when she was in her twenties. At a faculty meeting she proposed changing the way the school dealt with all the junk students left in lockers at the end of the year. She suggested that, on the last day, all teachers could take their students out of class twenty minutes early to empty lockers. "You would have thought I just committed a crime. They were up in arms that I would dare do such a thing," she told me. From that experience she learned that, if you are a newbie and you have a good idea, run it past a few of your superiors before you propose it in public.

Another benefit of the watch-and-listen approach is that some things that you find irritating or illogical will start to make sense. For instance, one young professor told me that after starting his new job he was puzzled by the distracted behavior and off-topic comments often made in meetings by a much older professor. What puzzled him more was the fact that other people at the meeting would respond to the off-topic comments, and the conversation would follow a very unproductive trail for a good chunk of time. In the beginning he found himself staring at the clock and trying to stop his legs from twitching. Over time, my friend heard various stories that made him realize that this older professor had been an excellent teacher for decades and had done considerable work that benefited the department. The new professor also suspected that the senior professor was suffering from hearing loss, although he wasn't certain. He realized that participating in the meandering conversations with this older person was a way that the faculty showed respect.

A community college teacher I interviewed told me that she was at first shocked by the arguments she often heard between two colleagues during department meetings. They clearly showed their anger and often interrupted each other. But after getting to know people in other departments, she came to realize that things could be much worse. Some people who have to work together have very significant disagreements about important issues. Arguing is not necessarily bad, as long as both people use professional language (i.e., they don't swear), don't insult each other, and don't yell. Yes, listening to an argument is difficult, but it is better than working with people who spread gossip about each other, go to war through e-mails sent to the entire department, and undermine each other's work.

Speaking of interrupting, you will probably notice plenty of this in meetings. Linguists study interrupting behavior as a strategy for asserting dominance. Watch how your co-workers deal with this. Do they raise their voices and keep talking until the other person backs down? Do they stare at the table until the other stops, then look up and say calmly, "May I finish?" You will probably be interrupted too, and during the first year you might just want to put up with it. But at some point you will need to assert yourself in a calm and professional way because you don't want to be seen as submissive.

Be Alert to Cultural Differences among Colleagues

Most of us have come through credential programs or graduate programs for the languages we teach. In these programs we don't always have significant interaction in potentially conflictive environments with people from other cultures. But if you start teaching in a department at a high school or university with instructors from Mexico, Japan, Germany, Sudan, and China, you will have to be open-minded about the way people talk and behave. Did you get your ego bruised because one of your co-workers looked you in the eyes at a meeting and said, "You're not being logical"? Maybe that is a perfectly polite way to talk in her homeland. Has a colleague started giving you the cold shoulder and even walks away every time you draw near? Maybe he was insulted by something you said that, in his culture, was an affront.

In both of these situations, it would be very good if you made the effort to bridge the divide, since you are the new kid on the block. In the first case, the person who felt affronted and might behave differently is you. Try to remember that the co-worker who "insulted" you might not have meant the comments as negatively as you took them. Also remember that we all need to grow thicker skins in order to survive workplace politics. Beyond that, you might try to talk to the person individually. Ask her a little bit more about her reasoning and, if the timing seems right, explain your point a little bit more. You might even say something like, "I simply don't want to be thought of as illogical." In the best-case scenario, your point will be better understood and your co-worker will realize that she should be more diplomatic.

The second situation is trickier. You probably want to know if you did or said something offensive, and you'd also like to let your colleague know that your intention was never to insult him. Some people might feel inclined to go to their chair or principal and ask, "Did I do something wrong? I'm really getting the cold shoulder." But chairs and principals usually prefer that people work things out on their own.

My recommendation is to be friendly and try to speak with the person you seem to have insulted. Go ask him or her for advice about something. If the coldness starts to melt, you might ask very directly, "Can I ask you very frankly, did I say something wrong?" In my experience, this direct approach works well. If the coldness does not start to melt and you don't feel that you can broach the subject directly, just keep being friendly. Whatever you did or said could not have been that bad, and he or she will have to let go eventually.

Make Friends with Staff

In every institution I've ever worked in, it has surprised me that administrative staff and teachers/professors appear to work in two different worlds. They can be friendly and get along great, but I never see them going to lunch together or hear of them socializing away from school. There are probably reasons for it that I don't quite understand, but I do know that developing workplace friendships with staff can have a very positive impact on how you feel about your job.

For one thing, it can make your morning much better if each day when you step into the office someone says "Good morning" and really means it. There is something about that positive interaction with the people who take care of the business end of the school that can make you feel connected. For another, the staff has knowledge and connections that you don't. They can stop that form you just filled out in error before it arrives at its destination, can change the room you teach in, and can tell you about funds that just came available for buying supplies.

Never underestimate the power of the people in the office.

Do Not Engage in Gossip

Some departments and schools have entrenched patterns of gossiping. I even heard of a department where criticisms of the physical attributes of students and other professors were considered appropriate workplace conversation. You alone cannot change that pattern, but you can do your best to stay out of it. Maybe you will want to clearly show your disapproval by walking away, but that will undoubtedly antagonize a person that you might end up working with for years. If you don't want to rock the boat you can use a trick I heard from a former colleague from grad school: wear a watch and pretend that you're in a hurry or that you've forgotten something. Pulling out a cell phone to check the time looks a bit contrived. However, if a colleague drops her voice and starts telling you about a humiliating moment for another colleague, it is easy to widen your eyes, look at your watch, and say, "Excuse me! I can't believe I forgot . . . (fill in the blank)."

A language supervisor told me that she tries not to antagonize gossips, in part because she doesn't want to be their next topic of conversation. But she also wants to send them the message that she doesn't want to play that game. "Instead of leaning forward and paying attention to what the person is gossiping about, I get busy and multitask, doing things like reading a student's paper. Then I dismiss the rumor with, 'Oh, that can happen to anybody,' and I change the subject. I don't want to antagonize the gossiper but I do want to send the message that I don't wish to engage in that kind of talk. They get the idea."

It is not simply participation in gossip that you want to avoid, but the hearing of it as well. Some potential friendships and positive working relationships can be ruined by gossip. Imagine you are sitting on a bench in the yard between classes with a colleague, bemoaning the impending finals and chuckling at the latest student fashion craze. You are really enjoying this moment in the sun when you look at her and think, "Is what they said true? Is she really a slacker?" It is best to be able to form your own opinions without those poisonous whisperings banging about in your head.

Another temptation will be to criticize somebody you really don't like to a new friend on the job. Maybe it has become clear to you that your new friend doesn't like this colleague either. But a professor I used to know at a very prestigious university told me that once she criticized a colleague to a person in her department that she considered to be a very good friend. That criticism became public and caused her considerable problems at work. Yes, you will probably see some outrageous behavior, and yes, you will probably make a friend who is equally critical of that behavior. With time, you might come to find that it really relieves tension to occasionally discuss the issue in private. Just be VERY careful about how and when you open your mouth.

Don't Hit "Send" When You're Angry

There have always been workplace conflicts, but they seem to have moved into a new realm since the advent of e-mails. With the touch of the "Send" key, people can now subject their entire department to their bad tempers, misconceptions, prejudices, sarcasms, and piousness. These eruptions and conflicts, and the feelings that spawned them, are natural. They have always happened in places of employment. But what is unnatural is the way they can be spread by e-mail. If humans simply interacted in person or through written correspondence, their words would be tempered by the physical presence of their co-workers or by the hassle of writing, printing, and sending out a memo. Plus, all those extra people who are part of the address list wouldn't get involved.

Be that as it may, you are going to get e-mails that make you really angry. My advice is to either not respond at all, or to wait twenty-four hours before you do, depending on the situation. When someone is really out of line, NOT replying is actually a kind of response, and one that many people respect. If you truly need to write a reply to get it out of your system, write a draft in a document and save it until the next day when you are calmer. The next day, consider pushing "delete." But if you think it is important that you respond, carefully craft your words to make the e-mail as objective and respectful as possible. Also, read through the address list if there is one. Don't include anybody who doesn't need to be part of this exchange.

Prioritize

You cannot do everything perfectly and you will run yourself into the ground if you try. I recommend coming up with a list of your three top priorities and checking in with that list every time you have to make a decision about your time. I truly hope that at least one thing on the list has to do with your new job. You don't need to put them in order, but you simply need to keep your eye on your goals.

Examples:

My family – My students – Getting tenure

My health – My significant other – My research

My students – My spirituality/religion – Getting along with my colleagues

Status in my job – My research – My teaching

Don't show this list to anybody: it's none of their business. But keep it in mind when you are pulled in two directions. For instance, let's say that your priorities are: your students, your family, and making friends at your new job. Let's also say that, since you arrived in town, you have arranged a schedule of picking up your daughter from school on Wednesdays and going to the park to play basketball. It is the best hour of your week. One afternoon the principal asks you to be the faculty advisor for the Model United Nations and the group meets Wednesdays after school. You could say, "Sorry, I play hoops with my kid." However, maybe it would be better to say something like, "I'm sorry. I have another commitment. But I noticed that the Multicultural Club has lots of students and that Julie Tran is the only advisor. Do you think she would like my help as an assistant?" If this works out, you get to keep your basketball time with your daughter, you are supporting extracurricular activities for the students, and maybe you will become friends with Julie Tran. You will be expected to volunteer for service, particularly in your first couple of years. But you can say no if you do it very strategically. Just keep your priorities in sight.

Another reason to keep your top priorities in mind is to constantly check to see if your behavior is in line with your priorities. One new professor told me that when she started her new job she just put her head down and worked like crazy. Two of her top priorities were teaching and getting tenure. She got excellent teaching evaluations, and her service was considered very good because she volunteered for everything. But during her personnel review, senior professors held her feet to the fire and told her, in so many words, "If you don't start getting published, you won't get tenure." Even though she had been working hard, she hadn't been necessarily working hard in the best way to keep her job. It dawned on her that the way she used her time was not necessarily lining up with her priorities. After that, she dropped one committee and set aside time to do research every week. Since teaching was her highest priority, that meant she had to come up with strategies such as sharing lesson plans with colleagues and preparing way in advance.

One final benefit of focusing on priorities is that it can help you be more forgiving. Let's say that one of your top priorities is the students. Let's also say that, after a semester honeymoon at your new job, the bloom is off the rose and there are a couple of people you really don't like. Maybe they are bossy and act superior. But maybe they bring some skills or experience or knowledge to the table that few other people have. Maybe one was educated in China and knows the Chinese writing system well, an achievement very hard to attain. In addition, she does an excellent job teaching writing. Or maybe one colleague was raised by farmworkers and got his bachelor's degree and teaching credential at night school while he worked full-time. And maybe he is an amazing mentor to Chicano students at the school, and helps them transition into community college. If the students are truly your priority, you might try to be more patient with their bad behavior because you see how much good they are doing for the students.

Avoid Doing Battle

But if you MUST go into battle, be respectful and channel Mr. Spock. If you have found a wonderful and supportive place to teach OR you are very skilled at getting along with everyone OR you are very lucky, you might have no political problems with people at work. But most of us come to a point sometime in our working lives where we find ourselves in conflict with somebody else. This could happen for a number of reasons. Maybe you have a legitimate disagreement with a reasonable person. Maybe you are being unreasonable. Maybe you are being treated unfairly.

Whatever the reason for the conflict, you should deal with it in a similar manner—logically, calmly, and with evidence to back yourself up. The way we handle ourselves when we argue with someone will greatly impact both our work environment and our colleagues' opinion of us. Following is some advice I have gathered from three seasoned professionals.

The first comes from a high school teacher with thirty years' experience who advises new teachers to prepare well before engaging in a potentially conflictive interaction: "When you go on the offensive, you must have all your ducks in a row. Then you say, 'Let's have a conference.'"

The second piece of advice comes from a professor at a research institution who told me that whenever she was about to blow her lid at her colleagues' behavior, she tried to imagine herself as Mr. Spock from the 1960s television show *Star Trek*. Spock was extremely logical and did not show any emotions. By "channeling Spock" and entering into disagreements in an objective and courteous way, she felt she was better able to handle her temperamental workmates, and she behaved in a way that, in hindsight, she never regretted.

The last piece of advice comes from a woman who for years was a public school teacher and then, after graduate school, taught at various colleges. "Avoid stepping into the ring. But if you do step in, don't back down," she said. "Stand firm and let them know that you're not weak. If you change your mind and slink away with your tail between your legs, you might get picked on again."

Allow me to expand on this advice by saying: don't pull your colleagues into disagreements. Do not walk down the hall asking, "Did I handle that OK? Do you think everything will be all right?" Just hold your head high and keep on doing your work with as cheerful a demeanor as possible. If you do get into an argument with one person, you need to make it clear that you don't hold on to differences, that you don't drag other people into your conflicts, and that you want to mend fences quickly.

TEACHERS AT JUNIOR HIGH OR HIGH SCHOOL

Respond to Complaints from Parents Immediately

All of the teachers I interviewed said they rarely have problems with parents, but when they do, things can get heated quickly and can become very stressful. These conflicts need to be approached slightly differently from conflicts with colleagues for a couple of reasons.

First of all, parents often behave emotionally because, after all, it's their *baby*. You don't want the emotions to escalate even further, so it will be up to you to try to diffuse that tension. (In contrast, with a colleague it should not necessarily be your responsibility to diffuse tension that you did not create.) By responding immediately you begin to diffuse the tension. Secondly, when parents don't hear right back from you, they have a tendency to contact the principal or the counselor to complain. It is best to try to resolve the situation without going up the ladder. Two teachers whom I respect greatly described their methods of handling angry parents. You will develop your own strategies, but these might be helpful.

The first teacher told me that when he receives a complaining or angry e-mail or phone call, the first thing he does is open a file on his computer where he stores all communication with that parent. Next, he responds with an e-mail acknowledging receipt of the message, assures the parent that he takes the issue seriously, and says that he will contact him again either later in the day or the following day. Sometimes a parent cools down considerably in twenty-four hours.

He then begins to draft a response, and he always does so in a Word document—not his e-mail account—because of one slip of the finger he made a few years ago. He was responding to an irrational e-mail from a parent with an angry tirade of his own (which he had no intention of sending—he just wanted to vent), when he accidently hit "Send" instead of "Save." Whoops! Now he always writes a document that he can later paste into an e-mail, in which he first says anything he wants. Then he goes back to it a few hours or a day later to respond in a professional and succinct way. If the accusation is, in his opinion, inaccurate, he tells the parent why by showing evidence: "I say, 'Have you looked at 1, 2, and 3?'" However, if he believes that he did make a mistake or, after reflecting, is handling something incorrectly, he says that he understands what the parent is saying and will probably handle the situation in a new way. "If I am in the wrong, I fix it," he said. Either way, the teacher offers to meet with the parent and the student.

The second teacher told me that she makes it clear to parents from the beginning that she does not respond to e-mails because she prefers the telephone. "I don't use e-mail," she said. "I need to talk to them, to hear the tone of their voice." The back-and-forth interaction of a conversation also helps clear up miscommunication immediately.

Also important, she found, is to call after five p.m., when parents are more likely to be at home. "If they don't answer, I don't leave any information about the problem in the message. I just tell them I will call them back and that they can leave me a message at my work number."

It should be noted that this teacher has had no substantial conflicts with parents in her fifteen years of teaching. When she does talk to parents it is usually initiated by her, to deal with a problem she has had with the student. She begins the conversation by saying two or three positive things about their son or daughter, then states the "concern" and asks the parent, "What can we do to help Michael?"

UNIVERSITY PROFESSORS AND LECTURERS

Handling Competition within the Department

One inherent difference between teaching at the secondary and postsecondary level is the institutional structure that sometimes puts colleagues in competition with one another for funding, teaching assistants, or administrative positions that come with benefits. For instance, most professors work in language departments where they might have between two and seven majors and twice the number of minors. Since there is one budget for the entire department, there is constantly a push and pull over which classes will get funded. With the cuts to education that have been implemented throughout the country during the last decade, the tensions are growing. "Budget cuts are constantly part of the dialogue," said one professor. "We have to compete with other languages."

Another issue is the competition at some research institutions between linguistics and literature. Many universities that offer graduate degrees offer the option between specializing in linguistics or literature, with research universities offering even more focused specialization. They accept a certain number of applicants into each field, and those students become the teaching assistants for the department. "There is always the juggling over who gets the TA-ships because there is a limited number they can fund. We in linguistics were only allotted two this year, but literature got ten," said one full professor.

A final issue that can drive a wedge between colleagues is competition for administrative positions that offer higher pay or release time from teaching. The position as department chair is the most obvious example, but some departments also pay extra for professors to be in charge of computer laboratories, assessment, or study abroad programs.

How will you deal with these conflicts? You probably will have limited involvement in your first two years. You will simply do your best no matter what decisions are made about class funding, TAs, and administrative positions. But you can learn during this period by watching how others handle themselves and, after two or three years, reflect back on who came out better in the long run. Did the Russian professor move very aggressively to protect her minor at the expense of the Italian minor? Did it work? Or did her minor get cut as well and was she left with a number of enemies? How did things turn out for the professor who stepped back from the responsibility of running the computer laboratory and turned the position (and additional salary) over to a colleague who expressed interest? Did he end up teaching summer school in order to pay for his daughter's college tuition? Or did he end up being appointed associate dean, an appointment spurred in part because of his ability to get along with colleagues? Emulate those that you admire and that are successful.

◊   ◊   ◊

The idea of handling workplace politics can be daunting to new teachers and professors, and possibly some of the suggestions in this chapter did nothing to allay worries you might have. The truth is that it can be very stressful learning the ropes of dealing with your colleagues in the beginning, especially at universities.

But please remember two other things as well. First of all, almost everyone figures it out and does just fine. The issues that seem so stressful in the beginning about department or school politics get put into perspective with time. The kinds of things that used to keep me up at night barely register on my stress-o-meter these days. Also, I have never known of a new teacher or new professor to leave a department only because of politics. I have heard of experienced teachers coming into a new environment, getting into fights, and then leaving. But people new to the profession almost always figure out how to fall into the hierarchy and get along.

The second thing to remember is that even if politics are stressful in the beginning, the difficulty is worthwhile because teaching a language is one of the most enjoyable professions there is. If you infuse your classes with high energy, become good at the communicative approach, and build a supportive community among your students, you will love your job. Every language teacher I have known who is good at what he or she does has told me that teaching is a natural high and that they would not change jobs for the world .

Beyond keeping the big issues in perspective, also keep in mind the importance of establishing some good relationships with other teachers and staff at your job, with particular focus on finding a mentor. Set your priorities and always check in with them when you are making decisions about time and effort. Never engage in gossip or criticize your colleagues, and if you do get into a conflict with someone, stay as calm and objective as you can.

Finally: enjoy! Welcome to the world of language teaching.

Summary Questions

1. Can you imagine an ideal professional mentor? What would he or she be like? Why would you choose this person?

_____

_____

2. What are your top three or four priorities for your first year in teaching? Why? Do you imagine that those priorities will change in your second or third year?

_____

_____

3. In this chapter there are two techniques presented for avoiding gossip. Do you think either of them would work for you, or could you imagine a different approach?

_____

_____

4. For high school or junior high teachers, how would you handle angry e-mails from parents? Do either of the methods listed here sound like they would work for you?

_____

_____

Scenarios

Scenario 1

It is your second semester in your new job. Last weekend was the new student orientation, and you informed your principal / department chair that you could not attend because it was your mother's birthday. This morning a senior teacher / professor in your department sent an e-mail scolding you for not being at the orientation. What's worse, she copied everyone in your department. After reading the e-mail, you headed to your supervisor's office to ask his advice. However, when you saw him in the hall, he glanced in your direction, then walked away. Everyone else you passed in the hallway seemed to be intentionally ignoring you. What should you do?

Scenario 2

At this new job you are beginning to develop a friendship with a more experienced teacher/professor. He invites you to go for coffee but says that he only has about fifteen minutes to talk. You want to ask him about so many things, including the problematic professor / teacher who likes to gossip. But also, you have been very stressed about a couple of rude and disruptive students in one class, and you are having all kinds of "extra" responsibilities shuffled in your direction. Which one of these issues are you going to talk to your mentor about and why?

Appendix A

Chapter 3 • Sample Task Activities

Worksheet 3.1: What Do You Do?

Do you shave your legs?	Do you wash your hands after going to the bathroom?	Do you go to sleep before 10:00 p.m.?	Do you have fun dancing on weekends?
Do you comb your hair several times a day?	Do you sometimes sleep less than five hours a night?	Do you like getting up early?	Do you wear the same clothes two days in a row?
Do you bathe every other day?	Do you wear clothes when you sleep?	Do you fall in love easily?	Do you dress nicely to go to school?
Are you in love with a movie star?	Do you shower with cold water?	Do you fall asleep in class?	Do you get up after noon on weekends?

Worksheet 3.2: Who Is This Person?

Names

Descriptions

Britney Spears	tall, strong, conservative
Beyoncé	short, fat, funny
Danny DeVito	tall, beautiful, thin
Kanye West	intelligent, thin, handsome
Barack Obama	immature, pretty, rich
Arnold Schwarzenegger	aggressive, impulsive, talented

Worksheet 3.3: Family Reunion

Family #1

Your name is **Tom.**
You are a professor at Stanford.
You are from Reno.
Your grandchild does not like to study.
Your grandchild is 14 years old.

Your name is **Tracy.**
You are a medical doctor.
You are from Reno.
Your husband is a professor at Stanford.
Your spouse is from Reno.

Your name is **Vinny.**
Your family is rich, but you are poor.
You live in the New York City subway.
Your mother is a medical doctor.
Your mother lives in Reno.

Your name is **Victoria.**
You work in a library.
You live in New Jersey.
Your brother lives in New York.
Your brother is poor.

Your name is **Edmund.**
You live in New Jersey.
You are an actor.
Your wife works in a library.
Your wife lives in New Jersey.

Your name is **Charles.**
You are 13 years old.
You don't like to study.
Your father is an actor.
You live with your father in New Jersey.
Your sister likes to read.

Your name is **Carmen.**
You are 11 years old.
Your brother is 13 years old.
You like to read the *Twilight* books.
Your grandfather is from Reno.

Your name is **Jonah.**
You are an artist.
You are from Montana.
Your brother is a professor at Stanford.
Your nephew is poor and lives in the New York City subway.

Family #2

Your name is **Raymond**.
You are the CEO of American Express.
You are from San Francisco.
Your granddaughter is 10 years old.
Your granddaughter likes to watch TV.

Your name is **Mary**.
You don't work, but you are rich.
You like exotic animals.
Your husband is from San Francisco.
Your granddaughter likes to drink lemonade.
Your husband is the CEO of American Express.

Your name is **George**.
You study chimpanzees in Africa.
You are an anthropologist.
Your mother is rich.
Your mother likes exotic animals.

Your name is **Susan**.
You drink a lot of rum.
You are from Los Angeles.
Your brother is an anthropologist.
Your brother studies chimpanzees in Africa.

Your name is **David**.
You are from Los Angeles.
You work at Burger King.
Your wife is an alcoholic.
Your wife is from Los Angeles.

Your name is **Rachel**.
You like to watch TV.
You are 10 years old.
Your grandmother is rich.
Your grandmother likes exotic animals.

Your name is **Alexandra**.
You like to drink lemonade.
You are 5 years old.
Your grandmother is rich.
Your grandmother likes exotic animals.

Your name is **Javier**.
You are a professional athlete.
You live in Indianapolis, Indiana.
Your sister is an alcoholic.
Your niece is 10 years old.

Family #3

Your name is **Chachi**.
You have a ranch.
You are from Amarillo, Texas.
Your son lives in Austin, Texas.
Your son studies medicine.

Your name is **Peter**.
You are a photographer.
You live in Amarillo, Texas.
Your wife has a ranch.
Your wife is from Amarillo.

Your name is **Mary**.
You are a music teacher.
You are from Austin, Texas.
Your husband lives in Austin.
Your husband studies medicine.

Your name is **Manny**.
You live in Austin, Texas.
You study medicine.
Your sister lives in Austin.
Your sister works with
    computers.

Your name is **Helen**.
You live in Austin, Texas.
You work with computers.
Your father is from Amarillo,
    Texas.
Your father is very intelligent.

Your name is **Steve**.
You like plastic cars.
You are 4 years old.
You live with your mother in
    Austin, Texas.

Your name is **Jane**.
You like to ride bikes.
You are 8 years old.
Your grandfather is very
    intelligent.
Your grandfather is a
    photographer.
Your uncle plays the guitar.

Your name is **Johnny**.
You are tall and thin.
You play the guitar with a band.
You like rock music.
Your niece likes to ride bikes.
Your sister works with
    computers.

Worksheet 3.4: Warm-up Questions

Did you use to suck your thumb? Until when?
What TV programs did you watch when you were little?
Did you have good grades in elementary school? Why (not)?
Were you fat or skinny when you were in middle school? Was that tough?
Describe your favorite middle school teacher.
What was your favorite place in the house where you grew up?
Did you use to sing in a choir?
Did you like middle school? Why (not)?
What were your favorite foods when you were in kindergarten?
Did you speak another language when you were little? Which?
Describe your personality when you were 5 to 10 years old.
What cereals did you eat when you were in elementary school?
Were you terrible or good when you were 10 years old? What did you do?
Did you play a musical instrument in middle school? Do you still play it?
Did you play with toy cars when you were little? Why (not)?

Did you play with dolls when you were little? Why (not)?
What was your favorite toy when you were in kindergarten?
Did you use to fight with your siblings?
Did you work after school when you were in high school?
Where did you live when you were 10 years old?
Did you have pets when you were growing up? What were their names?
Did you have a nickname in middle school? Did you like it?
Did you have a favorite blanket when you were little?
What was your best friend's name in middle school? Describe your friend.
Were you afraid of the dark when you were little? What else are you afraid of?
What type of games did you play when you were in elementary school?
What type of music did you like to listen to in middle school?
Did you play with your food when you were little?
What books did you read in middle school?
Do you remember your elementary school teachers' names?

Worksheet 3.5: Speed Dating

Interview questions:

- What is your name?
- What is your favorite pastime?
- Where do you work?
- What do you do for a living?
- What type of music do you like?
- Do you have any pets? What are their names?
- Who in your family are you closest to?
- Are you a morning person?
- Who do you admire the most?
- What is your biggest achievement so far?

Worksheet 3.6: Bargaining

Sample dialogue:

Seller: This way, this way, I have a good price for you today. Everything is very cheap.
Client: How much is this _____?
Seller: For you, 300 euros.
Client: It is too expensive. / It is too much. / I don't like it that much. / It doesn't fit me well. / I was not planning on spending that much.
Seller: Well, just because it is such a nice day and you are a nice lady, I'll part with it for 250 euros.
Client: I'll take it.

Worksheet 3.7: Defend Your Side

To give an opinion:

- The way I see it . . .
- I imagine that . . .
- I suspect that . . .
- I am sure that . . .
- Honestly, I think . . .
- Without a doubt . . .

To disagree:

- It is hard to believe that . . .
- What do you mean by . . .
- I am afraid I don't agree with you . . .
- Really, I doubt that if . . .
- The problem with your point of view is . . .

Worksheet 3.8: Family Tree

- What is your father's/mother's/grandparent's name?
- How many brothers and sisters do they have?
- What are their last names?
- Who is older/younger?
- Do you have any children?

Worksheet 3.9: Mini-Biography

- How old are you?
- When is your birthday?
- What is your personality like?
- Describe yourself physically.
- How many siblings do you have?
- How many classes do you have?
- What is your favorite class?
- What do you like to do in your free time?

Appendix B

Chapter 12 · Sample Lab Exercises

Worksheet 12.1: Famous Person

I. Search activity: I have assigned you a famous person and you have to find an image of this person on the Internet and describe him/her verbally to your partner or group. It is important that you keep the name secret and not share it with the rest of the class.

My famous person is _____.

To find images, go to Google.com and click on the images link to the right.

II. Writing activity: Write seven or more sentences about this person.

1. This person is _____ (gender).

2. His/her eyes are _____.

3. His/her hair is _____.

4. Describe this person physically. Use at least three adjectives.

5. He/she is from _____ (country of origin).

6. His/her favorite activity is _____.

7. Describe his/her personality using at least three adjectives.

_____

_____

_____

III. Pair activity chat: Describe your famous person. Using your headphones, ask and provide information. Talk about your famous person without mentioning his/her name. And finally, guess who this person might be.

1. Is your person a man or a woman?
2. What color are his/her eyes?
3. What activities does your person do?
4. Is s(he) young or old?
5. Where is (s)he from?
6. Is your famous person _____?

Worksheet 12.2: More Information on the Famous

I. Writing: Assume the personality of someone famous. Describe your character in three sentences and add more information about him/her.

1.   He/She is _____ (physical description).
2. He/She was born _____.
3. He/She likes _____.

II. Converse: Using your headphones, try to find out who your partner's character is and vice versa. Use question words like: What, When, Who, Where, How much, Which, and How. Cover the following topics:

- Country of origin
- Work
- Talents
- Sports
- Physical description
- Personality
- Family
- Languages the person speaks
- Likes and dislikes on: foods, friends, music, women/men, cars, books, countries to visit, etc.

III. Search: Pick one of the two characters you have been talking about with your partner and together search for more information. Use the links I provide here (Teacher: include your target language links).

IV. Writing: Using the chat room, collaborate with your partner to write a paragraph about your character using the information gathered together. Write at least three sentences each. Be ready to read your work to the class.

Worksheet 12.3: What Is the Weather Like?

(Student A)

I. Writing: What are you going to do next weekend? Write a total of nine sentences describing your plans for the weekend: three about what you are going to do if it is cold, three about if it is sunny, and three about if it is raining. Then, read your sentences to your nearest classmate.

   Example: *If it rains, I will watch a movie.*

II. Conversation: Use your headphones to converse with your classmate about the weather. Your classmate will have some questions for you. Use the following questions:

1. How is the weather in the city where you live?
2. What type of weather do you prefer?
3. What are you going to do next weekend if it is sunny?
4. Do you like the snow?
5. Do you think the climate of the world is changing?

III. Search the weather in other countries: Use the link I provide here (Teacher: include your target language links) to search for the climate patterns in different cities. Select a country in South America and a country in the Caribbean. (Select an area suitable for your language that is different than the area for Student B.)

Country in South America: _____

City: _____

What is the weather like today? _____

What is the temperature? _____

What is the forecast for tomorrow? _____

What is the forecast for the next few days? _____

Country in the Caribbean: _____

City: _____

What is the weather like today? _____

What is the temperature? _____

What is the forecast for tomorrow? _____

What is the forecast for the next few days? _____

IV. Conversation: Using your headphones, ask your classmate about the weather he/she searched—in this case, a city in Europe and a city in Central America—and fill in the information below:

Country in Europe: _____

City: _____

What is the weather like today? _____

What is the temperature? _____

What is the forecast for tomorrow? _____

What is the forecast for the next few days? _____

Country in Central America: _____

City: _____

What is the weather like today? _____

What is the temperature? _____

What is the forecast for tomorrow? _____

What is the forecast for the next few days? _____

V. Writing: Using the chat room, collaborate in the writing of a paragraph about what both of you are going to do on a rainy day and on a sunny day.

(Student B)

I. Writing: What are you going to do next weekend? Write a total of nine sentences describing your plans for the weekend: three about what you are going to do if it is cold, three about if it is sunny, and three about if it is raining. Then, read your sentences to your nearest classmate.

    Example: *If it rains, I will watch a movie.*

II. Conversation: Use your headphones to converse with your classmate about the weather. Your classmate will have some questions for you. Use the following questions:

1. How is the weather in the city where you live?

2. What type of weather do you prefer?

3. What are you going to do next weekend if it is sunny?

4. Do you like the snow?

5. Do you think the climate of the world is changing?

III. Search the weather in other countries: Use the link I provide here (Teacher: include your target language links) to search for the climate patterns in different cities. Select a country in Europe and a country in Central America. (Select an area suitable for your language that is different than the area for Student A).

Country in Europe: _____

City: _____

What is the weather like today? _____

What is the temperature? _____

What is the forecast for tomorrow? _____

What is the forecast for the next few days? _____

Country in Central America: _____

City: _____

What is the weather like today? _____

What is the temperature? _____

What is the forecast for tomorrow? _____

What is the forecast for the next few days? _____

IV. Conversation: Using your headphones, ask your classmate about the weather he/she searched—in this case, a city in South America and a city in the Caribbean—and fill in the information below:

Country in South America: _____

City: _____

What is the weather like today? _____

What is the temperature? _____

What is the forecast for tomorrow? _____

What is the forecast for the next few days? _____

Country in the Europe: _____

City: _____

What is the weather like today? _____

What is the temperature? _____

What is the forecast for tomorrow? _____

What is the forecast for the next few days? _____

V. Writing: Using the chat room, collaborate in writing a paragraph about what both of you are going to do on a rainy day and on a sunny day.

Worksheet 12.4: World of Foods

I. Search

a. Using the link provided (the one I use is http://cocinadelmundo.com), look for a recipe. What country is the recipe from? _____

b. Look at the ingredients and answer the following questions:

    1. Does it have healthy ingredients?

    2. Does it have a lot of calories?

    3. What do you like and not like?

    4. What is the main ingredient?

II. Conversation

Using your headphones, talk to your partner about:

a. what country each of you visited, what recipe you liked, and what the ingredients are.

_____

_____

b. what foods s(he) prepares well in real life, and what the ingredients are.

_____

_____

III. Writing

In the chat room, together write a step-by-step description of the way to make:

a. a salad.

_____

_____

_____

b. scrambled eggs.

_____

_____

Worksheet 12.5: Let's Go Shopping

I. Search: Using the link provided (I picked a very big department store in Spain called *El Corte Inglés*), search for three things you would like to buy for yourself.

I am going to give myself:

_____

_____

My partner is buying:

_____

_____

II. Conversation: Using the headphones, collaborate and come to an agreement with your partner to buy a gift for the people listed below. You only have 200 euros.

1. A classmate you both like: _____
2. A classmate whose birthday is coming up or who is sick: _____
3. Your teacher: _____

III. Writing: In the chat room together, write a get-well message for the classmate who was recently sick (your teacher will give you his or her e-mail).
Go to the link provided to send an electronic card.

Sample message:
Hi Jackie:
Jim and I noticed you were not in class. The teacher told us you were sick. Class was a lot of fun without you, ha, ha. No, we really missed you.
Hope you feel better soon. Don't forget to do the homework.
Love, Jim and Andy

Bibliography

ACTFL Proficiency Guidelines, American Council on the Teaching of Foreign Languages, http://www.actfl.org.

Bateman, B. E., and S. L. Wilkinson (2010). "Spanish for Heritage Speakers: A Statewide Survey of Secondary School Teachers." *Foreign Language Annals* 43: 324–53.

Bjork, D. W. (1997). *B. F. Skinner: A Life*. Washington, DC: American Psychological Association.

Blanco-Iglesias, S., J. Broner, and E. Tarone (1995). "Observations of language use in Spanish immersion classroom interaction." In L. Eubank, L. Selinker, and M. Sharwood Smith (eds.), *The Current State of Interlanguage: Studies in Honor of William E. Rutherford*. Philadelphia: John Benjamins.

Bley-Vroman, R. (1989). "What Is the Logical Problem of Foreign Language Learning?" Chapter 2 in S. Gass and J. Schachter (eds.), *Linguistics Perspectives on Second Language Acquisition*. Cambridge, UK: Cambridge University Press.

Broner, M. A. (2012). "English and Spanish Language Use by Three Fifth Graders in a Full Immersion Classroom." An Internet publication by the Center for Advanced Research on Language Acquisition, http://wwwcarla.acad.umn.edu/immersion/broner.html.

Brophy, J. (2006). "History in Research." In C. Evertson and C. Weinstein (eds.), *Handbook of Classroom Management: Research, Practice, and Contemporary Issues*. Mahwah, NJ: Lawrence Erlbaum.

California Department of Education (2003). "Foreign Language Framework for California Public Schools Kindergarten through Grade Twelve." Sacramento: California Department of Education.

Canale, M. (1983). "From communicative competence to communicative language pedagogy." In J. Richard and R. Schmidt (eds.), *Language and Communication*. London: Longman.

Canale, M., and M. Swain (1980). "Theoretical Bases of Communicative Approaches to Second Language Teaching and Testing." *Applied Linguistics* 1: 1–47.

Carranza, I. (1995). "Multilevel analysis of two-way immersion classroom discourse." Georgetown University Round Table of Languages and Linguistics. Washington, DC: Georgetown University.

Cazabon, M. T., E. Nicoladis, and W. E. Lambert (1998). "Becoming Bilingual in the Amigos Two-Way Immersion Program." An Internet publication by CREDE (Center for Research in Education, Diversity and Excellence), http://crede.berkeley.edu/products/print/reports/rr3.html.

Chomsky, N. (2002). *Syntactic Structures*. (First published in 1957.) Berlin–New York: Mouton de Gruyter.

Clunies-Ross, P., E. Little, and M. Kiehuis (2008). "Self-reported and actual use of proactive and reactive classroom management strategies and their relationship with teacher stress and student behaviour." *Educational Psychology* 28: 693–710.

Colombi, M. C. (2006). "Grammatical metaphor: Academic language in Latino students in Spanish." In H. Byrnes (ed.), *Advanced Language Learning: The Contribution of Halliday and Vygotsky*. London: Continuum.

Colombi, M. C. (2009). "A systemic functional approach to teaching Spanish for heritage speakers in the United States." *Linguistics and Education* 20: 39–49.

Dörnyei, Z. (2005). *The Psychology of the Language Learner: Individual Differences in Second Language Acquisition*. Mahwah, NJ: Lawrence Erlbaum.

Doughty, C., and E. Varela (1998). "Communicative focus on form." In C. Doughty and J. Williams (eds.), *Focus on Form in Classroom Second Language Acquisition*. New York: Cambridge University Press.

Ellis, R. (1985). *Understanding Second Language Acquisition*. Oxford, UK: Oxford University Press.

Evertson, C., and E. Emmer (1982). "Effective management at the beginning of the school year in junior high classes." *Journal of Educational Psychology* 74: 485–98.

Evertson, C. M., and K. W. Neal (2006). "Looking into learning-centered classrooms: Implications for classroom management." Working paper. Washington, DC: National Education Association.

Fishman, J. A. (2001). "300-plus years of heritage language education in the United States." In J. K. Peyton, D. A. Ranard, and S. McGinnis (eds.), *Heritage Languages in America: Preserving a National Resource*. Washington, DC: Delta Systems; and McHenry, IL: Center for Applied Linguistics.

Fox, M. (2007). *Talking Hands*. New York: Simon and Schuster.

Galloway, V., and A. Labarca (1990). "From Student to Learner: Style, Process, and Strategy." In D. Birchbichler (ed.), *New Perspectives and New Directions in Foreign Language Education*. The ACTFL Foreign Language Education Series. Lincolnwood, IL: National Textbook.

Gass, S. (1997). *Input, Interaction and the Second Language Learner*. Mahwah, NJ: Lawrence Erlbaum.

Gass, S., and L. Selinker (1994). *Second Language Acquisition: An Introductory Course*. Hillsdale, NJ: Lawrence Erlbaum.

Gass, S., and E. Varonis (1989). "Incorporated repairs in NNS discourse." In M. Eisenstein (ed.), *The Dynamic Interlanguage*. New York: Plenum.

Goodman, K. (1967). "Reading: A Psycholinguistic Guessing Game." *Journal of the Reading Specialist* 6 (4): 126–35.

Gutiérrez, J. (1997). "Teaching Spanish As a Heritage Language: A Case for Language Awareness." *ADFL Bulletin* 29 (1): 33–36.

Jackson Hardin, C. (2011). *Effective Classroom Management: Models and Strategies for Today's Classrooms*. Boston: Pearson.

Jelinek, Frederick (1997). *Statistical Methods for Speech Recognition*. Cambridge, MA: MIT Press.

Koike, D. A., and C. A. Klee (2003). *Lingüística aplicada: Adquisición de español como segunda lengua*. New York: John Wiley & Sons.

Krashen, S. (1982). *Principles and Practice in Second Language Acquisition*. New York: Pergamon Press.

Lantolf, J., and W. Frawley (1988). "Proficiency—Understanding the Construct." *Studies in Second Language Acquisition* 10 (2): 181–95.

Larsen-Freedman, D. (1991). "Second Language Acquisition Research: Staking Out the Territory." *TESOL Quarterly* 25: 315–50.

Larsen-Freeman, D., and M. H. Long (1991). *An Introduction to Second Language Acquisition Research*. New York: Longman.

Leavitt, S. E., and S. A. Stoudemire (1942). *Concise Spanish Grammar*. New York: Henry Holt and Company.

Lennenburg, Eric (1967). *Biological Foundations of Language*. New York: Wiley.

Lightbrown, P. M., and N. Spada (2006). *How Languages Are Learned*. Oxford, UK: Oxford University Press.

Long, Michael (1983). "Does Second Language Instruction Make a Difference? A Review of the Research." *TESOL Quarterly* 1: 359–82.

Lynch, A. (2003). "Towards a theory of heritage language acquisition." In A. Roca and M. C. Colombi (eds.), *Mi lengua: Spanish as a Heritage Language in the United States* (pp. 25–50). Washington, DC: Georgetown University Press.

MacWhinney, B. (1997). "Implicit and Explicit Processes." *Studies in Second Language Acquisition* 19: 277–81.

MacWhinney, B. (2008). "A Unified Model." In N. Ellis and P. Robinson (eds.), *Handbook of Cognitive Linguistics and Second Language Acquisition*. Hillsdale, NJ: Lawrence Erlbaum.

Martinez, G. A. (2006). *Mexican Americans and Language*. Tucson: University of Arizona Press.

Marzano, E. J., J. S. Marzano, and D. J. Pickering (2003). *Classroom Management That Works: Research-based Strategies for Every Teacher*. Alexandria, VA: Association for Supervision and Curriculum Development.

McKay, S. L., and S. C. Wong (1996). "Multiple discourses, multiple identities: Investment and agency in second-language learning among Chinese adolescent immigrant students." *Harvard Educational Review* 66 (3): 577–608.

McLaughlin, B. (1987). *Second-Language Acquisition in Childhood*, vol. 1, *Preschool Children*. Hillsdale, NJ: Lawrence Erlbaum.

McNamara, T. F. (1999). "'Interaction' in Second Language Performance Assessment: Whose Performance?" *Linguistics* 18 (4).

Met, M., and E. B. Lorenz (1997). "Lessons from U.S. immersion programs: Two decades of experience." In R. K. Johnson and M. Swain (eds.), *Immersion Education: International Perspectives*. Cambridge, UK: Cambridge University Press.

Minor, D. (2009). "Bring the Rebels Aboard: Language Choices and Motivational Systems in Elementary Immersion Education." *Notos: The Journal of Second Languages and Intercultural Council* 9 (2): 5–16.

National Center for Education Statistics, http://nces.ed.gov.

Norton, B. (2000). *Identity and Language Learning: Gender, Ethnicity and Educational Change*. Essex, UK: Pearson Education Ltd.

Norvig, Peter (2009). "Natural Language Corpus Data." In T. Segaran and J. Hammerbacher (eds.), *Beautiful Data*. Sebastopol, CA: O'Reilly.

Omaggio Hadley, A. (2001). *Teaching Language in Context*. Boston: Heinle and Heinle.

Phillips, J. K., and M. Abbott (2011). "A Decade of Foreign Language Standards: Impact, Influence, and Future Directions." American Council on the Teaching of Foreign Languages, http://www.actfl.org/files/public/national-standards-2001.pdf.

Phillips, J. K., and M. Abbott (2011). "A Decade of Foreign Language Standards: Impact, Influence, and Future Directions. Survey Results." American Council on the Teaching of Foreign Languages, http:www.actfl.org/files/public/StandardsImpact SurveyApr2011.pdf.

Pica, T. (1994). "Research on negotiation: What does it reveal about second-language learning conditions, processes, and outcomes?" *Language Learning* 44: 493–527.

Pienemann, M. (1999). *Language Processing and Second Language Development: Processability Theory*. Amsterdam: John Benjamins.

Pienemann, M., ed. (2005). *Cross-Linguistics Aspects of Processability Theory*. Amsterdam: John Benjamins.

Pinker, S. (1995). *The Language Instinct: How the Mind Creates Language*. New York: HarperCollins.

Polinsky, M., and O. Kagan (2007). "Heritage Languages: In the 'Wild' and in the Classroom." *Language and Linguistics Compass* 1 (5): 368–95.

Potowski, K. (2004). "Student Spanish Use and Investment in a Dual Immersion Classroom: Implications for Second Language Acquisition and Heritage Language Maintenance." *Modern Language Journal* 88: 75–79.

Potowski, K., and M. Carreira (2004). "Towards teacher development and national standards for Spanish as a heritage language." *Foreign Language Annals* 37: 427–37.

Rogers, P. (1957). *Spanish for the Second Year*. New York: Macmillan.

Rymer, R. (1993). *Genie: A Scientific Tragedy*. New York: Harper Collins.

Sanchez, R. (1994). *Chicano Discourse: Socio-historic Perspectives*. Houston: Arte Público Press.

Sanz, C. (2000). "What Form to Focus On? Linguistics, Language Awareness, and the Education of L2 Teachers." In J. F. Lee and A. Valdman (eds.), *Form and Meaning: Multiple Perspectives*. AAUSC Issues in Language Program Direction. Boston: Heinle and Heinle.

Schleppegress. M. J. (2004). *The Language of Schooling: A Functional Linguistics Perspective*. Mahwah, NJ: Lawrence Erlbaum.

Shen, H. (2003). "A Comparison of Written Chinese Achievement Among Heritage Learners in Homogenous and Heterogeneous Groups." *Foreign Language Annals* 36: 258–66.

Shohamy, E. (1988). "A Proposed Framework for Testing the Oral Language of Second/Foreign Language Learners." *Studies in Second Language Acquisition* 10: 165–79.

Silva-Corvalán, C. (2001). *Sociolingüística y pragmática del español*. Washington, DC: Georgetown University Press.

Swain, M. (1985). "Communicative competence: Some roles of comprehensible input and comprehensible output in its development." In S. Gass and C. Madden (eds.), *Input in Second Language Acquisition*. Rowley, MA: Newbury House.

Swain, M. (1995). "Three functions of output in second language learning." In G. Cook and B. Seidlhofer (eds.), *Principle and Practice in Applied Linguistics: Studies in Honour of H. G. Widdowson*. Oxford, UK: Oxford University Press.

Swain, M., and M. Kowal (1997). "From semantic to syntactic processing." In R. K. Johnson and M. Swain (eds.), *Immersion Education: International Perspectives*. Cambridge, UK: Cambridge University Press.

Tarone, E. (1982). "Systematicity and Attention in Interlanguage." *Language Learning* 32: 69–84.

"Teaching Foreign Languages K–12: A Library of Classroom Practices." Annenberg Learner Produced by WGBH Educational Foundation with the American Council on the Teaching of Foreign Languages, http://www.learner.org/resources/series185.html.

Terrell, T. D. (1977). "A Natural Approach to Second Language Acquisition and Learning." *Modern Language Journal* 61: 325–37.

Terrell, T. D. (1982). "The Natural Approach to Language Teaching: An Update." *Modern Language Journal* 66: 121–32.

Thornberg, R. (2008). "School children's reasoning about school rules." *Research Papers in Education* 23: 37–52.

Tomlinson, C. (1999). *The Differentiated Classroom: Responding to the Needs of All Learners.* Alexandria, VA: Association for Supervision and Curriculum Development.

Tungseth-Faber, K. (1998). "Strategies for Motivation of L2 Output in a Linguistically Homogeneous Language Classroom: A 4th Grade Spanish Immersion Model." A Master of Arts thesis in the Linguistics Department at the University of California, Davis.

United States Department of Education Index of Educational Statistics, www.edu.gov.

Valdés, G. (1997). "The teaching of Spanish to bilingual Spanish-speaking students: Outstanding issues and unanswered questions." In M. C. Colombi and F. X. Alarcón (eds.), *La enseñanza del español a hispanohablantes: Praxis y teoría* (pp. 8–44). Boston: Houghton Mifflin.

Valdés, G., J. A. Fishman, R. Chávez, and W. Pérez (2006). *Developing Minority Language Resources: The Case of Spanish in California.* Clavedon, UK: Multilingual Matters.

van Lier, L. (1988). *The Classroom and the Language Learner: Ethnography and Second Language Classroom Research.* New York: Longman.

Wallace, E., G. Tucker, and R. Lambert (1972). *Bilingual Education of Children: The St. Lambert Experiment.* Rowley, MA: Newbury House.

Webb, J. B., and B. L. Miller (2000). *Teaching Heritage Learners: Voices from the Classroom.* ACTFL Foreign Language Education Series. Yonkers, NY: ACTFL.

Weger-Guntharp, H. (2006). "Voices from the Margin: Developing a Profile of Chinese Heritage Language Learners in the FL Classroom." *Heritage Language Journal.* National Heritage Language Resource Center, UCLA International Institute.

Wilkins, L. A. (1926). *New Second Spanish Book.* New York: Henry Holt.

Windholz, G. (1983). "Pavlov's position toward American behaviorism." *Journal of the History of Behavioral Sciences* 19 (4): 394–407.

Zentella, A. C. (1997). *Growing Up Bilingual.* Malden, MA: Blackwell.

Index

Illustration Credits

- Set up an online account with a digital dossier, a credentials file, and a letter of recommendation service, such as Interfolio. This may be a little pricey for some graduate students, but many swear by its convenience. Your university may also have a similar free service; check into that.

- Ask at least four professors for confidential letters of recommendation, and give them the information to upload to your chosen agency.

- Set up a personal website. Upload all your documents and show any favorable personal information you would like the committee to see.

- Draft and perfect two syllabi for courses you would like to teach. Make one of them a senior seminar.

- Shop for nice business attire ahead of time.

- Make sure your dissertation is at least halfway finished by the time you go to the MLA. Be prepared to talk about your goals and self-imposed deadlines to finish.

- Arrange for one or two mock interviews with your professors; it is important to practice.

- Adjust the content of your answers to the type of institution with which you are interviewing. Different research institutions will not only ask different questions and expect different answers, they will also focus on different aspects of your teaching or research.

- Rehearse for interviews on Skype. Make sure one of your mock interviews is online so you can work on your posture and background. Practice looking at the webcam instead of at the computer video image.

TEACHING PHILOSOPHY STATEMENT

What is the ideal teaching philosophy statement? The teaching philosophy statement is all about you as well as your teaching style, teaching goals, and teaching persona. Since this is the core of who you are, the overall content you will communicate to each institution doesn't change much. But that doesn't mean everybody gets the exact same application package from you; no, you have to tweak the statement a little to fit the institution. Look at your prospective employers' websites to find their areas of interest. See what textbooks they are using.

Here are a couple of examples of how to customize your teaching statement. A tenure-track research university will have top students who can be "pushed" a little more. So in your teaching philosophy, mention that you expect a lot from your students, you believe in maintaining high expectations, and your research will ensure that your students get exposed to the latest developments in their field. You might also mention all the technological tools you use in your teaching. Finally, convey that your love for research equals that of teaching, thus implying "don't worry, I also plan to publish."

In contrast, students in community colleges may be somewhat older, have families, or may not be as academically oriented as those at research institutions. Remember, in this environment research is secondary to excellence in teaching, and so that is what you should emphasize.

Note that in the two above examples, the core of the teaching philosophy is the same, and it reflects you and your style, but adding or deleting key sentences that reflect the institution to which you are applying really could make the difference in whether you get the fat acceptance package in the mail, or the thin, polite rejection letter.

The basic elements that I recommend you **do include** in your teaching philosophy are: the most important skills you want students to learn in class and why this is important to you; what you have taught and how many years of experience you have; your passion, happiness, and enthusiasm for the profession of teaching; the fact that teaching matches your personality and that it is personally rewarding to teach; how you are able to relate to your students; your teaching approach or rationale of why you do what you do at each of the levels (elementary, intermediate, advanced, and lower division), including specific examples; your feelings about the importance of culture (how you make it come alive); and the use of technology to enhance your teaching and professional development.

You could also include: the name of a very effective professor who influenced your teaching, and the qualities you have adopted from him or